Approaches to
Teaching Fitzgerald's
The Great Gatsby

Approaches to Teaching
World Literature
Joseph Gibaldi, series editor

For a complete listing of titles,
see the last pages of this book.

Approaches to Teaching Fitzgerald's *The Great Gatsby*

Edited by

Jackson R. Bryer

and

Nancy P. VanArsdale

The Modern Language Association of America
New York 2009

© 2009 by The Modern Language Association of America
All rights reserved
Printed in the United States of America

For information about obtaining permission to reprint material from
MLA book publications, send your request by mail (see address below),
e-mail (permissions@mla.org), or fax (646 458-0030).

Library of Congress Cataloging-in-Publication Data

Approaches to teaching Fitzgerald's The great Gatsby /
edited by Jacskon R. Bryer and Nancy P. VanArsdale.
p. cm.—(Approaches to teaching world literature ; 108)
Includes bibliographical references (p.   ) and index.
ISBN 978-1-60329-020-3 (alk. paper)—
ISBN 978-1-60329-021-0 (pbk. : alk. paper)
1. Fitzgerald, F. Scott (Francis Scott), 1896–1940. Great Gatsby.
2. Fitzgerald, F. Scott (Francis Scott), 1896–1940—Study and teaching.
I. Bryer, Jackson R.   II. VanArsdale, Nancy P., 1957–
PS3511.I9G8226 2008
813'.52—dc22   2008028809

Approaches to Teaching World Literature 108
ISSN 1059–1133

Cover illustration of the paperback edition: Watch, by Gerald Murphy. 1925.
Oil on canvas. 78½" × 78⅞". Dallas Museum of Art.
© Estate of Honoria Murphy Donnelly, licensed by VAGA, New York, NY

Printed on recycled paper

Published by The Modern Language Association of America
26 Broadway, New York, New York 10004-1789
www.mla.org

CONTENTS

PREFACE TO THE SERIES

In *The Art of Teaching* Gilbert Highet wrote, "Bad teaching wastes a great deal of effort, and spoils many lives which might have been full of energy and happiness." All too many teachers have failed in their work, Highet argued, simply "because they have not thought about it." We hope that the Approaches to Teaching World Literature series, sponsored by the Modern Language Association's Publications Committee, will not only improve the craft—as well as the art—of teaching but also encourage serious and continuing discussion of the aims and methods of teaching literature.

The principal objective of the series is to collect within each volume different points of view on teaching a specific literary work, a literary tradition, or a writer widely taught at the undergraduate level. The preparation of each volume begins with a wide-ranging survey of instructors, thus enabling us to include in the volume the philosophies and approaches, thoughts and methods of scores of experienced teachers. The result is a sourcebook of material, information, and ideas on teaching the subject of the volume to undergraduates.

The series is intended to serve nonspecialists as well as specialists, inexperienced as well as experienced teachers, graduate students who wish to learn effective ways of teaching as well as senior professors who wish to compare their own approaches with the approaches of colleagues in other schools. Of course, no volume in the series can ever substitute for erudition, intelligence, creativity, and sensitivity in teaching. We hope merely that each book will point readers in useful directions; at most each will offer only a first step in the long journey to successful teaching.

Joseph Gibaldi
Series Editor

PREFACE TO THE VOLUME

> "Who is this Gatsby anyhow?" demanded Tom suddenly. "Some big
> bootlegger?"
> "Where'd you hear that?" I inquired.
> "I didn't hear it. I imagined it. A lot of these newly rich people are just
> big bootleggers, you know."
> "Not Gatsby," I said shortly. (*The Great Gatsby* 107)

"Who is this Gatsby anyhow?" Answering that question is fundamental to teaching F. Scott Fitzgerald's *The Great Gatsby*. Inevitably, students find no simple
answer, but classroom analysis of this classic American novel repeatedly leads to
a rich exploration of the complexities of character, the bias of point of view, the
structure and language of the text, and, eventually, the dimensions of an evolving
modern American culture. With limited time to analyze and interpret a text during a semester, instructors strive to find techniques that help students understand a specific text, make connections between literature and history, and
develop critical thinking skills transferable to the world outside the academy.
The purpose of this volume is to help instructors effectively teach this great
novel.

Although close to 400,000 copies of *The Great Gatsby* are reportedly sold an-
nually and the novel is taught in countless secondary school, undergraduate,
and graduate courses throughout the world, there is little commentary that directly addresses how to teach it. To be sure, the implication that lies behind
Jackson R. Bryer's essay in the "Materials" section of this book is that much of
the voluminous scholarship and criticism on the novel and its author can be
useful as one prepares to teach it. Nonetheless, one of the few explicit accounts
of teaching the novel is the fascinating description Azar Nafisi provides in her
2003 best seller, *Reading* Lolita *in Tehran*. Nafisi tells how she literally had to
put the book and its characters on trial in her class, because her students had
such divergent views on it. We hope that some of the essays in our collection
will be as stimulating as Nafisi's.

The dialogue between the millionaire Tom Buchanan and the narrator,
Nick Carraway, quoted in the passage above points to several of the thematic
dichotomies students are likely to encounter in studying the novel: between
money and power, truth and illusion, image and identity, one social class and
another, crime and morality, and mistrust and loyalty, to name just a few. *The
Great Gatsby*, originally published in 1925, provocatively depicts the historical era known as both the period of Prohibition and the Jazz Age. Moreover,
it is a great American novel, portraying the traits, admirable and ugly, of an

emerging and modern American character and American culture, influenced by the postwar era, the rise of a new generation of business and criminal tycoons, and the modernist movement in the arts. This volume provides instructors with dozens of approaches that are attentive to teaching the novel in a limited time frame while maximizing learning outcomes. In his essay, Kirk Curnutt perhaps speaks for many of us when he admits, "Balancing between text and context when teaching *The Great Gatsby* can be a daunting task." The twenty-five other contributors share their instructional starting points or show how their research interests inform their teaching, with the purpose of assisting others to find meaningful teaching approaches for their own classrooms.

The volume is organized in two parts. Part 1 presents a range of scholarly resources related to *The Great Gatsby*. Jackson R. Bryer's essay offers an overview of bibliographical, biographical, and critical publications related to Fitzgerald and the novel. Nancy P. VanArsdale supplements Bryer's account by giving a brief annotated listing of Internet sources useful for studying *Gatsby*. James L. W. West III presents a concise history of the drafting processes used by Fitzgerald in conceiving and revising the narrative. He identifies three texts integral to his study—the handwritten draft now housed at Princeton University (and available in a facsimile edition), an intermediate version entitled *Trimalchio*, and the 1925 Scribner's edition—and shows how these versions can be used by instructors to demonstrate the artistry of Fitzgerald's novel. Part 2 presents teaching approaches used by instructors throughout North America, as well as one essay contributed by Swedish scholars who teach both the film and the novel to European students. The twenty-one essays in part 2 cover a variety of critical and theoretical perspectives, from the new historicism to narrative theory to feminist criticism.

Like other volumes in the series, *Approaches to Teaching Fitzgerald's The Great Gatsby* intends to provide new instructors with interesting ideas for devising comprehensive lesson plans. Perhaps it will also intrigue experienced instructors to try alternative approaches and new technologies to stimulate today's media-savvy students.

The editors of this volume are grateful to everyone who contributed ideas and essays. We thank the many teachers and scholars who responded to our initial survey and calls for proposals as well as those who made constructive suggestions as the project evolved. We appreciated the patience of our contributors, since the project took a long time to complete. Joseph Gibaldi, general editor of the Approaches series, saw the initial promise of this volume and helped us get it started. Most important, we express our sincere gratitude to Sonia Kane, assistant director of book publications; without her guidance and encouragement, this volume never would have been completed.

We remain indebted to our students, who help us continue to be passionate about teaching, and we hope this volume inspires a new generation of students and instructors to enjoy reading, analyzing, and interpreting *The Great Gatsby*.

JRB and NPVA

NOTE

Controlling time and recapturing the past are important themes in *The Great Gatsby*. As editors, we selected the painting *Watch*, by Gerald Murphy, as the cover image for the paperback edition of this book (the painting is currently owned by the Dallas Museum of Art). During the summer and early fall of 1924 on the French Riviera, F. Scott Fitzgerald worked on the later drafts of the manuscript for *The Great Gatsby* while he and Zelda frequented the company of Gerald Murphy and Sara Murphy. Gerald Murphy had started to paint in the 1920s, and he exhibited the painting *Watch* in Paris in 1925, the same year *The Great Gatsby* was published. Murphy's painting uses a cubist style to present the mechanisms and cases of timepieces, including a pocket watch, demonstrating his shared interest with Fitzgerald in the theme of time.

Part One

MATERIALS

The Great Gatsby:
A Survey of Scholarship and Criticism

Jackson R. Bryer

Readers, students, and teachers of *The Great Gatsby* have available to them what well may be more bibliographical, textual, biographical, and critical information than on any other single work of twentieth-century American literature. What follows is an attempt both to organize this vast amount of material into manageable categories and to highlight what is most useful and insightful.

Editions

Between 1992 and 2004, the only paperback edition of *The Great Gatsby* available in the United States was based on what is the most textually reliable version of the novel. *The Great Gatsby* was first scheduled to come out of copyright in 2000, seventy-five years after its original publication in 1925, but the Sonny Bono Copyright Extension Act of 1998 moved that date to 2020, and Scribner's has steadfastly refused to permit any other American publisher to issue editions of the text. In 1991, however, they did allow Cambridge University Press, technically based in Great Britain, to inaugurate their multivolume Cambridge Edition of the Works of F. Scott Fitzgerald with Matthew J. Bruccoli's definitive scholarly edition of *The Great Gatsby*. The text of the subsequent Scribner's paperback edition published in 1992 and in circulation for the next twelve years was identical to that in Bruccoli's Cambridge edition; the major difference was the absence of the elaborate editorial apparatus present in the Cambridge volume and Bruccoli's detailed introduction. Teachers and students thus could rely on this Scribner's paperback to incorporate Bruccoli's editorial alterations, such as his restoration of Fitzgerald's original spelling of Wolfshiem (changed to "Wolfsheim," probably by Scribner's copyeditors, and retained in that form from 1925 until 1991); but if they wanted to learn the rationales for such alterations they had to consult the 1991 Cambridge edition.

Then, in 2004, Scribner, in its paperback edition published that year, abandoned Bruccoli's text and produced a version of Fitzgerald's novel that retained (without explanation) some of the changes Bruccoli had made in the 1925 original for the Cambridge edition, rejected others (most notably, it restored Scribner's "Wolfsheim"), and instituted other alterations present neither in Bruccoli's Cambridge text nor in the 1925 edition. Bruccoli registered his detailed objections to this paperback in a privately printed pamphlet, *Getting It Right: Resetting* The Great Gatsby. Yet despite the questions regarding its flaws, the 2004 Scribner paperback edition of *The Great Gatsby* is the one most likely to be accessible now and in the future to teachers and students, and thus references to *Gatsby* throughout this volume are to that edition.

Because the style of *The Great Gatsby* is often seen as one of its greatest virtues, the process of the novel's composition has come under considerable scrutiny. Once again, persons interested in this process are very fortunate in the resources available to them. A facsimile of Fitzgerald's handwritten draft was published in 1973 as The Great Gatsby: *A Facsimile of the Manuscript*, edited by Bruccoli in an edition limited to two thousand numbered copies. Also available in two forms is the first version of the novel Fitzgerald had set in type, which he called *Trimalchio*. A facsimile version of the unrevised galley proofs of *Trimalchio* was published in 2000 as *Trimalchio by F. Scott Fitzgerald: A Facsimile Edition of the Original Galley Proofs for* The Great Gatsby; in the same year, *Trimalchio: An Early Version of* The Great Gatsby appeared as a volume in the Cambridge edition, edited by James L. W. West III. The facsimile edition reproduces the galleys exactly; in his edition, West makes a very few editorial emendations, all of which he explains in his notes. Fitzgerald then extensively revised the *Trimalchio* galleys, retitling the novel *The Great Gatsby*. These revised galleys, which, with a very few minor exceptions (Bruccoli, in his 1991 Cambridge edition, discusses these), became the text of the first edition of the published novel, are reproduced in volume 3 of *F. Scott Fitzgerald: Manuscripts*, edited by Bruccoli. Thus, while vital steps in *Gatsby*'s composition process are missing—most notably the typescript or typescripts that followed the handwritten manuscript and preceded the *Trimalchio* galleys and the reset final galleys—there is ample material present through which to discern in detail the crucial stylistic and structural decisions Fitzgerald made as he shaped his carefully crafted masterpiece.

Considering the importance of this composition process and the resources available to examine it, it is remarkable that there is no book-length composition study of *Gatsby*—as there are for the composition of three of Fitzgerald's four other novels. Bruccoli's introductions to his 1991 Cambridge edition and to the 1973 facsimile are useful brief summaries, and Kenneth Eble's "The Craft of Revision: *The Great Gatsby*" is a more extensive treatment of the subject. Of corollary interest is the famous dust-jacket illustration for the original edition of *Gatsby*, a representation of the eyes of Doctor T. J. Eckleburg, which is reproduced on the cover of the current Scribner paperback; its history is traced in detail by Charles Scribner III in "Celestial Eyes: From Metamorphosis to Masterpiece." Andrew T. Crosland's *A Concordance to F. Scott Fitzgerald's* The Great Gatsby can be used to determine recurrent words and images in the novel and thus is helpful for stylistic studies.

Bibliographies

The basic bibliographic tools for the study of Fitzgerald are the revised edition of Bruccoli's *F. Scott Fitzgerald: A Descriptive Bibliography*, the definitive listing of Fitzgerald's publications, and Jackson R. Bryer's two annotated listings of secondary sources, *The Critical Reputation of F. Scott Fitzgerald: A Bibliographical Study* and *The Critical Reputation of F. Scott Fitzgerald: A Bibliographical Study, Supplement One through 1981*. Linda C. Stanley's *The Foreign Critical Reputation of F. Scott Fitzgerald: An Analysis and Annotated Bibliography* and *The Foreign Critical Reputation of F. Scott Fitzgerald, 1980–2000: An Analysis and Annotated Bibliography* summarize a great deal of difficult-to-locate commentary in languages other than English, and Mary Jo Tate's *F. Scott Fitzgerald A to Z: The Essential Reference to His Life and Work* is a valuable and authoritative general reference volume with numerous entries relevant to *The Great Gatsby*.

Those wishing to update Bruccoli's, Bryer's, and Stanley's listings should consult the annual *MLA International Bibliography* and the evaluative essay on Fitzgerald and Hemingway scholarship and criticism in *American Literary Scholarship: An Annual*, published each year by Duke University Press. Other helpful surveys of Fitzgerald scholarship and criticism that include sections on *Gatsby* are Jackson R. Bryer's Fitzgerald chapters in his editions *Sixteen Modern American Authors: A Review of Research and Criticism* and *Sixteen Modern American Authors: Volume 2, a Survey of Research and Criticism since 1972* and his essays "Four Decades of Fitzgerald Studies: The Best and the Brightest" and "The Critical Reputation of F. Scott Fitzgerald."

Primary Texts

Information about and insight into *The Great Gatsby* can be gleaned from the Fitzgerald primary texts that have been published in the years since his death. His letters, especially those to his Scribner's editor, Maxwell E. Perkins, with whom he worked extremely closely on *Gatsby*, contain much of interest. *Dear Scott / Dear Max: The Fitzgerald-Perkins Correspondence*, edited by John Kuehl and Jackson R. Bryer, includes most of both sides of their correspondence. Many of Fitzgerald's letters to Perkins are in Andrew Turnbull's edition *The Letters of F. Scott Fitzgerald*, as well as in *Correspondence of F. Scott Fitzgerald*, edited by Bruccoli and Margaret M. Duggan, with Susan Walker, and *F. Scott Fitzgerald: A Life in Letters*, edited by Bruccoli, with Judith S. Baughman. These last three volumes also include letters to and from persons other than Perkins, some with valuable comments on *Gatsby*. Typical of these is Fitzgerald's remark, in a 1924 letter to his friend Ludlow Fowler, written shortly after Zelda Fitzgerald's involvement with a young French aviator, that the "whole burden" of the novel was "the loss of those illusions that give such color to the world so that you don't care whether things are true or false as long as they partake of the magical glory" (*F. Scott Fitzgerald: A Life* 78).

Other such nuggets may be found in Bruccoli's edition *The Notebooks of F. Scott Fitzgerald*, Bruccoli and Jennifer McCabe Atkinson's edition *As Ever, Scott Fitz—: Letters between F. Scott Fitzgerald and His Literary Agent Harold*

Ober, 1919–1940, Bruccoli and Judith S. Baughman's edition *F. Scott Fitzgerald on Authorship*, Fitzgerald's *Afternoon of an Author: A Selection of Uncollected Stories and Essays*, and the first half of Bruccoli and Bryer's edition of Fitzgerald's humorous essays, book reviews, and poetry, *F. Scott Fitzgerald in His Own Time*. Fitzgerald's undergraduate writings at Princeton, some of which foreshadow the themes of *Gatsby*, have been collected in Chip Deffaa's edition *F. Scott Fitzgerald: The Princeton Years: Selected Writings, 1914–1920* and in John Kuehl's edition *The Apprentice Fiction of F. Scott Fitzgerald, 1909–1917*.

A number of the short stories Fitzgerald published in commercial venues from 1919 to 1922 have been published as *Before* Gatsby*: The First Twenty-Six Stories*, edited by Bruccoli. Four essays that explicitly link early stories to *Gatsby* include three that deal with "Absolution," which was originally intended to be the novel's first chapter—Lawrence D. Stewart's " 'Absolution' and *The Great Gatsby*," Robert A. Martin's "The Hot Madness of Four O'Clock in Fitzgerald's 'Absolution' and *Gatsby*," and Ryan LaHurd's " 'Absolution': *Gatsby*'s Forgotten Front Door"—and one that focuses on *Gatsby* and "Winter Dreams," Akiko Ishikawa's "From 'Winter Dreams' to *The Great Gatsby*." Fitzgerald, who undeniably craved recognition as a major writer of his generation, inexplicably gave very few interviews to journalists and critics—and none of those he did give deal explicitly with *The Great Gatsby*. The interviews that have been located are reprinted as *Conversations with F. Scott Fitzgerald*, edited by Bruccoli and Judith S. Baughman.

Biographies

Because Fitzgerald's fiction was heavily inflected by events in his life, anyone studying *The Great Gatsby* should be familiar with the author's biography. Of the several full-length biographies that have appeared since his death, the first remains the best. Arthur Mizener's *The Far Side of Paradise: A Biography of F. Scott Fitzgerald*, originally published in 1951 and reissued in a revised edition in 1959, is the most readable and authoritative account of Fitzgerald's life and stands out as the best critical book on Fitzgerald. Of course, since its appearance a great deal of new information has surfaced; it is all gathered in the second revised edition of Bruccoli's *Some Sort of Epic Grandeur: The Life of F. Scott Fitzgerald*.

Among the other biographical studies, the most useful are Andrew Turnbull's *Scott Fitzgerald*, André Le Vot's *F. Scott Fitzgerald: A Biography*, and Scott Donaldson's *Fool for Love: F. Scott Fitzgerald*. The best of the biographies of Zelda Sayre Fitzgerald, the partial basis of many of her husband's fictional heroines including Daisy Buchanan, is Nancy Milford's *Zelda: A Biography*. James L. W. West III's *The Perfect Hour: The Romance of F. Scott Fitzgerald and Ginevra King, His First Love* provides a narrative, letters, and other materials documenting another possible model for Daisy. Greatly underrated as a source of biographical information on both Fitzgeralds is Bruccoli, Scottie Fitzgerald Smith (Scott and Zelda's only child), and Joan P. Kerr's beautifully organized selection of material from the voluminous scrapbooks the Fitzgeralds kept, *The Romantic Egoists: A Pictorial Autobiography from the Scrapbooks and Albums of Scott and Zelda Fitzgerald.*

Of the essays that speculate about the real-life models for characters in *The Great Gatsby*, the most extensively researched piece on the figure of Jay Gatsby is Horst Kruse's "The Real Jay Gatsby: Max von Gerlach, F. Scott Fitzgerald, and the Compositional History of *The Great Gatsby.*" Bruccoli explores the same topic in " 'How Are You and the Family Old Sport?' Gerlach and Gatsby," whereas Joseph Corso in "One Not-Forgotten Summer Night: Sources for Fictional Symbols of American Character in *The Great Gatsby*" focuses on models for Dan Cody as well as Gatsby and, more briefly, for the Buchanans and the owl-eyed man. John B. Humma's "Edward Russell Thomas: The Prototype for *Gatsby*'s Tom Buchanan?" cites parallels between Thomas and his wife (later to become Mrs. Cole Porter) and the Buchanans.

Criticism

Collections

There are numerous collections of material on *The Great Gatsby.* The only collection composed entirely of previously unpublished essays, Bruccoli's *New Essays on* The Great Gatsby, presents five excellent studies, by Richard Anderson, Roger Lewis, Susan Resneck Parr, Kenneth E. Eble, and George Garrett. Garrett's "Fire and Freshness: A Matter of Style in *The Great Gatsby*" is especially noteworthy for its acute observations on what sets *Gatsby* apart from other novels, the unique poetic quality of its style. The earliest collection of reprinted pieces was Ernest Lockridge's *Twentieth Century Interpretations of* The Great Gatsby, and the most recent is Katie de Koster's *Readings on* The Great Gatsby. Other collections of this kind are three volumes of Harold Bloom's massive Chelsea House project—*F. Scott Fitzgerald's* The Great Gatsby, *Major Literary Characters: Gatsby*, and *F. Scott Fitzgerald's* The Great Gatsby—and Henry Claridge's comprehensive but expensive (and thus difficult to find) four-volume *F. Scott Fitzgerald: Critical Assessments* (vols. 2 and 4 contain reprinted essays on and reviews of *Gatsby*). In his edition of *The Great Gatsby*, unfortunately not available in the United States, Michael Nowlin adds to the text of the novel his own extremely useful introduction, excerpts from Fitzgerald's 1920s letters, some contemporary reviews, advertisements of the day, and a selection of essays from the 1920s that illustrates the spirit of the Jazz Age and the racial issues raised by the novel.

Scott Donaldson's *Critical Essays on F. Scott Fitzgerald's* The Great Gatsby assembles some of the best essays of the 1970s and early 1980s, adds five new pieces, and reprints letters to and from Fitzgerald about *Gatsby*.

Frederick J. Hoffman's The Great Gatsby: A Study was the first collection to combine reprinted essays on the novel with relevant selections from Fitzgerald's other writings and background materials such as an excerpt from Joseph Conrad and a profile of Arnold Rothstein, generally thought to be the model for Meyer Wolfsheim; Henry Dan Piper's Fitzgerald's The Great Gatsby: The Novel, the Critics, the Background is a similarly eclectic volume. More recent collections of this kind are Nicolas Tredell's F. Scott Fitzgerald: The Great Gatsby, which skillfully imbeds excerpts from reviews, periodical articles, and book sections in a narrative of the novel's critical reception and interpretation from 1925 to 1996; Dalton Gross and Maryjean Gross's Understanding The Great Gatsby: A Student Casebook to Issues, Sources, and Historical Documents, which emphasizes the historical, social, and economic context of the 1920s by reprinting newspaper stories on such subjects as the Black Sox scandal, Texas Guinan, and the changing role of women during the decade; and an extraordinarily varied and comprehensive gathering of relevant documents edited by Bruccoli, F. Scott Fitzgerald's The Great Gatsby: A Literary Reference, which emphasizes the background of the novel's composition (with facsimiles of the manuscript and the galleys) and offers excerpts from the Perkins-Fitzgerald correspondence and a selection of contemporary reviews combined with a more modest selection of post-1925 commentary.

Full-Length Studies

Among the several good books on Gatsby is The Great Gatsby: The Limits of Wonder, by Richard Lehan, a longtime leading Fitzgerald scholar-critic who is also widely conversant with modern American literature generally. His book combines close textual analysis of the novel's style with an examination of the social, political, and economic contexts of its time, as well as its critical reception. Unlike Lehan, Ronald Berman had never published a word about Fitzgerald before the appearance of his two books on Gatsby (which may account for his fresh perspectives on this much-studied work), The Great Gatsby and Modern Times and The Great Gatsby and Fitzgerald's World of Ideas. The former places Fitzgerald's novel in the context of such mass culture items of the 1920s as newspaper columns and editorials, advertisements, and popular fiction, whereas the latter reads Gatsby in the light of what Berman calls "the firsthand cultural and intellectual sources" from which its author drew—principally, William James, H. L. Mencken, George Santayana, Josiah Royce, Walter Lippmann, and John Dewey (2).

Two books on Gatsby focus on it as a culmination of Fitzgerald's fiction before 1925. Robert Emmet Long's The Achieving of The Great Gatsby: F. Scott Fitzgerald, 1920–1925 begins by looking at how Fitzgerald's first two novels, This Side of Paradise and The Beautiful and Damned, and his early short stories lead thematically and stylistically to Gatsby and examines in detail the Conradian influences on the novel. The second half of Long's study provides a welcome close textual analysis of the novel's intricate stylistic and thematic patterns and places *Gatsby* in the culture of the 1920s. Robert Roulston and Helen H. Roulston, in *The Winding Road to West Egg: The Artistic Development of F. Scott Fitzgerald*, focus on Fitzgerald's first two novels and early short stories as revealing the evolution of the themes and techniques that would be present in *Gatsby*.

As its title suggests, Thomas A. Pendleton's *I'm Sorry about the Clock: Chronology, Composition, and Narrative Technique in* The Great Gatsby is concerned with and critical of Fitzgerald's handling of the novel's time sequences. John S. Whitley's *F. Scott Fitzgerald:* The Great Gatsby and Stephen Matterson's The Great Gatsby are both brief general introductions to the novel by British scholar-critics.

Chapters on *Gatsby* in Books about Fitzgerald

Useful commentary on *Gatsby* can be found in the chapters devoted to the novel in the major full-length critical studies of Fitzgerald. Besides Mizener's *The Far Side of Paradise*, these include James E. Miller, Jr.'s *F. Scott Fitzgerald: His Art and His Technique*, Sergio Perosa's *The Art of F. Scott Fitzgerald*, Henry Dan Piper's *F. Scott Fitzgerald: A Critical Portrait*, Richard D. Lehan's *F. Scott Fitzgerald and the Craft of Fiction*, Robert Sklar's *F. Scott Fitzgerald: The Last Laocoön*, Milton Hindus's *F. Scott Fitzgerald: An Introduction and Interpretation*, Milton R. Stern's *The Golden Moment: The Novels of F. Scott Fitzgerald*, John F. Callahan's *The Illusions of a Nation: Myth and History in the Novels of F. Scott Fitzgerald*, the revised edition of Kenneth Eble's *F. Scott Fitzgerald*, Joan M. Allen's *Candles and Carnival Lights: The Catholic Sensibility of F. Scott Fitzgerald*, Thomas J. Stavola's *Scott Fitzgerald: Crisis in an American Identity*, Brian Way's *F. Scott Fitzgerald and the Art of Social Fiction*, John B. Chambers's *The Novels of F. Scott Fitzgerald*, Andrew Hook's *F. Scott Fitzgerald*, and Michael Nowlin's *F. Scott Fitzgerald's Racial Angles and the Business of Literary Greatness*.

Contemporary Reviews

The first critical attention *The Great Gatsby* received were the newspaper and magazine reviews that greeted its publication in 1925. Some of these have been reprinted in the edited collections of reprinted commentary mentioned above; another useful resource is Jackson R. Bryer's collection *F. Scott Fitzgerald: The Critical Reception*, which contains the texts of forty-nine such reviews. G. Thomas Tanselle and Bryer, in *"The Great Gatsby*: A Study in Literary Reputation," provide a summary and analysis of the novel's reception and reputation between 1925 and the early 1960s, with an emphasis on the contemporary reviews.

Periodical Essays and Book Sections

Any attempt to organize the literally hundreds of essays and book sections on *Gatsby* is probably at best arbitrary and at worst foolish. Nonetheless, what follows is such an attempt, with a concomitant effort to highlight some of the most worthwhile pieces in each category.

Four of the very best essays on *Gatsby* are excellent places to begin a study of the novel: Arthur Mizener's "F. Scott Fitzgerald, *The Great Gatsby*," Kenneth Eble's "*The Great Gatsby*," James E. Miller, Jr.'s "Fitzgerald's *Gatsby*: The World as Ash Heap," and Norman Holmes Pearson's "Reading a Novel—*The Great Gatsby*." In her *Critical Theory Today: A User-Friendly Guide*, Lois Tyson provides brief essays on *The Great Gatsby* to illustrate each of the ten theoretical approaches to literary study she covers—psychoanalytic; Marxist; feminist; New Critical; reader-response; structuralist; deconstruction; new historicist and cultural; lesbian, gay, and queer; and postcolonial and African American.

A prevailing approach to *Gatsby*, seeing it as a criticism of the American success myth and stressing its universal themes and appeal, began with Lionel Trilling's chapter on Fitzgerald in his *Liberal Imagination* and can also be found in such important early essays as Marius Bewley's "Scott Fitzgerald's Criticism of America," Robert Ornstein's "Scott Fitzgerald's Fable of East and West," John Henry Raleigh's "Fitzgerald's *The Great Gatsby*" and "F. Scott Fitzgerald's *The Great Gatsby*: Legendary Bases and Allegorical Significances," and in the sections on *Gatsby* in Richard Chase's *The American Novel and Its Tradition*, Frederick J. Hoffman's *The Twenties*, John W. Aldridge's *After the Lost Generation*, and Wright Morris's *The Territory Ahead*.

Later good examples of this approach are Michael Millgate's "Scott Fitzgerald as Social Novelist: Statement and Technique in 'The Great Gatsby,'" Charles Thomas Samuels's "The Greatness of 'Gatsby,'" Kermit W. Moyer's "*The Great Gatsby*: Fitzgerald's Meditation on American History," Brian M. Barbour's "*The Great Gatsby* and the American Past," Ross Posnock's " 'A New World, Material without Being Real': Fitzgerald's Critique of Capitalism in *The Great Gatsby*," John Rohrkemper's "The Allusive Past: Historical Perspective in *The Great Gatsby*," Arnold Weinstein's "Fiction as Greatness: The Case of *Gatsby*," Joyce A. Rowe's chapter on *Gatsby* in her *Equivocal Endings in Classic American Novels*, Paul Giles's "Aquinas vs. Weber: Ideological Esthetics in *The Great Gatsby*," Rollo May's "Gatsby and the American Dream," John T. Irwin's "Compensating Visions: *The Great Gatsby*," Lois Tyson's "The Romance of the Commodity: The Cancellation of Identity in F. Scott Fitzgerald's *Great Gatsby*," Walter Benn Michaels's pages on *Gatsby* in his *Our America: Nativism, Modernism, and Pluralism*, Mitchell Breitwieser's "Jazz Fractures: F. Scott Fitzgerald and Epochal Representation," Scott Donaldson's "Possessions in *The Great Gatsby*," and John Lukacs's "*The Great Gatsby*? Yes, a Historical Novel."

The Great Gatsby has been linked to hundreds of other literary texts, ranging from Chaucer's *Troilus and Cresyde* and Milton's *Paradise Lost* to Raymond Chandler's *The Long Goodbye* and Theodore Dreiser's *An American Tragedy*. Some of these essays suggest influence; others merely cite parallels. Robert Roulston's "Something Borrowed, Something New: A Discussion of Literary Influences on *The Great Gatsby*" is a good summary of possible influences, and Lehan's "*The Great Gatsby* and Its Sources" is also useful. Because Fitzgerald acknowledged his indebtedness to John Keats, to Joseph Conrad, and to T. S. Eliot's *The Waste Land* and other Christian and pagan myths, pieces on these connections are both the most numerous and the most persuasive of the influence studies. For good work on the Keats-*Gatsby* links see Dan McCall's " 'The Self-Same Song That Found a Path': Keats and *The Great Gatsby*," George Monteiro's "James Gatz and John Keats," and Joseph B. Wagner's "*Gatsby* and John Keats: Another Version." The novel's debts to Conrad have been assessed by Robert Emmet Long in *The Achieving of* The Great Gatsby, by R. W. Stallman in "Conrad and *The Great Gatsby*," by Jerome Thale in "The Narrator as Hero," by Andrew Crosland in "*The Great Gatsby* and *The Secret Agent*," by John Skinner in "The Oral and the Written: Kurtz and Gatsby Revisited," by Peter L. Hays and Pamela Demory in "*Nostromo* and *The Great Gatsby*," and by Peter Mallios in "Undiscovering the Country: Conrad, Fitzgerald, and Meta-national Form."

Worthwhile early essays on the *Gatsby–Waste Land* connections are Philip Young's "Scott Fitzgerald's Waste Land," John W. Bicknell's "The Waste Land of F. Scott Fitzgerald," Robert Shulman's "Myth, Mr. Eliot, and the Comic Novel," and Letha Audhuy's "*The Waste Land*: Myth and Symbolism in *The Great Gatsby*." Douglas Taylor's "*The Great Gatsby*: Style and Myth," Wilfrid Louis Guerin's "Christian Myth and Naturalistic Deity: *The Great Gatsby*," Jeffrey Steinbrink's " 'Boats against the Current': Mortality and the Myth of Renewal in *The Great Gatsby*," Bruce Michelson's "The Myth of Gatsby," and D. G. Kehl and Allene Cooper's "Sangria in the Sangreal: *The Great Gatsby* as Grail Quest" are good articles on the novel's mythic elements. The definitive work on this topic, however, is Robert J. Emmitt's "Love, Death and Resurrection in *The Great Gatsby*," which examines closely and with great insight Fitzgerald's uses of the Grail legend, the wasteland myth, and "ancient Semitic and Egyptian resurrection myths."

Other essays compare *Gatsby* to a variety of literary texts: Norman Friedman's "Versions of Form in Fiction: 'Great Expectations' and 'The Great Gatsby,' " Steven Curry and Peter L. Hays's "Fitzgerald's *Vanity Fair*," Lawrence Thornton's "Ford Madox Ford and *The Great Gatsby*," Robert E. Morsberger's "The Romantic Ancestry of *The Great Gatsby*," Leslie F. Chard III's "Outward Forms and the Inner Life: Coleridge and Gatsby," Robert Roulston's "Traces of *Tono-Bungay* in *The Great Gatsby*," Kermit Vanderbilt's "James, Fitzgerald, and the American Self-Image," Leon Howard's "Raymond Chandler's Not-So-Great Gatsby," Tom Quirk's "Fitzgerald and Cather: *The*

Great Gatsby," Deborah Davis Schlacks's "Revising a Tribute: *The Great Gatsby*," Clyde Hermansson's " 'An Elusive Rhythm': *The Great Gatsby* Reclaims *Troilus and Criseyde*," André Le Vot's "Fitzgerald and Proust: Connoisseurs of Kisses," Robert Seguin's "*Ressentiment* and the Social Poetics of *The Great Gatsby*: Fitzgerald Reads Cather," D. G. Kehl's "Writing the Long Desire: The Function of *Sehnsucht* in *The Great Gatsby* and *Look Homeward, Angel*," James Plath's " 'What's in a Name, Old Sport?': Kipling's *The Story of the Gadsbys* as a Possible Source for Fitzgerald's *The Great Gatsby*," Horst Kruse's "*The Great Gatsby*: A View from Kant's Window—Transatlantic Crosscurrents," Clare Eby's "Of Gold Molars and Golden Girls: Fitzgerald's Reading of Norris," and J'aimé L. Sanders's "Discovering the Source of Gatsby's Greatness: Nick's Eulogy for a 'Great' Kierkegaardian Knight."

Gatsby is commonly linked with the two other major novelists of Fitzgerald's generation, Ernest Hemingway and William Faulkner. The Hemingway-*Gatsby* connection has usually been made with *The Sun Also Rises*—by Paul Lauter in "Plato's Stepchildren, Gatsby and Cohn," by Sister Mary Kathryn Grant in "The Search for Celebration in *The Sun Also Rises* and *The Great Gatsby*," by Peter L. Hays in "Hemingway and Fitzgerald," by M. A. Klug in "Horns of Manichaeus: The Conflict of Art and Experience in *The Great Gatsby* and *The Sun Also Rises*," and by James Plath in "*The Sun Also Rises* as 'a Greater Gatsby': 'Isn't It Pretty to Think So?' " Jacqueline Vaught Brogan's "Strange Fruits in *The Garden of Eden*: 'The Mysticism of Money,' *The Great Gatsby*—and *A Moveable Feast*" relates Fitzgerald's novel to the two Hemingway texts and to the expatriate Harold Loeb's essay "The Mysticism of Money."

The *Gatsby*-Faulkner relationship has been discussed by Cleanth Brooks in "The American 'Innocence' in James, Fitzgerald, and Faulkner," by F. A. Rodewald in "Faulkner's Possible Use of *The Great Gatsby*," and by Fran James Polek in "From Renegade to Solid Citizen: The Extraordinary Individual in the Community," who all look at *Gatsby* and *Absalom, Absalom!* Two essays linking *Gatsby* with both Hemingway and Faulkner are William T. Stafford's "Benjy Compson, Jake Barnes, and Nick Carraway—Replication in Three 'Innocent' American Narrators of the 1920s" and Ronald Gervais's "The Trains of Their Youth: The Aesthetics of Homecoming in 'The Great Gatsby,' 'The Sun Also Rises,' and 'The Sound and the Fury.' "

Of *Gatsby*'s characters by far the most attention has been directed at Nick Carraway and his role as the narrator of the novel. Early pieces include Thomas A. Hanzo's "The Theme and the Narrator of 'The Great Gatsby,' " E. Fred Carlisle's "The Triple Vision of Nick Carraway," and Peter Lisca's "Nick Carraway and the Imagery of Disorder." Gary J. Scrimgeour's provocatively titled "Against *The Great Gatsby*" was one of the earliest articles to question Nick's credibility and spurred much of the subsequent debate on the issue. That debate, the most contentious issue in *Gatsby* criticism, can be surveyed by looking at Oliver H. Evans's " 'A Sort of Moral Attention': The Narrator of *The Great*

Gatsby," Albert E. Elmore's "Nick Carraway's Self-Introduction," Ruth Betsy Tenenbaum's " 'The Gray-Turning Gold-Turning Consciousness' of Nick Carraway," Colin S. Cass's " 'Pandered in Whispers': Narrative Reliability in *The Great Gatsby*," Susan Resneck Parr's "Individual Responsibility in *The Great Gatsby*," Scott Donaldson's "The Trouble with Nick," Kent Cartwright's "Nick Carraway as an Unreliable Narrator," Ami M. Krumrey's "Nick Carraway's Process of Individuation," and James Phelan's "Reexamining Reality: The Multiple Functions of Nick Carraway."

Jay Gatsby has also been the subject of several essays: Giles Mitchell's "The Great Narcissist: A Study of Fitzgerald's Jay Gatsby," Philip Castille's "Jay Gatsby: The Smuggler as Frontier Hero," Thomas H. Pauly's "Gatsby as Gangster," Stephen Brauer's "Jay Gatsby and the Prohibition Gangster as Businessman," and Meredith Goldsmith's "White Skin, White Mask: Passing, Posing, and Performing in *The Great Gatsby*."

Judith Fetterley's "*The Great Gatsby*: Fitzgerald's *Droit de Seigneur*" is a feminist reading of the novel that calls Daisy Buchanan a "scapegoat" and an example of Fitzgerald's "hostility to women"; her reading is controversial but provocative and informed. Other good essays on Daisy are Leland S. Person, Jr.'s " 'Herstory' and Daisy Buchanan," Sarah Beebe Fryer's "Beneath the Mask: The Plight of Daisy Buchanan," Joan S. Korenman's " 'Only Her Hairdresser . . .': Another Look at Daisy Buchanan," and Glenn Settle's "Fitzgerald's Daisy: The Siren Voice."

The three substantial essays on Tom Buchanan are Robert Roulston's "Tom Buchanan: Patrician in Motley," Christian K. Messenger's "Tom Buchanan and the Demise of the Ivy League Athletic Hero," and Alberto Lena's "Deceitful Traces of Power: An Analysis of the Decadence of Tom Buchanan in *The Great Gatsby*." Myrtle Wilson is the subject of Barry Edward Gross's "Jay Gatsby and Myrtle Wilson: A Kinship," E. C. Bufkin's "A Pattern of Parallel and Double: The Function of Myrtle in *The Great Gatsby*," and Michel Viel's "Les lectures de Mrs. Wilson dans *The Great Gatsby*." The figure of Meyer Wolfsheim and how he reflects Fitzgerald's view of Jews is discussed in Josephine Z. Kopf's "Meyer Wolfsheim and Robert Cohn: A Study of a Jewish Type and Stereotype"; George Wilson is the subject of G. I. Hughes's "Sub Specie Doctor T. J. Eckleburg: Man and God in 'The Great Gatsby' "; and Dan Cody is analyzed in Alice Hall Petry's "James Gatz's Mentor: Traces of Warren G. Harding in *The Great Gatsby*."

The most frequently discussed of the novel's motifs and symbol patterns have been Doctor T. J. Eckleburg's eyes, color imagery, Gatsby's guest list, and automobiles. Doctor Eckleburg's eyes have been thoroughly examined in Tom Burnam's "The Eyes of Dr. Eckleburg: A Re-examination of 'The Great Gatsby,' " Milton Hindus's "The Mysterious Eyes of Dr. T. J. Eckleburg," Robert F. McDonnell's "Eggs and Eyes in *The Great Gatsby*," and Sanford Pinsker's "Seeing *The Great Gatsby* Eye to Eye." Daniel J. Schneider's "Color-Symbolism in *The Great Gatsby*" is one of the earliest and still one of the best studies of the topic, along with A. E. Elmore's "Color and Cosmos in *The Great Gatsby.*" Gatsby's guest list has been analyzed by Lottie R. Crim and Neal B. Houston in "The Catalogue of Names in *The Great Gatsby*," Robert Emmet Long in "The Vogue of Gatsby's Guest List," and Ruth Prigozy in "Gatsby's Guest List and Fitzgerald's Technique of Naming."

The automobile, boat, and train imagery in *Gatsby* have been traced in Rita Gollin's "The Automobiles of *The Great Gatsby*," John J. McNally's "Boats and Automobiles in *The Great Gatsby*: Symbols of Drift and Death," Laurence E. MacPhee's "*The Great Gatsby*'s 'Romance of Motoring': Nick Carraway and Jordan Baker," Kenneth S. Knodt's "The Gathering Darkness: A Study of the Effects of Technology in *The Great Gatsby*," Irving S. Saposnik's "The Passion and the Life: Technology as Pattern in *The Great Gatsby*," and Lauraleigh O'Meara's "Medium of Exchange: The Blue Coupé Dialogue in *The Great Gatsby*."

The houses in *Gatsby* are the subject of Richard Cohen's "The Inessential Houses of *The Great Gatsby*," W. T. Lhamon, Jr.'s "The Essential Houses of *The Great Gatsby*," and Hilton Anderson's "From the Wasteland to East Egg: Houses in *The Great Gatsby*." Sports as a motif in the novel, with particular emphasis on baseball, has occupied the attention of Christian K. Messenger in *Sport and the Spirit of Play in American Fiction: Hawthorne to Faulkner*, Michael Oriard in *Sporting with the Gods: The Rhetoric of Play and Game in American Culture*, Jarom Lyle McDonald in *Sports, Narrative, and Nation in the Fiction of F. Scott Fitzgerald*, John A. Lauricella in "The Black Sox Signature Baseball in *The Great Gatsby*," Richard Lessa in " 'Our Nervous, Sporadic Games': Sports in *The Great Gatsby*," and Robert Johnson, Jr., in "Say It Ain't So, Jay: Fitzgerald's Use of Baseball in *The Great Gatsby*."

Various aspects of gender and sexual issues in *Gatsby* have increasingly interested scholars and critics since the 1970s. The best of these essays are Georges-Michel Sarotte's "Francis Scott Fitzgerald: Self-Virilization and Its Failure," Patricia Pacey Thornton's "Sexual Roles in *The Great Gatsby*," Keath Fraser's "Another Reading of *The Great Gatsby*," A. S. Paulson's "*The Great Gatsby*: Oral Aggression and Splitting," Philip Sipiora's "Vampires of the Heart: Gender Trouble in *The Great Gatsby*," Edward Wasiolek's "The Sexual Drama of Nick and Gatsby," and Frances Kerr's "Feeling 'Half-Feminine': Modernism and the Politics of Emotion in *The Great Gatsby*."

Among the studies of other motifs and patterns in *Gatsby* are Howard S. Babb's " 'The Great Gatsby' and the Grotesque," David Stouck's "White Sheep on Fifth Avenue: *The Great Gatsby* as Pastoral," Peter L. Hays's "*Gatsby*, Myth, Fairy Tale, and Legend," John L. Kuhnle's "*The Great Gatsby* as Pastoral Elegy," Janet Giltrow and David Stouck's "Pastoral Mode and Language in *The Great Gatsby*," Lawrence Jay Dessner's "Photography and *The Great Gatsby*," Laura Barrett's " 'Material without Being Real': Photography and the End of Reality in *The Great Gatsby*," B. W. Wilson's "The Theatrical Motif in *The Great Gatsby*," and Kim Moreland's "Music in *The Great Gatsby* and *The Great Gatsby* as Music."

Victor A. Doyno's seminal essay, "Patterns in *The Great Gatsby*," inaugurated serious consideration of the narrative structure and style of the novel its author called "intricately patterned" (Bruccoli and Duggan 112) and "a consciously artistic achievment" (*F. Scott Fitzgerald: A Life* 67). Studies of *Gatsby*'s narrative structure include Dan Seiters's "*The Great Gatsby*," Ernest H. Lockridge's "F. Scott Fitzgerald's *Trompe l'Oeil* and *The Great Gatsby*'s Buried Plot," A. E. Elmore's "*The Great Gatsby* as Well-Wrought Urn," Barbara Gerber Sanders's "Structural Imagery in *The Great Gatsby*: Metaphor and Matrix," Dan Coleman's " 'A World Complete in Itself': *Gatsby*'s Elegaic Narration," and Richard Lehan's "*The Great Gatsby*—The Text as Construct: Narrative Knots and Narrative Unfolding."

Worthy stylistic studies include W. J. Harvey's "Theme and Texture in *The Great Gatsby*," Barbara Hochman's "Disembodied Voices and Narrating Bodies in *The Great Gatsby*," Janet Giltrow and David Stouck's "Style as Politics in *The Great Gatsby*," F. H. Langman's "Style and Shape in *The Great Gatsby*," Peter Messent's "Speech Representation, Focalization, and Narration in *The Great Gatsby*," Leonard A. Podis's " 'The Unreality of Reality': Metaphor in *The Great Gatsby*," Ruth E. Roberts's "Nonverbal Communication in *The Great Gatsby*," Guy Owen's "Imagery and Meaning in 'The Great Gatsby,' " and Jackson R. Bryer's "Style as Meaning in *The Great Gatsby*: Notes toward a New Approach."

Some of the best work on *Gatsby* has focused on close readings of specific sections of the novel, analyses that convincingly demonstrate the extent of Fitzgerald's artistry. Edwin Moses's "Tragic Inevitability in *The Great Gatsby*" explicates the first chapter, Christiane Johnson's "*The Great Gatsby*: The Final Vision" analyzes the famous last page, and Joan S. Korenman's "A View from the (Queensboro) Bridge" looks at the section of chapter 4 describing Nick and Gatsby's trip across the bridge. Bruce R. Stark's "The Intricate Pattern in *The Great Gatsby*" demonstrates, by looking at a seemingly disparate assortment of scenes and images, how "the words in *The Great Gatsby* participate in a multitude of complex patterns that link images, anomalous minor scenes, and even rather large units to one another in a variety of complex and subtle ways" (59).

The Great Gatsby has been adapted into a Broadway play, three Hollywood films, and numerous television versions. The best account of the play and the three films is Alan Margolies's "Novel to Play to Film: Four Versions of *The Great Gatsby*." Wheeler Winston Dixon's "The Three Film Versions of *The Great Gatsby*" is another useful essay.

The Great Gatsby in the Age of the Internet: Useful Web Sites for Instructors

Nancy P. VanArsdale

The promise of Web-based resources for instructors of *The Great Gatsby* was first realized in *F. Scott Fitgerald Centenary*, a site that drew on the Matthew J. and Arlyn Bruccoli Collection housed by the University of South Carolina. This site still exists, with updated entries, and is an outstanding starting point for students and instructors seeking relevant Web sites. Unfortunately, many general searches on *The Great Gatsby* lead students to exploitative sites attempting to sell term papers or abridged study guides. A number of sites devoted to the novel have been created by students as class projects, by teachers sharing lesson plans, or by other self-described authorities on Fitzgerald. While it can be interesting for students to peruse such sites, savvy teachers should remind their classes to question the credibility and the quality of information on them. During a unit on the novel, I find it useful to spend a portion of a class period displaying to students some of the quality sites listed below. Many contain rich visual and audio material that helps students and instructors develop an understanding of the cultural context of the Jazz Age. Some provide useful information or links to relevant texts, from primary texts of Fitzgerald's fiction to critical resources.

The F. Scott Fitgerald Centenary
  (http://www.sc.edu.fitzgerald/index.html)
Created in 1996 in honor of the hundredth anniversary of the birth of F. Scott Fitzgerald, the site shares the remarkable artifacts and resources of the Matthew J. and Arlyn Bruccoli Collection located at the University of South Carolina. The site features audio clips of Fitzgerald reading Keats's "Ode to a Nightingale" and passages from Shakespeare, as well as a brief film clip of Fitzgerald at a writing table. Photographs of objects such as Fitzgerald's flask and the image of the original dust jacket of the first edition of *The Great Gatsby* and other books can also be viewed. Text components of the site include a fundamental chronology of Fitzgerald's life and substantive critical articles.

The F. Scott Fitzgerald Society
  (http://www.fitzgeraldsociety.org/)
Another ideal starting point for Internet resources, the official site of the F. Scott Fitzgerald Society publishes an extensive bibliography, teaching resources, and links to digital resources. In addition to membership information about the society and its upcoming conferences, the site offers a number of links related to teaching specific works. Teachers of *The Great Gatsby* might be interested in the link to the painting by El Greco mentioned by Nick Carraway in the last chapter. Student researchers will find links to the F. Scott Fitzgerald Papers and the Zelda

Fitzgerald Papers at Princeton University, the *New York Times*, and the University of Memphis library. The site also includes links to online scholarly articles, professional reviews, other related professional societies, and cultural and historical background Web sites, a few of which are described below.

American Writers II: "F. Scott Fitzgerald: *The Great Gatsby*"
  (http://www.americanwriters.org/writers/fitzgerald.asp)
From March to July 2002, C-SPAN aired the series American Writers II: The Twentieth Century as part of a multiyear programming effort to highlight the lives and contributions of the great writers and thinkers who have shaped American culture since the seventeenth century, beginning with William Bradford. The companion Web site enables users to watch the program with *RealPlayer*, easily downloadable at the site. The program about F. Scott Fitzgerald lasts two hours. The site suggests lesson plans related to *The Great Gatsby*, the 1920s, and modern America. Edited clips, typically just a few minutes in length, are correlated with themes in the lesson plan and easily shown in a classroom. In the program about *The Great Gatsby*, the C-SPAN moderator interviews Matthew J. Bruccoli, a prominent scholar and leading expert on Fitzgerald. The Web site has brief clips of the interview, when Bruccoli summarizes the plot of the novel or when he responds to a question from an audience member about the device of the first-person narrator (the original show included a live interactive session with audience members who phoned in their questions). The companion site also has video archives of programs featuring other commentaries about Fitzgerald from scholars including Scott Donaldson and Dave Page, as well as the actor and author George Plimpton.

Jazz Age Culture, Part One
  (http://faculty.pittstate.edu/~knichols/jazzage.html)
Created by Kathleen L. Nichols, this Web site helps students of *The Great Gatsby* develop an overview of the emergence of jazz as a musical genre and the flapper as a cultural phenomenon. Links include magazine articles and illustrations featuring flapper fashion, background information on Prohibition, advertisements from the 1920s, and essays on the images of women. There are also links to music sites that play jazz from the period and to sites with background on the development of jazz in Harlem and other parts of the country.

The Jazz Age: Flapper Culture and Style
  (http://www.geocities.com/flapper_culture/)
Like Jazz Age Culture, this site gives students the opportunity to see images of flappers and to read about prototypical flappers. The site presents photographs and examines the life of the silent film star Louise Brooks. Easy links to period magazine articles are also pertinent. Students are often intrigued by the 1922 article from *Outlook* magazine entitled "A Flapper's Appeal to Parents."

American Literature on the Web: F. Scott Fitzgerald (1896–1940)
   (http://www.nagasaki-gaigo.ac.jp/ishikawa/amlit/f/fitzgerald20.htm)
A professor at Nagasaki University in Japan, Akihito Ishikawa developed this
site as part of American Literature on the Web, an ambitious project that organizes links to Web resources on classic American writers.

SimonSays.com: F. Scott Fitzgerald
   (http://www.simonsays.com/content/destination.cfm?sid=798&pid=349245)
Created by Simon and Schuster, this commercial site is a central page focused
on F. Scott Fitzgerald. The Image Gallery link features photos of F. Scott
Fitzgerald, starting with a portrait of the author as a three-year-old. Other images show the author with his parents, wife, and child. In addition, there is a
photograph of Fitzgerald's tombstone, with its inscription of the concluding
lines from *The Great Gatsby*.

The Jazz Age
   (http://www.btinternet.com/~dreklind/jazzhome.htm)
R. Richard Savill has compiled links and information on the Jazz Age, including
sound clips of jazz music from the 1920s. This site requires subscription and
log-in information.

The Fitzgeralds
   (http://www.zeldafitzgerald.com/fitzgeralds/index.asp)
This Web site promoting a 2004 production of the musical *Beautiful and
Damned* offers links to background information about the Fitzgeralds, particularly on Zelda. Students are often intrigued to find out how Fitzgerald's original
texts have inspired other writers and artists to create adaptations and new
works of art. The site displays some of Zelda's artwork and quotes passages from
her writing.

The Composition and Publication
of *The Great Gatsby*

James L. W. West III

The Great Gatsby has a fascinating, and very teachable, history of composition. Useful materials are available for study, and they reveal important things about the inception and gestation of the novel. The evidence survives in Fitzgerald's papers at the Princeton University Library: the two most significant documents are a full handwritten draft and a complete set of galley proofs bearing his revisions. Also extant is the correspondence between Fitzgerald and Maxwell E. Perkins, his editor at Charles Scribner's Sons, during the period of composition. All this material has been published in printed texts or in facsimile form; the words and images can be reproduced for lectures, either through photocopying or, more usefully, as slides or digital images. Such illustrated lectures are helpful to students and have important lessons to teach.

Three distinct texts of the novel are available for study: the handwritten draft (The Great Gatsby: *A Facsimile*), an intermediate version called *Trimalchio*, and the first edition of the novel (1925), reedited in 1991 by Cambridge University Press. Also in print is a facsimile of the revised galleys (*Trimalchio by F. Scott Fitzgerald*), which shows the handwritten changes Fitzgerald made when he revised the novel for page proofs.

These three versions of *The Great Gatsby* differ markedly from one another in characterization, mood, and language. By examining selected passages in the three forms, students will learn that the creation of the novel involved much more than spontaneous inspiration. (Some of the prose in the handwritten manuscript, in fact, is rather pedestrian.) The process of composition and revision required much rethinking by the author and a great many hours of restructuring, revising, and polishing. These are useful lessons for undergraduates to learn, since most of them believe that great literary works spring into being fully formed.

Some students will also believe (or have heard) that Fitzgerald was a poor caretaker of his talent and that he had a frivolous attitude toward authorship. A teacher of *The Great Gatsby* should disabuse them of this notion. Fitzgerald did live an irregular personal life, but at the worktable he was a serious professional, and never more so than during the creation of *Gatsby*. The period of its composition was his finest hour as an author, an extended moment during which he combined the magic ingredients of inspiration, talent, and hard work to produce a masterpiece.

Fitzgerald began to plan the composition of this novel in June 1922. He was then working on the proofs of *Tales of the Jazz Age* (published in September 1922), his second collection of short stories, and was living with his wife, Zelda Sayre Fitzgerald, at White Bear Lake in Minnesota, not far from his hometown, St. Paul. At the point of inception, Fitzgerald believed that his new novel would be set in "the middle west and New York of 1885" and would have "a catholic element" (Kuehl and Bryer 61). He labored for short periods on this ur-novel in 1922 and 1923 but never produced a full draft. What he did produce was written in the third person; Nick Carraway had not yet emerged as the narrator.

By spring 1924 he had scrapped his initial conception, salvaging only a short story from the material—"Absolution," published in the *American Mercury* in June 1924 and afterward collected in *All the Sad Young Men* (1926). "Absolution" is one of Fitzgerald's best works of short fiction and can be read as a preamble to *The Great Gatsby*. The story, set in the Midwest and involving a young boy and a Catholic priest, does not resemble *Gatsby* in plot or setting, but it does provide a character—the dreamy, yearning, imaginative Rudolph Miller—who is in many ways a youthful Jay Gatsby, longing for escape from the limited world of his boyhood.

Fitzgerald reconceived his novel during that spring. He and Zelda were then living in Great Neck, Long Island, and he decided to set his narrative in a fictional version of that locale. He based some of his characters on people he knew or had met. Ginevra King, a Chicago socialite with whom he had been infatuated as a teenager, provided a model for Daisy Buchanan (see West). Edith Cummings, an amateur golf champion, was the inspiration for Jordan Baker; Tommy Hitchcock, an investment banker and polo player, was the original for Tom Buchanan; Arnold Rothstein, a famous gambler, provided the template for Meyer Wolfsheim. Fitzgerald had high ambitions for the novel; he told Perkins that he wanted it to be "purely creative work," drawn from "the sustained imagination of a sincere and yet radiant world" (Kuehl and Bryer 70).

Fitzgerald began a handwritten draft of the narrative before he, Zelda, and their daughter, Scottie, moved to Europe that summer, and Fitzgerald continued to compose while living in Saint Raphaël on the French Riviera. By early September, he had completed the handwritten version; he spent the next two months restructuring and revising a succession of typescripts. He also fretted about the title, calling his novel "Trimalchio" for a time, after the ostentatious party-giver in *The Satyricon* of Petronius (*Trimalchio: An Early Version* 190). By 27 October, Fitzgerald was satisfied with the novel and put a final typescript in the transatlantic mail to Perkins.

These two early texts—the handwritten draft and the version submitted to Perkins—are available to teachers and students. The manuscript, which Fitzgerald preserved, was reproduced as The Great Gatsby: *A Facsimile of the Manuscript* in 1973; two thousand copies were printed, and most college and university libraries should have the volume or be able to acquire it on interlibrary loan. This draft shows, among other things, that Fitzgerald first composed the famous coda to the novel ("a fresh green breast of the new world") as the ending of chapter 1 (37–38). We learn also that Tom, Daisy, Gatsby, Jordan, and Nick—on their ill-fated trip to Manhattan—drove initially to the Polo Grounds (181–83). Students will find that the order of chapters was different in this holograph version and that Jay Gatsby was a more sentimental character than he is in the published novel.

The version that Fitzgerald mailed to Perkins from France in October 1924 was set into type, from Fitzgerald's final typescript (no longer extant), at the Scribner's printing plant on West 43rd Street late in December. Galley proofs were pulled, and these long sheets, each one containing enough text to fill three or more pages of the published book, were mailed to Fitzgerald. These are the sheets on which he revised and restructured the narrative. They were reproduced in facsimile in 1990 as The Great Gatsby: *The Revised and Rewritten Galleys* (vol. 3 of *F. Scott Fitzgerald: Manuscripts*). It was the underlying typeset text—which is as close as we can come to the lost typescript—that was published in 2000 as *Trimalchio*.

Before the galleys were mailed to Fitzgerald, he and Perkins corresponded about the novel. In his letters, Fitzgerald revealed some dissatisfaction with certain parts of the book. The necessity of moving the characters from Long Island to Manhattan for the face-off at the Plaza Hotel had involved some strong-arm work with the plot, he feared. He was also unhappy with the action in chapters 6 and 7 and displeased with his portrayal of Jay Gatsby: "*I myself didn't know what Gatsby looked like or was engaged in,*" he later confessed (Kuehl and Bryer 89). Perkins, in his letters, offered some criticisms of his own. He believed that Gatsby, in this penultimate version, was "somewhat vague." "The reader's eyes can never quite focus upon him," he complained. Fitzgerald had withheld the details of Gatsby's past from the reader until very nearly the end of the book; Perkins suggested a different method of character development. Perhaps Gatsby's background could be revealed "bit by bit in the course of actual narrative," he wrote (Kuehl and Bryer 82–84). These letters, and many more communications between the two men, appear in John Kuehl and Jackson R. Bryer's edition, *Dear Scott / Dear Max* (1971), a volume that repays close study by teachers. The quotations and summary above are only suggestive.

Fitzgerald took the criticisms from Perkins to heart, combining them with his own sense of what the novel needed. The result was a thorough revision of the text on the galley sheets. Fitzgerald rewrote chapters 6 and 7 entirely; he moved much material about Gatsby's past from the latter parts of the book into earlier chapters; he also added passages to account for (or at least hint at) the sources of Gatsby's money. He polished the text extensively, trimming out a few paragraphs that were not up to the mark and adding the famous description of Gatsby's smile in chapter 3 (48). This revision resulted in the same novel—and yet a different novel. Reading the two texts is like listening to two versions of the same work of music, one played in the key of C and the other in the more difficult key of F-sharp, each version with its distinctive structure and progression of themes, each adorned with similar (but not identical) leitmotifs and signature passages.

Fitzgerald's revisions had a strong effect on character and theme. Nick Carraway is more likable in the revised version, less snobbish and less obviously in control of the narrative. His relationship with Jordan Baker recedes from view, and we are not so conscious of their complicity in the affair between Daisy and Gatsby. The confrontation between Tom and Gatsby at the Plaza Hotel is presented differently (Gatsby is more thoroughly defeated), and the last party at Gatsby's—which began as a masquerade affair in *Trimalchio*—is entirely rewritten. Most important, the unfolding of Jay Gatsby's character is executed in a wholly different way. In *Trimalchio*, he remains shadowy and mysterious until almost the end of the book. In *Gatsby*, we begin to learn about him earlier; then more information is added, a little at a time, as we go along. As a consequence, the revelations about his past, late in the novel, come as less of a surprise.

Teachers of *The Great Gatsby* will almost surely not wish to assign both versions of the novel to be read by all members of a class, but they should read and be familiar with both *Trimalchio* and *Gatsby* to be able to explain to students the differences between the two texts. Teachers can assign both versions to be read by a team of three or four students. These students can give a joint oral report, then generate individual term papers of substance from what they have learned. Another good exercise is to assign a report on the chapter entitled "Trimalchio's Feast" from a translation of *The Satyricon* of Petronius. This account of domestic revelry from the reign of the emperor Nero, set in the house of a wealthy former slave and narrated by a character named Encolpius (who is eerily similar to Nick), was one of Fitzgerald's earliest inspirations for *The Great Gatsby*.

A fruitful project, for both teacher and student, is to read the short fiction that surrounds *The Great Gatsby*—that is, a selected group of stories written by Fitzgerald before and after he composed the novel. Fitzgerald regarded his short stories as opportunities to experiment with characters, plots, and themes that he would later reuse in his novels. Thus, in a handful of stories contiguous to *Gatsby*, one finds much material that has been reworked for the novel. "Absolution" has already been mentioned; students can also be sent to "Rags Martin-Jones and the Pr-nce of W-les" (1924) and "Love in the Night" (1924) for plot and character parallels (*Short Stories* 273–88, 302–16). In "Winter Dreams" (1922) and " 'The Sensible Thing' " (1924), they will find what amount to trial versions of *Gatsby* (*Short Stories* 217–36, 289–301). For a first-person narrator in the Nick Carraway mode, they should read "The Rich Boy" (1926), one of the finest stories Fitzgerald ever produced (*Short Stories* 317–49).

An intriguing exercise is to review the various titles that Fitzgerald considered for *The Great Gatsby*. What did each title have to offer? Fitzgerald worried about choosing the right title throughout the composition of the novel and was never really satisfied with the title under which the book was published. Among his working titles were "Trimalchio," "Trimalchio in West Egg," "Gold-Hatted Gatsby," "The High-Bouncing Lover," "On the Road to West Egg," and simply "Gatsby" (Kuehl and Bryer 81, 85). T. S. Eliot scholars sometimes amuse themselves by speculating about what would have been the fate of *The Waste*

Land had it been published under an early working title: "He Do the Police in Different Voices" (Eliot, The Waste Land: *A Facsimile* 4, 10). What if *The Great Gatsby* had been given Fitzgerald's final choice: "Under the Red, White and Blue" (Bruccoli and Duggan 153)?

This last exercise demonstrates to students how accomplished Fitzgerald was at revising his prose and, in particular, how sensitive his ear was for dialogue. Below are three passages: the first from the manuscript, the second from the unrevised galley proofs, and the third from the first edition. These are the lines in which Jay Gatsby utters his famous comment about Daisy's voice. Gatsby, Nick, and Tom are standing in the driveway outside the Buchanan house in East Egg; Daisy and Jordan are inside, gathering their belongings for the trip into Manhattan. Here is the passage from the handwritten manuscript:

> "Shall we take anything to drink?" called Daisy from an upper window.
> "I'll get some whiskey," answered Tom. He went inside. Gatsby turned to me, his eyes glittering with happiness.
> "She loves you," I agreed, "That voice is full of wonder."
> "It's full of money."   (The Great Gatsby: *A Facsimile* 169)

The sense is not quite right. Gatsby's happiness is not accounted for, and there is a non sequitur in Nick's line: with what or whom is he agreeing? Daisy's voice, to Nick, is only full of "wonder," a vague noun, and Gatsby's response—"It's full of money"—is blunt, flat, unprepared for.

Here is the same passage after Fitzgerald had revised it. This quotation is from the version Fitzgerald submitted to Perkins in October 1924, which was typeset in the galleys:

> "Shall we take anything to drink?" called Daisy from an upper window.
> "I'll get some whiskey," answered Tom. He went inside. Gatsby turned to me, his voice trembling:
> "I can't stand this," he said, "it's agony. I wanted to put my arms around her at luncheon when he began that talk. She's got to tell him the truth."
> "She loves you. Her voice is full of it."
> "Her voice is full of money," he said suddenly.
>   (*Trimalchio: An Early Version* 96)

Gatsby is emotional in this version. He has been watching Daisy throughout the luncheon, waiting for her to confront Tom and tell him that she is leaving him. She has not done so, and Gatsby is upset. Nick's words are soothing: "She loves you," he says, and then adds, "Her voice is full of it." Gatsby's answer—"Her voice is full of money"—now seems more appropriate, though the line is not set up properly. Gatsby blurts out the words, as if the insight has only just occurred to him. He even seems a little angry, as if he resents Daisy's background of wealth and gentility. Perhaps he senses that she will finally ally herself with Tom because of his money and social standing—a good insight, but one that we are not yet ready for.

Fitzgerald reworked the passage a final time on the galley sheets and produced the version below, which appears in the first edition and in all subsequent texts of the novel:

> "Shall we take anything to drink?" called Daisy from an upper window.
> "I'll get some whiskey," answered Tom. He went inside.
> Gatsby turned to me rigidly:
> "I can't say anything in his house, old sport."
> "She's got an indiscreet voice," I remarked. "It's full of—" I hesitated.
> "Her voice is full of money," he said suddenly.   (120)

All is changed by the revision. Gatsby is no longer emotionally overwrought; instead he is merely tense. He wants to behave properly and uses the locution "old sport," as he often does when he wants to appear casual and confident. "I can't say anything in his house, old sport," he tells Nick, who is sympathetic. "She's got an indiscreet voice," Nick says, but he (and his creator) both know that "indiscreet" is not exactly the word. "It's full of—" Nick begins, then pauses. "Her voice is full of money," says Gatsby in a level tone. This time the statement conveys an entirely different feeling, as if Gatsby has had the thought many times before, perhaps during his lonely, long nights of dreaming. For us, however, his remark is a surprise, a brilliant insight that we have been on the verge of having throughout the novel but that Gatsby, we can now see, has known all along.

The final passage seems perfect. Students will appreciate it the more because they will see that Fitzgerald did not simply toss it off. It took him three attempts; on the last try he got the lines just right.

Part Two

APPROACHES

Introduction

Nancy P. VanArsdale

Yet high over the city our line of yellow windows must have contributed their share of human secrecy to the casual watcher in the darkening streets, and I was him too, looking up and wondering. I was within and without, simultaneously enchanted and repelled by the inexhaustible variety of life.
(*The Great Gatsby* 35)

Nick Carraway repeatedly calls on the powers of vision, perspective, reflection, and introspection in his narration of *The Great Gatsby*, in his attempt to make sense of his summer living in West Egg and working in Manhattan. Nick doesn't just report on accompanying Tom Buchanan and Myrtle Wilson to the building where Tom rents an apartment for his mistress in chapter 2, nor does he simply narrate the events of the raucous party experienced there or fail to note his own inebriation that day. The narrator also identifies with the stranger walking the streets of the city, the stranger looking up at apartment windows imagining what lives are being lived therein. Nick is the stranger stimulated by all the people and possibilities offered by his summer in and near New York City; he is also the stranger overwhelmed by the recognition that good and evil so easily thrive in these environs peopled by the likes of Meyer Wolfsheim and Gatsby's party guests.

The lyrical language of the novel, the narrative stance of Nick Carraway, the symbolism of the East and West Egg settings, and the complex characterizations all provide instructors with rich material for motivating students to develop sophisticated critical reactions to the book. Ultimately, F. Scott Fitzgerald demands that the readers of his text, the students in our classrooms, consider what it means to be both "within and without, simultaneously enchanted and repelled by the inexhaustible variety of life," or, specifically, modern American life. Fitzgerald adeptly uses Nick Carraway's viewpoint, or, to use a Jungian concept, his "participation mystique," in the present moment of the plot's action and later in his reflections back on the summer's events as he records his experiences with Jay Gatsby, the Buchanans, the Wilsons, and others—the many others who flocked to Gatsby's mansion when the lights glared and the jazz roared. In doing so, the book requires the reader to consider larger questions of American identity and American destiny. Readers must participate with Nick in questioning whether Jay Gatsby achieved greatness by remaining steadfast to his dream of marrying Daisy, and why, in America, wealth appears to trump other core values: love, trust, friendship, and honesty.

The essays and materials in this book have been organized to give instructors of *The Great Gatsby* multiple tools and strategies for teaching the novel and for introducing students to the intricacies of the cultural changes after World War I that reshaped American life. The contributors demonstrate how a range of contextual, historical, and theoretical frameworks inform their teaching, from the new historicism to feminist and gender studies to narrative theory, among others. Not surprisingly, many of the essays carefully evaluate the role of Nick's point of view in presenting the life and dream of Jay Gatsby. Like Nick, Gatsby is a veteran of the war. Both men are attempting to create meaningful lives for themselves after resuming civilian status, engaged in the process of becoming, as several essayists suggest and explore. Other essays in part 2 examine the cultural and social contexts influencing the characters, symbols, and structures of the text, traditions ranging from classical philosophy to medieval courtly love.

As the original text of *The Great Gatsby* was being prepared to go to press, Fitzgerald sent a telegram to Maxwell E. Perkins, his editor, suggesting a new title for the book: "Under the Red, White and Blue." While my own students agree that Perkins was smart to reject the suggestion, the anecdote clarifies for them that indeed Fitzgerald believed he was writing an important novel about the United States, not just telling a summer tale of millionaires and lovers. I point out to students that Fitzgerald had also tried to write an important and entertaining play about American dreams, *The Vegetable*, a work he hoped would be a Broadway hit. Instead, the production failed miserably on its opening night in Atlantic City, just two years before the publication of *The Great Gatsby*. Despite the humiliation of such public failure, Fitzgerald did not give up on his artistic quest to write something significant about America. The spectacles mounted on the billboard of Doctor T. J. Eckleburg and those worn by the owl-eyed man are integral to the literary motifs of vision and retrospection woven throughout the text: this novel observes its 1920s New York setting and its inhabitants carefully and thoroughly. Nevertheless, the scope of its vision extends through time and far beyond the borders of New York, from the first impressions of colonial settlers arriving in the New World to Nick's recollection of trains rolling westward through the vast prairies of the expanded nation to the narrative's concluding contemplation of the merits of twentieth-century American life.

Respondents to the initial survey about the possible contents for this volume repeatedly noted that college teachers may often presume that large numbers of their students have read *The Great Gatsby* in high school. Consequently, instructors appreciate the opportunity to engage students in a deeper level of critical classroom interrogation since most students are rereading the novel.

Part 1 of this volume, "Materials," provides an overview of the bibliographic, biographical, critical, electronic, and textual resources related to *The Great Gatsby*. The twenty-one essays in part 2, "Approaches," are focused on classroom instruction of the novel and have been organized into three sections—"Cultural and Historical Contexts," "Narrative Structure and Style," and "Strategies and Resources."

The essays in "Cultural and Historical Contexts" provide extensive background on the era of the 1920s and the rise of American modernism as integral to approaches for teaching the novel. The opening essay examines how knowledge of World War I is critical to understanding *Gatsby* as a postwar text whose main characters are still recovering. Pearl James clusters Fitzgerald's 1925 novel with T. S. Eliot's *The Waste Land* and Hemingway's *The Sun Also Rises*: "These texts share a preoccupation with World War I as a fulcrum that shaped—and distorted—both masculine identity and literary production." She explains how she uses instructional time to help her students become more familiar with World War I history; her classes investigate archival artifacts, images, and film footage from the Imperial War Museum and from the Internet. James shows how the war and its aftermath influenced the writers of the Lost Generation; she requires her students to contrast the texts of Fitzgerald, Hemingway, and Eliot as "three alternative ways of writing after the war."

Fitzgerald coined the phrase "the Jazz Age" as a description of the time period, and the next two essays consider how the changing values of the 1920s illuminate study of the novel. Kirk Curnutt pays particular attention to the increasing importance of personality, mass culture, leisure culture, and youth culture. He also examines the pervasiveness of consumerism in a novel that is "richly textured with references to now obscure books and magazines, song lyrics, brand names, and sundry consumer goods." Michael Nowlin explores race in the 1920s, arguing for an examination of how "what we would today call a multicultural view of America develop[ed] alongside various movements and measures committed to a white supremacist view." Nowlin shows how he attempts to broaden his students' awareness of the racial stereotyping and theories of the novel's era, as well as of the changing racial attitudes and new opportunities of the period. From the anti-Semitic portrait of Meyer Wolfsheim to Tom Buchanan's references to a book about white superiority to the image of a limousine of successful black passengers driven by a white chauffeur, Nowlin offers a range of ways to explore the racial subtext of Fitzgerald's novel.

The essays by Jonathan N. Barron and Robert Beuka offer critical approaches to considering how the settings of the city and the rise of a new suburban culture are contrasted and linked to Fitzgerald's concern with depicting new national values and with the dichotomy of East versus West in America. Barron reflects on how his students at various points in his teaching career, in Minnesota and Mississippi, have brought dramatically different regional preconceptions of South, East, and West and thus to the geographic psychology of the novel. Cultural attitudes toward individualism, social class, and identity are also addressed in Veronica Makowsky's, Stephen Brauer's, and Kim Moreland's essays.

The next section focuses on approaches based on narrative structure and style. James Phelan investigates how narrative theory can be used to inform the teaching of the novel. He begins by asking how Fitzgerald persuades his audience to feel sorry ᵃ Gatsby, "a deluded and corrupt social climber." His essay presents table ᵃ ᵃe his students to analyze the sequence of events as conveyed in ᵃ ᵃnd to contrast them with the chronological order of the events. This process helps his students understand the complex accounting of the lives of Gatsby, Daisy, Tom, and Nick; question Nick's reliability as a narrator; and ultimately interrogate the audience's ethical response to the novel's characters as mediated through Nick's narrative. Also focused on Nick Carraway's perspective, Mark Shipman's piece considers how Heracleitus's teachings on logos, contradiction, and being and becoming can be useful to instructors.

Heidi M. Kunz posits that teaching the novel's chapters as bookend pairings (chs. 1 and 9, 2 and 8, 3 and 7, 4 and 6) helps students not only understand character and thematic development but also appreciate Fitzgerald's complex artistry in sequencing the novel's use of time and events. Kunz shows how chapter 1 introduces readers through Nick to the four principals (Jordan, Tom, Daisy, and Gatsby), whereas chapter 9, through Nick, dismisses them after Gatsby's death. She examines other instances of symmetry and parallelism in chapters 2 and 8, using themes of adultery, and in chapters 3 and 7, using motifs related to party gatherings. Ultimately, her essay analyzes how "Nick's modernist anxiety" attempts to impose order on his troubling memories of that chaotic summer by means of the structural choices the first-person narrator makes in retelling the story.

Jonathan P. Fegley's essay probes how Fitzgerald's youthful optimism and early belief in an individual's unlimited potential influence *This Side of Paradise*, his first novel, as well as *The Great Gatsby*, though in different ways. Remembering a student's preference for the first novel, Fegley acknowledges that many students in his classroom may be closer to their own first love experience and the idealism of the young Fitzgerald as well as of the transformed Jimmy Gatz than he is. His teaching strategy provokes students to question how Gatsby's motivation, first love and the quest for Daisy, causes him to transform his life and identity and to engage in becoming something more, regardless of whether Gatsby's effort is futile.

The nuances of Fitzgerald's rhetorical and linguistic style, from political inference to phraseology, are analyzed by Janet Giltrow and David Stouck and by Gail Sinclair. The symbolism associated with the Doctor T. J. Eckleburg billboard, Owl Eyes, and Gatsby's West Egg mansion is central to the teaching approach described in Ted Billy's contribution. Fitzgerald was an avid reader of medieval history and lore, an interest that prompts Deborah Davis Schlacks to trace connections between medievalism and modernism in her essay. Schlacks familiarizes her students with the tenets of courtly love and points out medieval allusions, such as "Fay," the maiden name of Daisy as well as a mythic supernatural figure in medieval literature, in Fitzgerald's novel.

The third section offers useful specific approaches for constructing lesson plans and incorporating other resource material in classroom teaching. The essays by Peter L. Hays and by Cecilia Konchar Farr reveal how experienced instructors train their students to become increasingly critical of the narrator's perspective and ultimately skeptical of Nick's view of morality and focus on teaching critical reading and thinking skills. Marilyn Elkins provides strategies for using a feminist teaching approach; in particular, she encourages her students to examine Daisy in the literary tradition of the "bitch-goddess" type. Danuta Fjellestad and Eleanor Wikborg describe how they begin their classroom unit by showing the 1974 movie version to their Swedish university students; they subsequently read and analyze the novel by comparing and contrasting it to the film adaptation. Anthony Berret's interest and extensive research in locating sheet music and recordings of the actual jazz and popular songs identified in the novel and of the period are integral to his teaching approach. The essays throughout part 2 illuminate the language, symbols, and structural ingenuity of the novel, providing instructors with numerous possibilities for their teaching.

The Great Gatsby remains an excellent book to teach because it weaves a tale of love and yearning with an examination of the promise and corruption of modern American culture. It is our hope that instructors will find the ideas and approaches presented here a welcome boost to their teaching of Fitzgerald's masterpiece.

Teaching *The Great Gatsby* in the Context of World War I

Pearl James

The Great Gatsby provides a useful opportunity to teach students to think and write about the complex relation between literature and history. I place *Gatsby* in a unit that focuses on World War I and on the ways in which writers translated aspects of war experience into literary form. This unit clusters *Gatsby* with T. S. Eliot's poem *The Waste Land* and Ernest Hemingway's *The Sun Also Rises* and is part of a larger course on American modernism. These texts share a preoccupation with World War I as a fulcrum that shaped—and distorted—both masculine identity and literary production. By making my students familiar with the history of World War I, I enable them to place literary texts in a larger historical context. Their ability to grasp that historical context, however, is not my ultimate goal; I expose them to contemporary sources and historical information to teach a practice of reading and interpretation—a practice that is historically informed but not historically determinist. This reading practice has been usefully described here:

> In order to gain insight into the significance and impact of the context on the text, the empirical context needs not just to be *known*, but to be *read*; to be read in conjunction with, and as part of, the reading of the text. . . . [T]he basic and legitimate critical demand for *contextualization of the text* itself needs to be complemented, simultaneously, by the less familiar and yet necessary work of *textualization of the context* . . . this shuttle reading in the critic's work—the very *tension between textualization and*

contextualization—might yield new avenues of insight, both into the texts at stake and into their context—the political, historical, and biographical realities with which the texts are dynamically involved and within which their particular creative possibilities are themselves inscribed.

(Felman and Laub xv)

To begin, I raise the need to put *Gatsby* in context. In my first class, I focus on Nick's introduction of himself as a narrator. Having already read writers with more difficult styles (Henry James and Gertrude Stein), my students often find Fitzgerald's opening pages refreshingly transparent—we seem safely within the bounds of realism. But I ask them to consider: How old does Nick seem? What is his tone? Why has he come east? I want them to be skeptical of Nick and to think about him as a narrator with a particular history. I ask, How does Nick describe his experience as a soldier in the Great War? I point out that he gives more detail about his great-uncle, who "sent a substitute to the Civil War," than he gives about his own, more direct, war experience (3). I ask them to use what they know about the war to interpret his ironic way of describing it and his participation in it. Some students may notice that the Great War—a name Nick draws attention to as a misnomer (3)—echoes the novel's title and that Fitzgerald's choice invites us to compare these two "great" entities. Before we can use this insight, however, we need to become more informed about World War I.

Keeping in mind my intent to show a reciprocal relation, a "shuttle," between text and context, I give a historical overview of the war that unfolds through primary texts. Following Fitzgerald's example, I focus on the western front: from the assassination of the Prussian archduke to the blissful summer of 1914 to the outbreak of war in August to the mythic war enthusiasm in England and in Germany to the raising of civilian armies. I quote letters from Rupert Brooke that voice his enthusiasm for adventure and his belief that the war was what he had been waiting for all his life ("I've never been quite so happy in my life . . . I suddenly realize that the ambition of my life has been—since I was two—to go on a military expedition. . . ." [cxxxvii]). Then I read Winston Churchill's obituary of Brooke, noticing its language of heroism and martyrdom ("he was willing to die for the dear England he knew" and had "absolute conviction of the rightness of his country's cause" [Brooke clvii]). Is this propaganda?, I ask.

I also expose students to some of the visual records of World War I, photographs and especially recruitment posters that deploy traditional images of masculinity. "BE READY! JOIN NOW," reads the caption around a boldly silhouetted soldier with phallic gun and bayonet; "Daddy, what did YOU do in the Great War?" reads the caption below a patriarchal triangle of pensive father, inquisitive daughter, and younger son playing with toy soldiers (visual material can be obtained by visiting the Web site of the Imperial War Museum in London, www.iwm.org.uk). I remind my students that these appeals to traditional masculinity come in the crisis of war but also at a cultural moment when the practical differences between men and women have been undermined (particularly in the processes of urbanization and industrialization) and contested (particularly by the women's suffragist movement and—as they know—in new literary representations of women). Having already noticed the representation of gender by other modernist writers, I hope that my students see the traditional masculinity of these posters and of Churchill's letter with more than anachronistic distance (for perspectives on modernism and gender, see Gilbert and Gubar; Koestenbaum; and DeKoven). Returning to *Gatsby*, I ask them to relate these evocations of traditional masculinity to Nick's self-description. On the one hand, he frames his identity in similarly traditional masculine terms: he places himself in a patriarchal line of descent, he desires adventure, he imagines himself as a pioneering "pathfinder" with a role in history (4). But, on the other hand, Nick undercuts these traditions with irony and omits stories of his own heroism. He denies the war's place as a superlative experience in his life or in history. Moreover, despite Nick's participation in the war, Fitzgerald makes it nearly impossible for us to imagine him in either of the stances evoked by the recruitment posters we have seen: Nick is neither an athletically assertive man nor the patriarchal founder of a family. In the novel, those ideals are fulfilled—only parodically—by Tom Buchanan. Tom's masculine parody, though not heroic, does make him a compelling character in Nick's narrative. As Keath Fraser has pointed out, the "cruel" power of Tom's body "fascinates" Nick (145).

Having suggested that ideals of traditional masculinity were central to soldiers and to recruitment campaigns and remain central—in ambivalent ways— to *Gatsby*'s narrator, I begin to contrast them (along with the models of warfare to which they refer) with the conditions on the western front. I explain how, after the German army failed to reach Paris, the war of movement came to a halt. By 1915, the western front was established: German, French, and British troops had taken their places in lines of entrenched opposition. The war became a battle of attrition. I show my students photographs of the trenches and of no-man's-land and give them numbers of wounded and casualties. I emphasize the replacement of hand-to-hand combat and cavalry battles with "total war": mechanization, mass slaughter, the mobilization of and attack on civilian populations, the advent of chemical warfare. The considerable ferocity and costliness of its battles (such as the Meuse-Argonne, in which—as Richard Lehan points out—Nick and Gatsby would have taken part [*Great Gatsby: The Limits* 4–5]) defy description.

I quote contradictory letters from soldiers in which they describe the conditions in the trenches in realistic language (the presence of lice, rats, mud, terror, noise, wounded and dead bodies) while insisting that they lack the words to do their experience justice. I also show the British army-issue Field Service postcard for infantrymen, with preprinted items soldiers could circle: "I am quite well"; "I have been admitted into hospital"; "{sick, wounded}"; "and am going on quite well"; "and hope to be discharged soon"—emphasizing the limited parameters of these narrative possibilities (reproduced in Fussell 184).

I explain that letters from soldiers were censored. I ask my students to think about the ways in which speech and writing were limited, both by literal historical conditions and, just as profoundly, by an awareness that this kind of warfare had not been experienced or described before. I describe a pandemic sense that the extreme experience of this war fell outside the bounds of traditional lexicons.

As I present the broad context of World War I, my goal is to provide my students with a sense of how the war reads as a text: the images, tropes, and plot lines that participants in the war—both official and unofficial, combatant and noncombatant—used to shape and describe the experience. Paul Fussell's *The Great War and Modern Memory* is a touchstone here. He explores some organizing tropes of, particularly, the British experience of the war: the predominance of sport metaphors, the use of the pastoral, the organizing rhetorical figure of irony, and so on (also useful is Modris Eksteins's *Rites of Spring*). I describe the discourse that framed the American experience of the war: the invocations of American exceptionalism, Wilson's moral justification of the United States's neutrality and then its entrance into the war, and the repeated rhetoric of America's coming of age in the context of modern war. These notions frame not only the Great War but also *The Great Gatsby*. By understanding the profound historical consequences of such ideas, students gain a better sense of the ideological stakes in Fitzgerald's novel. Moreover, I want them to understand that the war, even—or especially—while it was being fought, posed a dilemma with ethical, cognitive, and semiotic dimensions. Postwar writers inherited this dilemma and responded to it long after the armistice in 1918.

I conclude this historical overview by focusing on two issues central to the war and to *Gatsby*: the use of masculine coming of age as an organizing motif and the use of realism as a lens. As I present wartime visuals and quotations, I ask my students to consider how themes and images of traditional masculinity (adventure, heroism, bravery, and individual exploit) are alternately invoked for purposes of memorialization and of propaganda. (Again, Churchill's obituary of Brooke honors his sacrifice, but it does so in terms that invite other young men to follow his example. Dying a soldier's death for one's country becomes a ritualized means of proving one's manhood and of becoming immortal, either in heaven or in the grateful memory of a great nation.) Because of this dual imperative, images and narratives of masculinity become central in a more general problem of wartime and postwar aesthetic representation: how can writers and artists recognize the sacrifice made by millions of men without glorifying, excusing, or justifying the war's destruction? How can they represent the war? Through the experience of the war, an aesthetic problem comes to bear the burden of an ideological problem. The historical experience of World War I, particularly that of mass death, put enormous pressure on traditional masculinity as a coherent ideal and on realism as a signifying practice, creating a profound aesthetic problem for writers and artists. (For an analysis of the ideological conflict surrounding the use of realism in British war writing, see

Cobley; for a broader discussion of literary and artistic representations of the war, see Winter.)

Propaganda performed an essential function in the war machine, keeping war enthusiasm alive while casualties grew to appalling numbers. Especially in the context of total war, the lines between art, propaganda, and journalism blurred. War documentaries (such as the British *Battle of the Somme*, available on videotape from the Imperial War Museum) often attempt to strike a balance between images of heroism (brave faces, charging horses, mechanical skill) and images of dehumanizing destruction (particularly wounded and dead bodies). Given the rich visual archives available from the Imperial War Museum and the Web, it is easy to show students pictures and video clips of actual war footage. Seeing photographic and filmed images of destroyed landscapes, muddy soldiers, and dead bodies allows students to visualize *Gatsby*'s "valley of ashes" (23) in a new way.

As we turn to consider the literary texts by Fitzgerald, Eliot, and Hemingway in more detail, my students are prepared to think of them as postwar texts, with a fuller understanding of what that term means. While a phrase or two in reference to World War I might have conjured up images, stories, and other information in the minds of earlier generations of readers, today's students often lack basic associative familiarity with the conflict. Access to the events and devastation of World War I gives students a richer perspective on these three texts.

I frame Fitzgerald's, Eliot's, and Hemingway's texts as three alternative ways of writing after the war, of using writing in the wake of its destruction. We return to the deceptively simple narration of *Gatsby*. Having provided some context for the novel and for Nick's character, I ask my students to write a reading response or short paper that critically considers Nick's (un)reliability. They must use specific evidence and consider why Fitzgerald puts so much emphasis on Nick's "honesty." After collecting these responses, I outline the parameters of this debate in the critical record: that Nick is reliable (Parker); that Fitzgerald wanted but failed to make Nick reliable (Neuhaus); that Nick's unreliability suggests a latent gay desire (Fraser); and so on. Then I suggest another reading, one that has grown out of our classwork (and one that their papers may reflect): that Nick's unreliability as a narrator is one way in which Fitzgerald represents the historical experience of World War I. Nick's claims to naïveté deny the war's importance in his past, and this same denial characterizes him throughout the novel. His euphemisms, his forgetfulness about Jordan's dishonesty (a reflection of his own dishonesty), his unvoiced but enacted willingness to act as a pander for Gatsby, and his inability to confront Tom in the end testify to Nick's almost willful blindness.

His subtle fallibility—his omissions and his self-serving vacillations in loyalty—should alert us to the fact that narration, despite its pretenses to the contrary, is prejudiced and limited. Nick's repeated insistence on his trustworthiness is a symptom of his distorted point of view of himself and his world; as a narrator, he cannot afford to be honest. His conscious acknowledgment of what he knows would be too costly, too destructive. Such an acknowledgment would make the whole world seem—as his own Middle West seemed after the war—like "the ragged edge of the universe": a place of devastation, a wasteland (3). The novel represents a failed attempt to keep painful knowledge at bay. Banished memories of war experience continually resurface in the novel. Nick and Gatsby met in France but cannot say exactly where ("Your face is familiar. . . . Weren't you in the Third Division during the war?" [47]). The valley of ashes looks like the western front. Nick's foreboding anticipations of violence and death suggest that his past has been marked by war experience. Most important, his fantasies become reality when Myrtle is mowed down by a machine and Gatsby is shot dead; as he puts it, "[T]he holocaust was complete" (162). Nick's narration has the telltale shape of a war story: he has to memorialize a comrade whose story will otherwise remain untold, all the while wondering if he died for nothing, for a dream (for interpretations of *Gatsby* as an act of mourning, see Breitwieser, *"Great Gatsby"*; Forter).

I then turn to *Gatsby's* depiction of gender. I ask my students to describe masculinity in *Gatsby*: how does Fitzgerald shape the reader's attitude toward each of the novel's masculine characters? Nick, Gatsby, Tom Buchanan, Meyer Wolfsheim, George Wilson, Mr. McKee—these characters each embody elements of masculine ideals and failures. Tom Buchanan's violence, paranoia, and racism all come under consideration here as limits and symptoms of his desire to epitomize and to exert masculine power. Fitzgerald divides incompatible expectations about what it means to be a man among his characters and, in doing so, undermines the notion of a consistent or coherent masculine ideal. At the same time, femininity in the novel seems equally problematic: Myrtle and Jordan both disrupt stereotypic ideals of femininity. And, like her husband, Daisy parodies her gender; she makes the reader conscious of the feminine ideal of "the angel in the house" as a (poorly) staged performance. The historical background of the war permits us to see these disruptive representations of gender in a broader context. Cultural definitions of gender were used to mobilize consent for and participation in the war. *Gatsby* both mourns the failure of gendered ideals (heroism, bravery, honesty; purity, docility, domesticity) and questions their authenticity. The novel's equivocation and nostalgia condense, in novelistic terms, pressing questions about masculinity (and its necessary antithesis, femininity) in the aftermath of World War I.

From this discussion of *Gatsby*, we turn to *The Waste Land*. I ask my students to compare *Gatsby's* attempt to romance its "holocaust" with the poem's (arguably) similar task. I suggest an analogy between Nick's unreliable point of view and the poem's multiple voices. We listen to Eliot's reading of the poem (*The Waste Land* [1988]), and I ask students to note when he seems to give voice to different speakers. I draw attention to the poem's disjunctive form, its unwillingness to conform to the expectations of narrative, lyric, elegy, or sermon. Like Fitzgerald, I argue, Eliot plays with the illusion of mimesis, as the poem abruptly moves between realistic and imaginary images, narrators, memories, and admonitions. Narrative, like Marie's beautiful memories of times before the war (sledding, hearing German before it was the language of "the enemy," the youthful sensuality distilled in a phrase: "They called me the hyacinth girl"), emerges in fragments. Like "the dead tree," romantic writing "gives no shelter" (*The Waste Land* [1980] 38). I draw attention to the poem's critiques of ideal masculinity, its emphasis on memory and loss, and its translation of that loss into the reader's loss (and, if you like, potential recovery) of poetic intelligibility and tradition.

The poem's elegiac evocations of a lost world are disrupted, our attention repeatedly brought back to death in its most corporeal forms. These familiar ways of thinking about Eliot's poem are more accessible to students with some historical background: although the poem is inexhaustible in its meanings, its evocations, and its formal implications, it would not have been written in the same way without the war. As with *Gatsby*, I suggest not that the poem is strictly (or even primarily) referential but, rather, that the whole question of referentiality, to which the poem calls attention, has been profoundly inflected by the recent war and its representations. In the face of the poem's self-conscious difficulty, contextual knowledge provides students a set of concerns with which to begin their investigations.

I conclude this unit with a discussion of Hemingway's novel *The Sun Also Rises*. Like Eliot's poem, it can be difficult to teach, but for precisely the opposite reasons. Hemingway's prose style has been imitated to such an extent that it can seem, to many students, entirely natural or mimetic. Again, knowledge of both *Gatsby* and the war helps students look deeper. I contrast Nick Carraway's introduction of himself to Jake Barnes's: "I mistrust all frank and simple people, especially when their stories hold together" (12). One can almost imagine that Jake has Nick in mind. Despite this ostensible difference between them, I ask, how are these narrators alike? Jake's ironic attitude toward the war bears some resemblance to Nick's. Unlike Nick, however, Hemingway's first-person narrator admits to knowing something about the war and how the war has changed him. For Jake, writing offers some solution; he is a journalist. Experience of the war has ostensibly trained him to be a realist. And yet I ask my students to question his journalistic style and its implicit reliability. Might his status as a spectator be, like Nick's, more complicated? How involved is Jake in the novel's violence?

I pose these questions alongside an excerpt from Hemingway's *A Farewell to Arms*: "Abstract words such as glory, honor, courage, or hallow were obscene beside the concrete names of villages, the numbers of roads, the names of rivers, the numbers of regiments and the dates" (185). I ask students to evaluate *The Sun Also Rises* according to the aesthetic injunction of this passage, in which Hemingway privileges realism as *the* postwar signifying practice. To what extent does *The Sun Also Rises* follow this injunction? To what extent does it valorize "glory, honor, courage"—the very notions of traditional masculinity that *A Farewell to Arms* puts in quotation marks? As we have already seen,

Fitzgerald and Eliot use writing to enact, rather than announce, limitations of point of view and of narrative. Hemingway's choice to make such questions explicit, however, does not merely do away with them. Although Jake and Bill banter about clichéd postwar aesthetics, "pity and irony," they cannot avoid them. Students have a tendency to take Hemingway at face value because of this stylistic choice. Yet familiarity with the context of the war helps my students critically question the novel's realistic aesthetic and its insistence on the reality of appearances, seeing both as potential shelter from the reality of destruction rather than the means of access to it. Hemingway makes Jake's wound explicit, as if that disclosure is medicine enough. But, in *Gatsby*, *The Waste Land*, and especially *The Sun Also Rises*, questions of wounds and of trauma are decidedly more complicated.

The Great Gatsby provides a useful link between pre- and postwar themes and aesthetics, either in American literature or in an international modernism course. The novel works well as a bridge between expatriate texts and the work of other important American writers such as Willa Cather and Sherwood Anderson. *Gatsby* makes the experience of European war relevant in an American context and connects the experience of loss associated with the war to American evocations of loss: loss of the frontier, loss of innocence, loss of the American dream. Fitzgerald expresses these themes in a new postwar idiom that he, along with other writers and artists, developed in the wake of the war. Giving students access to this idiom and some of its nuances enables them, I hope, to read this novel in a historically informed way.

All That Jazz:
Defining Modernity and Milieu
in *The Great Gatsby*

Kirk Curnutt

Balancing between text and context when teaching *The Great Gatsby* can be a daunting task. Because the novel's central conflicts (hard work versus easy money, character versus personality, aristocratic privilege versus middle-class striving, even eastern versus midwestern values) readily lend themselves to formalist analysis, class time is easily spent explicating the rich body of symbolism by which Fitzgerald limned his themes. Yet focusing solely on the figural significance of the green light at the end of Daisy Buchanan's dock or the billboard spectacles of Doctor T. J. Eckleburg elides the historical background necessary to appreciate the story's take on the sweeping cultural changes associated with the advent of modernity. Historicizing *Gatsby* by reading it in the context of the 1920s poses its own problems, however. Discussion of the era's newfound prosperity and its resulting reverence for fun and frivolity often leaves students with simplistic images of flappers, bathtub gin, and decadent fetes that do a disservice to the novel's essential tragedy. A biographical approach, meanwhile, often roots that tragedy too deeply in Fitzgerald's own life, so that the book seems only his story and not a story of his time. One way to bridge this gap between plot and time period is to examine how the decade's new attitudes toward identity, consumerism, leisure, and aging compel the drama. These four particular issues are certainly not the only touchstones by which to illustrate the shifting values of the modern age; nevertheless, their thematic centrality can lend students a deeper understanding of the Jazz Age as a milieu by providing teachers productive tools for decoding the history behind the story.

The Rise of Personality

Critics have long argued that identity is a core theme in *Gatsby*. In particular, the novel is said to explore the illusoriness of the American dream of self-making, which promises people the freedom to determine their own destiny and realize the potential of their unique capabilities. Yet Jay Gatsby's doomed efforts to win the heart of the debutante Daisy Fay—a quest symbolizing his desire to escape his working-class roots and enter the upper-class world of privilege and prestige—is more than a simple critique of this ideal. The book documents a profound shift in cultural conceptions of identity. As Warren I. Susman has noted, the modern age defined selfhood less as a matter of character than of personality. Victorian-era definitions of *character* used terms such as *duty*, *citizenship*, *work*, and *integrity*, and "the stress was clearly moral and the interest was almost always in some sort of higher moral law." The discourse of *personality*, by contrast, was built around adjectives such as *"fascinating, stunning, attractive, magnetic . . .* words [that would] seldom if ever be used to modify the word *character"* (274). As an antidote to the growing threat of anonymity in mass society, personality emphasized the mechanics of performance and display and created a demand for what Susman calls "modes of externalization," new forms of expression to provide "ways [by which] people could gain the attention of others." Not surprisingly, the prerogative of "being a Somebody" raised fears of rhetorical manipulation and ignited debate over whether personality was a mask or guise rather than an expression of a true, inner self (281–82). By investing so much significance in exterior concerns such as "proper methods of conversation or public speaking—clothing, personal appearance, and 'good manners,'" personality advocates unwittingly implied that it was not natural but something to "be learned and practiced, through exercise and by study of guidebooks to success" (280).

Gatsby dramatizes this concern over the authenticity of personality by contrasting characters who revel in the self-conscious theatricality of their modes of externalization and those who naively assume that their gestures create their real selves. On visiting Daisy Buchanan in East Egg, Nick Carraway notices his cousin's tendency to murmur when speaking, a habit that he has "heard it said" is designed "to make people lean toward her" (9). Daisy has also cultivated her elocutionary skills; her intonation and rhythm project "an excitement . . . that men who had cared for her found difficult to forget." Her speech patterns are hypnotic because they convey the "promise that she had done gay, exciting things just a while since and that there were gay, exciting things hovering in the next hour" (9). But Nick also recognizes "the basic insincerity" of Daisy's behavior, in no small part because of the "absolute smirk" that occupies her face whenever she says or does something outrageous; as he tells himself, her comportment seems "a trick of some sort to exact a contributary emotion from me" (17). Nick understands that her behavior is designed to make her the center of attention.

He sees a similar tendency in other characters. Jordan Baker may not aspire to the same level of outlandishness as Daisy, yet she still constructs a performative facade to create a mystique about herself. Nick finds himself attracted to her "bored haughty face" precisely because he is convinced it conceals "something—most affectations conceal something eventually, even though they don't in the beginning" (57). A coarser but no less captivating exemplar of personality is Myrtle Wilson, Tom Buchanan's mistress. Over the course of a Manhattan sojourn with Tom and Nick, Myrtle changes clothes three times; with each new costume a different identity emerges. When she finally dons chiffon to entertain guests at the love nest that Tom maintains for her, Nick describes the transformations in her demeanor:

> With the influence of the dress her personality had also undergone a change. The intense vitality that had been so remarkable in [her husband's]

garage was converted into impressive hauteur. Her laughter, her gestures, her assertions became more violently affected moment by moment.

(30–31)

In the drive to garner attention and certify oneself a "Somebody," Nick implies, one's sincerity is not a concern; rather, the display of personality is of paramount importance, for if the gestures are not vivid and dramatic, they will not engage the attentions of the audience.

Of course, the character whose personality is most contrived is Jay Gatsby. In the novel's introductory paragraphs, Nick describes the peculiar appeal of his enigmatic friend: "If personality is an unbroken series of successful gestures, then there was something gorgeous about him, some heightened sensitivity to the promises of life" (2). "Successful" is a curious word to apply to Gatsby, for throughout their brief acquaintanceship, Nick repeatedly notes the utter transparency of the man's expressive nuances. On meeting Gatsby, Nick is struck by the superciliousness of his smile: "It understood you just as far as you wanted to be understood, believed in you as you would like to believe in yourself, and assured you that it had precisely the impression of you that, at your best, you hoped to convey" (48). Yet, at certain moments, Gatsby's drive to win Daisy undermines the slick performance of his persona. When the couple reunites at Nick's house five years after their abbreviated courtship, Gatsby leans against the mantelpiece in "a strained counterfeit of perfect ease, even of boredom"—a facade disrupted only when his nervousness leads him to inadvertently knock a clock off the shelf (86).

Despite the flagrancy of Gatsby's affectations, Nick never denounces him as "Mr. Nobody from Nowhere," as Tom Buchanan does (130). Indeed, Nick finds his "incredulity . . . submerged in fascination" (66) because, unlike other characters, Gatsby believes wholeheartedly that the image he constructs for himself is his self. As Ronald Berman puts it, he "is not a very good actor because he often gives way to sincerity" (Great Gatsby *and Modern Times* 113). By constructing an identity grounded in what Nick calls "his Platonic conception of himself" (98), Gatsby presumes an organic connection between his mannerisms and the aristocratic spirit he believes to be the essence of his character. His naïveté about the nature of personality is revealed after George Wilson murders him, mistakenly believing that Gatsby drove the car that killed Myrtle.

Gatsby's father shows Nick a boyhood book of his son's on whose flyleaf the ambitious young man recorded his self-improvement schedule, including such directives as "Practice elocution, poise and how to attain it." "Jimmy was bound to get ahead," his father proudly declares. "He always had some resolves like this or something" (173). At first glance, Gatsby's resolves are characteristic of the perfectionist impulse that motivates most self-improvement programs. Yet the areas targeted for improvement in Gatsby's schedule differ from the resolves that Benjamin Franklin prescribes in his autobiography. Whereas Franklin endorses values tied to character (temperance, humility, chastity), Gatsby is exclusively concerned with external surfaces of personality (elocution, physical fitness, appearance). Even his professed goal ("I didn't want you to think I was just some nobody," he tells Nick [67]) suggests that his ultimate goal is to have his existence validated by the recognition of others. What he fails to comprehend is that the attention that the mystique of personality generates is transitory; he may inspire "whispers . . . from those who had found little that it was necessary to whisper about in this world" (44), but his real desire—to be accepted by the wealthy world that Daisy represents—cannot be achieved through personality. To the rich, his affectations are (as Tom puts it) just so much "dust [thrown] into your eyes" (178).

The Rise of Mass Culture and Personal Style

As students quickly realize, *Gatsby* is richly textured with references to now ob-scure books and magazines, song lyrics, brand names, and sundry consumer goods. While these material artifacts convey the spendthrift impulsiveness of the Jazz Age, they also allude to the event responsible for its gaudy temper—namely, the rise of mass culture, the large-scale manufacturing of what Stuart Ewen calls "style objects," commodities marketed as "images and symbols of luxury, abundance, and distinction, [with] powerful suggestions of privilege and franchise" (75). In conjunction with such ancillary phenomena as advertising, brand diversification, consumer credit, and planned obsolescence, mass culture encouraged conspicuous consumption by functioning as a network of identifica-tion; it allowed individuals to construct a sense of self through the medium of style. Ewen explains:

> A central appeal of style was its ability to create an illusory transcendence of class or background. While hierarchy and inequities of wealth and power were—in many ways—increasing, the free and open market in style offered a symbolic ability to name oneself; to become a "lady" or a "gentleman," a "Sir" or a "Madam." Mass-produced, often shoddy, style seemed to subvert ancient monopolies.   (77)

Fitzgerald does not just dramatize the allure of personality; he also shows how the consumer marketplace, through the promise of prefabricated style, pro-vided the resources by which the performing self constructed its identity.

Because she expresses her social aspirations so nakedly, Myrtle Wilson stands as an obvious example of this consumer attitude. On arriving in New York with Tom and Nick, she purchases "a copy of *Town Tattle* and a moving-picture mag-azine, and in the station drug-store some cold cream and a small flask of per-fume" (27). Later, in the cramped apartment Tom keeps for Myrtle, Nick discovers "[s]everal old copies of *Town Tattle* [lying] on the table together with a copy of *Simon Called Peter*, and some of the small scandal magazines of

Broadway" (29). Presumably, Myrtle is not an aficionado of gossip magazines because she idolizes stage and screen stars; nothing in her conversation suggests an infatuation with Fairbanks or Valentino. Celebrity-oriented publications, in addition to profiling the rich and famous, analyzed the attributes that made stars worthy of attention, even offering readers advice on externalizing "what it took to rise [to fame]—'star quality,' 'charisma,' 'appeal,' 'personality,' or simply 'It' . . . [that] indefinable internal quality of the self" (Gamson 32). Perusing *Town Tattle* is Myrtle's effort to convince herself that she possesses "It" and deserves a better fate than George Wilson can offer.

As for *Simon Called Peter*, Fitzgerald undoubtedly alludes to this salacious 1921 novel to underscore the vulgarity of Mrs. Wilson's tastes. The book's overheated romances, however, also suggest Myrtle's desire to confer the excitement of melodrama on her own love life. As with Gustave Flaubert's Emma Bovary, it is not hard to imagine Myrtle's scouring tawdry love stories for the standard of eros she hopes to achieve with her ideal lover. Berman identifies what he calls "shopgirl films" as another source for this compulsion. Dozens of two-reelers in the 1920s, he notes, perpetuated the quasi-Cinderella fantasy of "the Poor But Honest Girl entrapped into marriage by A Man Beneath Her and then finding eventually Her One True Love," eventually "Triumph[ing] Over Adversity" (Great Gatsby *and Modern Times* 114). Myrtle's panting description of how she and Tom first met—their bodies pressed together on a crowded train ride—suggests this tendency to articulate personal experience through the narrative conventions of such popular-culture texts: "When we came into the station he was next to me, and his white shirt-front pressed against my arm, and so I told him I'd have to call a policeman, but he knew I lied," Myrtle confesses. "All I kept thinking about, over and over, was 'You can't live forever; you can't live forever' " (36). By promising to instill the thrill and throb of romance into mundane lives, mass-culture artifacts, whether magazines or films, shifted consumer purchasing preferences from utility toward emulation; instead of its usefulness, a product was valued for the aura that its style projected.

Intriguingly, the middle-class characters are not the only ones who define their identities through mass culture. Despite their old-money stock, Tom and Daisy Buchanan also draw from popular commodities to construct their attitudes and ideas. In the opening chapter, Jordan Baker entertains Tom, Daisy, and Nick by reading aloud from the *Saturday Evening Post* (17). Although Fitzgerald declines to specify the exact article read, the placement of this particular magazine in the Buchanan's East Egg estate is itself significant. As the veritable bible of bourgeois mores, the *Post* (to which Fitzgerald contributed dozens of short stories throughout his career) established itself in the early 1920s as the arbiter of middlebrow refinement. Both the magazine's editorial matter and advertising conferred a sense of noblesse oblige on the middle class, modeling sophisticated manners for readers while introducing them to stylish consumer accoutrements. As André Le Vot writes, the editor George Horace Lorimer's "strategy was based on respect for the American Way of Life. To encourage individual initiative in the young, in businessmen and ad-men was at once honorable, moral and profitable" (*F. Scott Fitzgerald* 79). What the *Post* aimed to create, in other words, was an egalitarian aristocracy of readers who believed in cultural elevation through better living. The unspoken irony in *Gatsby* is that Tom Buchanan, who complains that his social stature is eroding at the hands of the "Colored Empires" (12), would turn to this source for solace. Because the *Post* represented the embourgeoisement of upper-class entitlement, assuring readers that disposable income could compensate for the lack of a birthright, it was every bit as responsible for the devaluation of old-money influence as was immigration, intermarriage, and the other phenomena that Tom blames. The reference to the *Post* confirms Nick's estimation of Tom ("There is no confusion like the confusion of a simple mind" [125]), for it proves that Tom is an unwitting agent of his own cultural diminishment.

Daisy evinces similar contradictions. In Gatsby's view, she embodies the ro-manticism of wealth, the "ripe mystery . . . of bedrooms upstairs more beautiful and cool than other bedrooms" (148). Yet, like Myrtle, Daisy reveals through her actions the influence of mass culture. During the climactic confrontation between Gatsby and Tom over her, she tells her lover, "You always look so cool. . . . You resemble the advertisement of the man. . . . You know the adver-tisement of the man—" (119). The particular advertisement she refers to is less important than the fact that her romantic fantasies are articulated through mass-marketed images; linking Gatsby to an icon of style reveals the superfi-ciality of her feelings by suggesting that she seeks the peculiar quality both he and the man in the ad project rather than mature love and commitment. And just what is that quality? In singling out Gatsby's "coolness," Daisy notes not just his indifference to the stifling summer humidity but his unflappable de-meanor. In a tense environment in which, as she complains, "everything's so confused" (118), Gatsby radiates insistent but controlled determination. As Ewen writes, a central appeal of "consumable style" is initiative. When "the principle of *having* [is] a surrogate for *doing*," commodities "are depicted as fix-tures in the lives of people who thrive on a life of total satisfaction," people who "are spared the limits of everyday life" (107). That self-directing aura is exactly what Gatsby's pursuit of her conveys, and it is appealing to Daisy, whose mar-riage was motivated by "unquestionable practicality" because she is essentially passive (151). If she is to leave Tom, she must be taken. Thus, when Gatsby de-mands she declare that she never loved Tom, she falters: "[Y]ou want too much!" she cries. "I did love him once—but I loved you too"—words that "seemed to bite physically into Gatsby" (132). She is incapable of making a de-cisive choice because she sees herself as the object of conflict, not the agent of its resolution.

The Rise of Leisure Culture

In classroom discussions of *Gatsby*, teachers often introduce students to Thorstein Veblen's phrase "conspicuous consumption" to place the protagonists' materialism in its sociohistorical context. Veblen's closely related concept of "conspicuous leisure" likewise helps illuminate Gatsby's attraction. But the type of leisure dramatized in the book also departs from Veblen's definition in ways that reflect the 1920s. For Veblen, leisure was not a synonym for "indolence or quiescence" but a substitute form of labor. It demonstrated that, while the "gentleman of leisure" enjoyed the "pecuniary ability to afford a life of idleness," he, "for the sake of his good name," must be able to exhibit "some tangible, lasting result of the leisure so spent." But Tom Buchanan's polo playing and horsemanship are the lone remnants of this social pressure to place into public view what Veblen calls "the mark of exploit" (28). Instead, *Gatsby* dramatizes an ethos in which leisure symbolically enacts the pleasure of consumption through prodigious displays of wastage. Rather than channel leisure into a disciplined cultivation of a skill, the new attitude celebrates elaborate squandering and quasi forms of self-destruction as privileges of abundance.

The public intoxication at Gatsby's parties is the most overt example of this new consumerist attitude. Not only do attendees get wasted but their drunkenness becomes a curious form of entertainment. One red-haired chorus girl slurs her way through several popular songs, weeping and crying, her tears coming "into contact with her heavily beaded eyelashes," thus assuming "an inky color" and running "in slow black rivulets" down her cheeks: "A humorous suggestion was made that she sing the notes on her face, whereupon she threw up her hands, sank into a chair, and went off into a deep vinous sleep" (51). A short time later, Nick comes across the same crowd of partygoers gaping at a new coupé lying in a ditch, one wheel snapped off in a collision with a wall. Much to the crowd's dismay, the drunken driver declares he has run out of gas and attempts to maneuver the wreck back into the street. In neither case does the excessive drinking inspire more than mild rebuke. Even the sudden surge of domestic quarrels ("[T]he remaining women were now having fights with men said to be their husbands," Nick notes as the party draws to a close [51]) is part of the festivity's fun. Those present seem captivated, if not titillated, by the overt loss of control and the visible expenditure of resources, both mental and material; ultimately, the passed-out woman and wrecked coupé hold the same fascination as the "pyramid of pulpless halves" of oranges and lemons generated by Gatsby's electric juicer (39)—they demonstrate the sheer efficiency of the modern propensity for wastage.

The motif of wastage as leisure is not confined to incidents of tipsy revelry. It is also present in the aura of ennui that blankets both East and West Egg in sleepy passivity. Canny students will note that, with the exception of Gatsby and Nick, characters are frequently seen yawning. When Nick first meets

Jordan Baker, she is stretched across a divan and greets him with a yawn. Moments later, as the pair prepare to dine with Tom and Daisy, she yawns again, "sitting down at the table as if she were getting into bed" (11). During Myrtle Wilson's impromptu party a few days later, Tom audibly expresses his boredom as Mr. McKee pontificates on his photography (32). (Whenever his wife speaks to him, Mr. McKee himself "nod[s] in a bored way" [33].) Even after Jordan has learned the "tantalizing" story of Gatsby and Daisy's Louisville romance, teasing Nick with its gossipy appeal, she "yawn[s] gracefully in [his] face" (52). The point, obviously, is not that these characters are narcoleptic or even tired; their enervation in no way compares with the sickness that eats away at George Wilson, who complains of being "all run down" by the physical depletion of working-class labor (123). Instead, when upper-class characters display their lethargy, they boast that they have consumed experience to the point where their flagrant lassitude is the sole activity for which they can muster enthusiasm. They are effectively reveling in their "been there, done that" dolorousness. "I've been everywhere and seen everything and done everything," Daisy assures Nick, explaining her cynicism: "Sophisticated—God, I'm sophisticated!" (17). At the ripe old age of twenty-three, Daisy insists that because life holds no more surprises for her, she has nothing better to do than waste away her days.

The Rise of Youth Culture

The 1920s were also the first decade in which American popular culture was dominated by images of youth. As an index of passion and vitality, youthfulness provided advertisers, fashion experts, and health-care and beauty advisers with a powerful appeal for promoting countless Ponce de Léon–style remedies for the importunate fact of senescence. Equally important, young people were a topic of intense cultural debate, inspiring endless editorializing over what their self-consciously modern manners and pastimes said about the state of the nation's morality. Paula Fass suggests why youth generated such controversy throughout the Jazz Age:

> The young of the twenties were less a threat to former stability than an ongoing reminder that it had passed. Portrayed as responding to modern life with frivolous unconcern for the sterner ways of their predecessors, the young epitomized both what America had lost and what America had become. The ways of youth fascinated the twenties . . . because they teased and tantalized, telling readers what they most feared but wanted to hear again and again in different and ever more alarming ways. (28)

No writer in this era performed this service as diligently as Fitzgerald. His early novels, *This Side of Paradise* and *The Beautiful and Damned*, exposed the carpe diem mentality of a postwar, under-thirty generation that equated aging with a dissipating enthusiasm for life. In them, Fitzgerald advanced the idea that young people would rather throw themselves into experience than conserve their innocence. Explaining the openness with which youth indulged in drink, eros, and other forms of stimulation, he insisted that youth was intent on maximizing the fun of being young—in a sense, using it up (or wasting it) before it naturally gave way to middle age.

The Great Gatsby marks a significant departure from the attitude of these early works, however. Indeed, one suspects that it is celebrated as Fitzgerald's first mature effort not just for the oft-cited reasons (its style is more streamlined and controlled than in his first two novels) but also because it represents a newfound acceptance of maturity itself. Nick best articulates the awareness that one must relinquish adolescent ideals of romance. Shortly after Daisy acknowledges that she once loved Tom as well as Gatsby, Nick remembers that the day marks a significant milestone: "I was thirty," he recalls. "Before me stretched the portentous, menacing road of a new decade" (135). Throughout his career, Fitzgerald was obsessed by the meaning of different age markers, thirty in particular. As he drafted Gatsby in mid-1924, his own thirtieth birthday was barely two years away, and he seems to have imbued Nick with many of his anxieties toward that passage: "Thirty—the promise of a decade of loneliness, a thinning list of single men to know, a thinning briefcase of enthusiasm, thinning hair" (135). But whereas previous Fitzgerald protagonists were content to view this "menacing road" as entirely negative, Nick challenges himself to find something positive about it. Ultimately, he comes to equate thirty with the realization that one must grow up. Once he decides that "unlike Daisy," he will not "carry well-forgotten dreams from age to age," his fear of aging subsides, and he feels "the formidable stroke of thirty [die] away" (135–36). Later, when Jordan Baker accuses Nick of treating her unjustly, he admits to his callousness, defending himself only by noting, "I'm thirty. . . . I'm five years too old to lie to myself and call it honor" (177).

The insistence that with age comes the acceptance of responsibility and complicity stands in marked contrast to both Gatsby and Daisy, neither of whom can admit that ideals conceived in youth eventually must accommodate the pragmatic realities of adulthood. Fitzgerald even underscores his titular hero's arrested development with another age reference: "[H]e invented just the sort of Jay Gatsby that a seventeen-year-old boy would be likely to invent, and to this conception he was faithful to the end" (98). As for Daisy, her unwillingness to mature is most apparent when she suddenly becomes nostalgic for the carefree carelessness of youth. At the Plaza Hotel, as Tom and Gatsby square off over her, Daisy overhears music from a nearby ballroom: "We're getting old," she says. "If we were young we'd rise and dance" (128). The statement reflects Daisy's desire to elude the consequences of the situation; if the group could just revert to its teenage years, she implies, the events inveigling it would not seem so serious and consequential.

These four contextual concerns—personality, mass culture, leisure, and youth—represent only a few of the most obvious topics by which *The Great Gatsby* dramatizes the transformations of modernity. Several other issues can be raised in class to suggest how the novel illuminates Fitzgerald's historical milieu: technology, celebrity, the growth of suburbs, and even organized crime are all present to differing degrees in the text, offering substantive insight into the otherwise superficial catchphrase "the Jazz Age." (Because it examines a plethora of such themes, Berman's The Great Gatsby *and Modern Times* is an invaluable resource for any teacher.) Exploring *Gatsby* from a contextual perspective also adds further dimension to Fitzgerald's formalist elements. Analyzing Doctor Eckleburg's spectacles apropos of mass culture allows students to see the billboard as a symbol of the pervasive gaze of advertising in the 1920s. Discussing the pleasures of wastage in the party scenes, meanwhile, offers an opportunity to reflect on how planned obsolescence affects attitudes toward thrift—a phenomenon to which students easily relate as they interrogate their own social construction as consumers. Of course, when *Gatsby* was published in April 1925, many reviewers (most prominently, H. L. Mencken ["As H. L. M. Sees It"]) found the book too topical to be admitted to that rarefied category of literature, a judgment that damaged its reputation for years to come. In the pedagogical effort to bridge the gap between history and fiction, however, this topicality can prove *Gatsby*'s greatest asset. It allows students to view the story as a living link to a past decade whose confluence of changing values and ideals continues to influence our own time.

Teaching the Racial Subtext
of *The Great Gatsby*
Michael Nowlin

It is difficult to teach *The Great Gatsby* these days without reference to its troubling racial stereotypes. Some students will raise questions about, and perhaps openly object to, Nick Carraway's casually racist description of a limousine, "driven by a white chauffeur, in which sat three modish negroes, two bucks and a girl. I laughed aloud as the yolks of their eyeballs rolled toward us in haughty rivalry" (69). And many students will recognize as anti-Semitic the portrait of Jay Gatsby's mobster-mentor Meyer Wolfsheim. The more astute might even begin detecting an unsettling pattern. Blacks being driven by whites and a powerful Jew who fixed the World Series are part of a pervasive immigrant presence—funereal southeastern Europeans (68–69), "a gray, scrawny Italian child" celebrating the Fourth of July (26), and a number of more subtle indications. Cumulatively, they seem to underscore the novel's topos of cultural decay, its apparent implication that there is something deeply awry about the modern American scene.

Can we dismiss these details as accidental to the novel's meaning and to Fitzgerald's larger artistic purpose or apologize for them by acknowledging that, like all great writers, Fitzgerald did not always rise above some now damning prejudices of his time and place? I think not, though teachers have presumably long done so if the novel's critical history is any indicator. Until relatively recently, most criticism of the novel—with noteworthy exceptions (Hindus, "F. Scott Fitzgerald"; Forrey; Gidley; Slater)—has evaded its racial signposts, in keeping with the still dominant liberal-humanistic view among Fitzgerald scholars that his art transcends divisive social and political positions. But the race-oriented criticism that emerged in the context of 1980s debates about cultural pluralism has caught up with the novel, and if few have gone so far as Felipe Smith in arguing that the novel is fundamentally racist (142–99), a consensus is evidently growing that *The Great Gatsby* is very much about racialized American selves and desires (see Michaels, "Souls" 193–206; Marren 70–107; Clymer; Gleason 211–14, 238–58; and Goldsmith).

The liberal reading of *The Great Gatsby* has always relied on Fitzgerald's characterization of Tom Buchanan, the novel's overt racist, as an intellectual lightweight and a bad guy. Fitzgerald's heart, from this perspective, was always in the right place. But this argument does not sufficiently explain other things in the text. How do we help students explore the contradiction between the ironic view of Tom's racism, which is obvious to most of them, and the novel's tendency to confirm his belief that "[c]ivilization's going to pieces" (12), that "the white race ... will be utterly submerged" (13) by others, that "intermarriage between black and white" could become socially acceptable (130)?

This contradiction is crucial to the novel; it stems from Fitzgerald's sense of himself as a distinctly modern American writer and artistic novelist who, like his narrator Nick Carraway, could live "within and without" his historical moment, what he dubbed the Jazz Age, which "simultaneously enchanted and repelled" him with its "inexhaustible variety" (35).

Let me suggest three potentially interrelated approaches to guiding students in their responses to the racial subtext of the novel. First, the instructor can present them with accounts of the historical and cultural context from which it partly derives and suggest ways in which the novel engages this context. Second, students can be asked to think about the function more generally of racial stereotypes as literary figures—particularly in demonstrably sophisticated art. And third, they can be reminded of the always equivocal nature of self-consciously literary statements: anything this novel seems to say, of course, is formally mediated by Fitzgerald's aesthetic decision to have things registered or said by the complexly drawn narrator, Nick Carraway.

The Great Gatsby emerged from a historical context fraught with discussions about race that were generally inseparable from debates about national identity. The 1920s witnessed what we would today call a multicultural view of America develop alongside various movements and measures committed to a white supremacist view of America as the rightful property of Nordics, Aryans, or, more commonly, Anglo-Saxons. (Fitzgerald was an undergraduate at Princeton University when the modern concept of cultural pluralism was coined by the New York–based, Jewish American intellectual Horace Kallen in 1915, the same year in which D. W. Griffith's historic pro–Ku Klux Klan film, *The Birth of a Nation*, was released to popular and critical acclaim over the protests of African Americans.)[1] If the pluralist view ultimately seems to have triumphed from the standpoint of cultural history, the white supremacist view was clearly ascendant on political terrain. Klan membership rose in the 1920s to a level it had not reached since the days of Reconstruction, and Klansmen exercised considerable political clout; at the same time, African Americans could not get a federal antilynching bill passed in the Senate (Perrett 72–75, 186–87, 245). Anti-Semitism was intensified by the imaginary threat posed to the United States by the Bolshevik-led revolution in Russia, as well as by rising anti-Semitism in Europe. Henry Ford's *Dearborn Independent* became a widely read vehicle for spreading hatred and suspicion of Jews. Such vulgar anti-Semitism was abetted by a long-standing and largely class-based "genteel" mode of anti-Semitism (one that undoubtedly inflected Fitzgerald's outlook). This form manifested itself in the routine practice of social discrimination, including the implementation by the early 1920s of restrictive quota systems at elite universities (including Princeton) determined to reduce the number of Jewish students (Dinnerstein 79–104).

Students today may tend to think of the "scientific" book Tom Buchanan passionately cites—Goddard's "The Rise of the Colored Empires" (12)—as an aberrant, possibly underground tract. But the book Fitzgerald likely had in mind, Lothrop Stoddard's *The Rising Tide of Color*, and others like it, such as Madison Grant's *The Passing of the Great Race*, were published by the respectable, conservative house of Charles Scribner's Sons, Fitzgerald's own publisher; along the same lines, Kenneth Roberts's *Why Europe Leaves Home* first appeared as a series of articles in the *Saturday Evening Post*, which had become Fitzgerald's venue of choice for his stories (Berman, Great Gatsby *and Modern Times* 24–27). Such books were written largely in response to what were perceived to be the decadent, "mongrelizing" effects of America's open-door immigration policy, which had resulted in the huge wave of immigration between 1880 and the early 1920s, substantially composed of southern and eastern European immigrants, many of them Jewish. A trope of Nordic or Anglo-Saxon "race suicide" was given pseudoscientific dignity by the likes of Grant and his follower Stoddard and taken seriously by America's political leaders; it reached fruition in the passage of the 1921 Immigration Act, which set quotas according to national origin, and of the even more restrictive 1924 Johnson-Reed Immigration Act, heavily influenced by Grant (Perrett 82–83, 183–84; Jacobson 78–90). *The Great Gatsby* appeared one year after the Johnson-Reed Act became law, and the conflict the novel draws between a triumphant Nordic elite (including a white, southern belle) and the racially ambiguous stranger cast from its midst seems to resonate with the putative cultural crisis that act was meant to resolve.

But if the early 1920s culminated in a public policy aimed at ensuring Anglo-Saxon control of America, the changing face of modern America's cultural center—New York City—suggested something else. And it was toward New York City that Fitzgerald migrated, like his returning veteran Nick Carraway and many other young, middle-class Americans revolting against the village, when he aimed to make his name as a writer. New York, of course, had for the past decades been the final destination of many of the European immigrants that racist Americans were worried about. By 1920, only one New York resident in six was a white, native-born Protestant (Douglas 304). And since 1910 and well into the 1920s, a quarter of the population had been Jewish; indeed, New York had "the largest concentration of Jews in the world," the historian Hasia Diner tells us, and "functioned as the hub of American Jewish life" (105; cf. Dinnerstein 89). It would have been very much in keeping with popular perception that the first person Nick meets when he accompanies Gatsby into the city is a Jew—the uncouth, obsequious, and yet dangerously powerful Meyer Wolfsheim. But students should especially attend to the romantic haze through which Nick sees New York before he enters it: "The city seen from the Queensboro Bridge is always the city seen for the first time, in its first wild promise of all the mystery and the beauty in the world" (68). A young man from the American provinces, he approaches the city in the romanticized spirit of the immigrant coming to partake of the American dream. He may have more in common than he wants to acknowledge with those southeastern European mourners crossing his path or those "modish Negroes" rolling their eyeballs in "haughty rivalry" at him.

"Anything can happen now that we've slid over this bridge," he thinks (69). Even a New Negro could happen, given Nick and Gatsby's proximity at this moment to Harlem, the "black city," in James Weldon Johnson's words, "located within the heart of white Manhattan, and containing more Negroes to the square mile than any other spot on earth." This might appear "a miracle straight out of the skies" to an "uninformed observer" such as we might assume Nick to be (*Black Manhattan* 4), but as Alain Locke's landmark 1925 anthology *The New Negro* would make clear, modern Harlem was the outgrowth of national (and transnational) trends and owed much of its contemporary vitality to another tide of migration—largely from the American South. Nick initially finds Gatsby's spectacular success incomprehensible outside the terms of the kind of immigrant or migrant success stories that New York would foster: "I would have accepted without question the information that Gatsby sprang from the swamps of Louisiana or from the lower East Side of New York" (49). And we might urge students to follow Fitzgerald's cue here, as recent scholarship working with a broadened canon has done, and trace out affinities between Gatsby's story—of spurious success, of successful imitation followed by exposure, of failed assimilation—and immigrant narratives like Abraham Cahan's *The Rise of David Levinsky* and Anzia Yezierska's *Salome of the Tenements* or Harlem Renaissance narratives like Johnson's *The Autobiography of an Ex-Colored Man* and Nella Larsen's *Passing* (see esp. Gleason 211–58; Goldsmith).

When Fitzgerald thought of the cultural resources and possibilities of New York City, he had less in mind the avant-garde literary milieu of Greenwich Village than the "entertainment that city poured forth into the nation" ("My Lost City" 28): the popular music, the Broadway shows, the big publishing houses, the publicity machines, even the residual presence of movie people. Though Fitzgerald trusted that *The Great Gatsby* would establish him as a distinguished literary artist (he wrote most of it in France), he was deeply drawn to the celebrity culture attached to America's popular entertainment industry. *The Great Gatsby* followed on the heels of *The Vegetable*, the comic play he wrote in the hopes of making a fortune on Broadway but which flopped miserably. Students should learn that modern America's entertainment industry and popular culture would be unimaginable apart from the contributions made to it by Jewish immigrants and African Americans, and Jewish membership in the industry (in the Broadway theater, in songwriting, in the movies) was legion (Most 32–65; Melnick 95–140; Douglas 346–76; Gabler 1–183). Gatsby first describes Wolfsheim as "a denizen of Broadway," which leads Nick to mistake him for "an actor" (73). This was also the era of the African American revues like *Shuffle Along* and *Runnin' Wild*, which gave the Jazz Age some of its more renowned songs and dances. "It's getting very dark on old Broadway," went a 1922 show tune sung by the *Follies* star Gilda Gray—née Marianne Michalski—whose understudy is presumed to be putting on a jazzy dance performance at Gatsby's (41; see Goldsmith 452).

Gatsby's parties are a destination for all kinds of theater people, musicians, and even a "moving-picture director and his Star" (106–07); his guests include "a whole clan named Blackbuck" and men named "Eckhaust and Clyde Cohen and Don S. Schwartze . . . all connected with the movies in one way or another" (62). Gatsby is compared with one of the major Jewish American Broadway producers of the day ("a regular Belasco" [45]) and in the manuscripts is associated with Tin Pan Alley songwriters (Great Gatsby: A Facsimile 162–63). He hosts a performance of Vladimir Tostoff's "Jazz History of the World" (Les Epstein's in the earlier versions), which might recall the work of George Gershwin.[2] Allusions to a distinctly modern and distinctly American popular culture created by African Americans and immigrants ("The Beale Street Blues" [151], "The Sheik of Araby" [78]) pervade the novel, and Fitzgerald's hero, who suggests going to Coney Island (81) even though his house already operates like an amusement park (41, 81), is squarely identified with it. Fitzgerald's title itself finally resonates with American show business, betraying how much of his own creative inspiration and ambition was drawn from its products and possibilities.

This kind of historical background should enrich students' appreciation of the novel's relation to its milieu, but it should not be approached in a misleading way. The Great Gatsby aspires to be more than social realism; Fitzgerald expressly aimed to write an "intricately patterned" work of literary art rather than a "document novel" (Bruccoli and Duggan 112, 126). It is less thickly descriptive than elliptical and allusive, and this style has implications for how ethnic and black Americans are represented. Edith Wharton's compliment to Fitzgerald on his "perfect Jew" arguably refers less to any measure of verisimilitude than to the vividness he gave to a symbolically resonant type ("Three Letters" 309). Regardless of the extent to which Fitzgerald had in mind the real gambler and gangster Arnold Rothstein when he created Wolfsheim, his "perfect Jew" functions as a trope around which the novel's motifs of disillusionment, corruption, lost belief, infidelity, overmastering ambition, and unbridled materialism organize themselves. The stereotype is consistent with the billboard featuring the face of T. J. Eckleburg overlooking the ash heaps; and among the echoes from T. S. Eliot's poetry that we hear in the novel, we might remember "the Jew" in "Gerontion," who "squats on the window sill, the owner" of "a decayed house," figuring forth a dying nation (21).

Rather than encourage our students to denounce the novel on such grounds, or to explain it away as part of what Milton Hindus calls the "fashionable anti-Semitism" of 1920s writers ("F. Scott Fitzgerald" 510), we should suggest they think more deeply about why such figuration seems an almost necessary component of the novel's appeal. Why should such a "perfect Jew" shadow Gatsby? If we read in a realist vein too determined by the historical context, the answer would seem to be that Gatsby is a Jew (despite the detail about his attending a Lutheran college [99]). What we have, quite plausibly, is a passing novel, in which the "gonnegtion" to Wolfsheim always threatens to betray Gatsby's true identity as an undesirable racial alien.[3] But if we attend more to the fact that

Fitzgerald never lets us know for certain what his Mr. Nobody is passing from, only that he came so close to becoming what he set out to become, then Wolfsheim's presence deepens into a romantic trope, a "double," as Murray Baumgarten sees it (44–45), embodying an idea of Jewishness connoting marginality, pariah-hood, and criminality and underscoring the corrupt worldly means that must inevitably undo Gatsby's "Platonic conception of himself" (98).

I am suggesting we approach "the Jew" here in ways analogous to the approach opened up to "the Negro" by the African American writer-critics Ralph Ellison, James Baldwin, and Toni Morrison, all of whom worked (or are still working) to unravel the imaginative hold on American writers of a figurative "Negro" through which, as writers, they can express, contain, and explore a national pathology intrinsic to the nationalist narratives they are writing—a deep psychological investment in America as a white nation and a concomitant fear of the implications of freedom. "The story of the Negro in America," wrote Baldwin, "is the story of America—or, more precisely, it is the story of Americans"; more precisely still, it is the story of Americans embattled by a "Negro" that "does not really exist except in the darkness of our minds" (19). This is the "Africanist presence," as Morrison calls it, indispensable to the national literary project of creating "a new white man" (14–17). It is a presence Ellison detected in *The Great Gatsby* in the figure of the lone, African American witness to the collision that kills Myrtle Wilson and leads to Gatsby's murder: that his testimony cannot save Gatsby betrays "some of the problems and possibilities of artistic communication in the U.S.A." (13–15).

This "Africanist presence," finally, is manifest in several of Fitzgerald's pre-*Gatsby* stories—most notably, "The Offshore Pirate" and "Dice, Brass Knuckles, and Guitar" (*Short Stories* 70–96, 237–58), which both deal, as does *Gatsby*, with competing styles of white, American masculinity (see Nowlin, "F. Scott Fitzgerald's Elite Syncopations" 419–25; Clymer 170–82). Inasmuch as *The Great Gatsby* takes as its most obvious subject an American romance of white masculine self-making, the presence of the black or Jewish other seems almost inevitable. For in a culture with a long-standing racial caste system and a tradition of anti-Semitism, what else is more readily correlative of the economic, social, and sexual impurity—the "foul dust" (2)—ever threatening that romance at its core? Gatsby "took what he could get, ravenously and unscrupulously," we might recall from Nick's second, far less romantic account of Gatsby's seduction of Daisy: "he took Daisy one still October night, took her because he had no real right to touch her hand" (149). Brutal as this sounds, the romance's ideally unattainable white, southern belle seems to have let herself be taken quite willingly.

The presence of the black or Jewish other seems almost inevitable from another standpoint: Fitzgerald's literary ambition. While Fitzgerald was announcing his intention "to write something *new*—something extraordinary and beautiful and simple + intricately patterned," "to be a pure artist + experiment in form and emotion" (Bruccoli and Duggan 112, 126), to do "purely creative work" showcasing "the sustained imagination of a sincere and yet radiant world" (Kuehl and Bryer 70), he was incorporating in that pattern and in that radiant world the threatening presence of literature's other. Although this other includes popular novels such as Robert Keable's *Simon Called Peter* and (perhaps his own) *Saturday Evening Post* fiction, it also consists of the expressive forms that owed so much to the creative energies of African and Jewish Americans. Those energies fueled the American entertainment that was becoming crucial to the experience of being American, and without them a coinage like "the Jazz Age" would be inconceivable.

As "the sustained imagination of a sincere yet radiant world," *The Great Gatsby* is a romance about romance, but one organized in the light of what Fitzgerald took to be the boldest (and most novel) experiment in modern poetry—Eliot's *The Waste Land*. It may be mere coincidence that one of the novel's most racially freighted passages is also a stylistic tour de force. But we should return students to the form of that troubling passage over the Queensboro Bridge and recall that what an enchanted Nick first sees is "the city rising up across the river in white heaps and sugar lumps all built with a wish out of non-olfactory money" (68). The "first wild promise of all the mystery and the beauty in the world" is quickly exploded by a kind of paratactic notation: first a "dead man" and a train of southeastern European immigrant mourners (68–69); then the "three modish negroes" with their "haughty rivalry"; then Nick's sense that "[a]nything can happen. . . . Even Gatsby could happen, without any particular wonder"; then an abrupt shift of scene, to the restaurant where we first encounter Wolfsheim, a "small, flat-nosed Jew" (69). That image of a white city built with "non-olfactory" money might be considered an ironic reflection on the romantic aim Fitzgerald set himself of creating a pure aesthetic object, a "sincere and radiant world," unpolluted by the olfactory commerce that nonetheless must underwrite art as much as it underwrites the more ephemeral cultural trends putting talented black "bucks" into the backs of limousines.

For all its attention to the energies of an urbane, multiethnic American popular culture, *The Great Gatsby* exudes literariness and indeed pretends to be written by its white, solidly bourgeois narrator after he has turned his back on the modern American scene and returned to the world of his staid, third-generation father. Nick's testimony about his riotous excursion into the hub of Jazz Age America becomes elevated to a lofty aesthetic representation of his times and an elegy for "the last and greatest of all human dreams" (180), an America no sooner grasped for than lost. The novel lays America's misappropriation at the hands of the Meyer Wolfsheims, at one end of the socioeconomic power spectrum, and the Tom Buchanans, at the other. Only the safely dead Gatsby gets enshrined for (over)reaching, by virtue of the purity of his belief or his will to believe. What Nick recovers in the course of writing Gatsby's story, after wanting "the world to be in uniform and at a sort of moral attention forever" (2), is his capacity for "reserv[ing] all judgments" (1), for a disinterested openness to the other (he "who represent[s] everything for which I have an unaffected scorn" [2]). And his achievement in this respect is Fitzgerald's. "You adopted exactly the right method of telling it," Fitzgerald's editor Maxwell E. Perkins wrote him, "that of employing a narrator who is more of a spectator than an actor: this puts the reader upon a point of observation on a higher level than that on which the characters stand and at a distance that gives perspective" (Kuehl and Bryer 82).

Through Nick, Fitzgerald acquired the authorial position that eluded him in his earlier novels, the disinterested position espoused by modernism's forerunner Gustave Flaubert, and a legacy from the American romance tradition linking Fitzgerald to Henry James and back to Nathaniel Hawthorne. Small wonder that Eliot called the novel "the first step that American fiction has taken since Henry James" ("Three Letters" 310). Students should be invited to explore critically the relation between Nick's distant connection to the novel's white supremacist elite and Nick's capacity for disinterestedness, for occupying the position "within and without" (35), for the self-deprecating irony of someone who knows exactly who he is. Why is it more difficult to imagine this capacity wielded by someone like the "pale well-dressed negro" witness (139), who becomes an invisible man? or by someone like "the little kike" (34) we hear about offhandedly, who almost married Myrtle's sister—someone like Gatsby, in effect, whose "heightened sensitivity to the promises of life" (2) becomes tainted by lust, ambition, greed, opportunism, and probably the experience of oppression?

The Great Gatsby is surely predicated at some level on the trope of the passing of the white American "race." But the sense of displacement this trope fosters in that race's sensitive witnesses, like Nick, only enhances their cultural authority to go on representing that displacement in a literary language (at once mythic, poetic, and vernacular) that might survive. Whatever racial message we might look for in *Gatsby*, we cannot make too little of Fitzgerald's masterful narrator, who, by virtue of his own self-displacing desire, knows that the "great race" he belongs to is always already passing, knows its paradise ("a fresh, green breast of the new world" [180]) is always already lost, and accepts the empowering aesthetic challenges and compensations that flow from that understanding.

NOTES

[1] Two landmark articulations of a multiculturalist view of America were Horace Kallen's "Democracy versus the Melting-Pot," which appeared in two parts in the *Nation* in February 1915, and Randolph Bourne's "Trans-national America," which appeared in the *Atlantic Monthly* in summer 1916. It is unlikely that Fitzgerald knew nothing of these essays, given his friendship with Edmund Wilson. *The Birth of a Nation* (initially titled *The Clansmen*) was first shown in New York in March 1915. We know that Fitzgerald greatly admired Griffith, and a reference to *The Birth of a Nation* suggests that he, like so many others, admired the film (see Fitzgerald, "My Lost City" 28). On the African American reaction to the film, see D. L. Lewis 506–09.

[2] For insightful commentary on Fitzgerald's specific range of reference here, see Berman, Great Gatsby *and Modern Times* 116–21; Breitwieser, *"Great Gatsby"* 61–68; and Goldsmith 451–56. Breitwieser and Goldsmith draw especial attention to significant revisions and cuts Fitzgerald made to the still extant manuscripts.

[3] Under the influence of Michaels's reading of the novel in *Our America*, Jacobson, in his own influential work, refers to Gatsby as a "Hebrew," as though this is self-evidently established in the text (97).

Teaching Regionalism and Class in *The Great Gatsby*

Jonathan N. Barron

In this essay on *The Great Gatsby*, I offer some reflections and suggestions for teaching the link between region and class. I come to this connection after teaching the novel in two distinct and distinctly different American regions, both monocultures, where issues of class are bound inextricably to issues of region: Northfield, Minnesota, home of St. Olaf College, and Hattiesburg, Mississippi, home of the University of Southern Mississippi. In the novel, as Jay Gatsby's biography unfolds, we learn that "[a]n instinct toward his future glory had led him . . . to the small Lutheran college of St. Olaf's in southern Minnesota" (99). It was a brief stay, often forgotten but significant enough for Nick to tell us that "[h]e stayed there two weeks, dismayed at its ferocious indifference to the drums of his destiny, to destiny itself, and despising the janitor's work with which he was to pay his way through" (99). These are, if not among the least remarked, then at least among the most forgotten set of sentences concerning Gatsby's life before New York.

When I taught this novel at the actual St. Olaf College, however, these sentences proved to be among the most vivid and memorable in the novel. Yet after the excitement of seeing their school mentioned in a great novel passed, the students could not help being somewhat surprised to learn that Gatsby has to pay his way through school by working as a janitor. When I taught the novel there in the 1990s, no student, no matter what form of financial aid he or she received, worked on campus as a janitor. In fact, the overwhelming majority of students there did not work full-time at all while attending college, saving that hardship only for summer vacations. The dissonance between their and Gatsby's experience accentuated even more dramatically the novel's second paragraph: "just remember that all the people in this world haven't had the advantages that you've had" (1).

The point of this anecdote is to underline just how fundamental to the stories of Nick and Gatsby the problem of class and region becomes; while Nick goes east to Yale, Gatsby goes slightly east and a bit south from a farm in the Dakotas to a college in rural Minnesota—only to work as a janitor to pay for his education. Realizing his impossible social situation—particularly with regard to his ambition and sense of self—Gatsby decides to leave St. Olaf. It may be that in teaching the novel elsewhere, this scene's story of social class is easily missed; but in Northfield, Minnesota, the social story proved impossible to ignore.

In Mississippi, the St. Olaf episode also stands out to my students, for weirdly similar yet dissonant reasons. Thanks to reruns, they cannot help recalling the television situation comedy *The Golden Girls*. This long-running program took as its premise the incompatible social class and regional identities of a group of retired women living together in Florida. The least wealthy and by far the most ignorant, if not stupid, of them was a woman said to be from the small town of St. Olaf, Minnesota. My students in Mississippi are always surprised to discover that St. Olaf is not just a television invention but a real enough place to warrant mention in a 1925 novel. In their opinion, after watching a few seasons of *The Golden Girls*, no town could be as slow or as ridiculous as the television world of rural St. Olaf, Minnesota. To my students in Mississippi, then, Gatsby's flight from that place makes perfect sense, and his desire to leave is less about class and more about region: who would not want to leave so slow and boring a town? Interestingly, the students who trade this regional story for the class story are, for the most part, themselves working full-time while going to college; some even work as janitors, groundskeepers, and the like on campus. Nevertheless, what captures their attention in the college experience of Gatsby and Nick tends to be the regional rather than the class dimension.

My own view when comparing these divergent experiences is to find in the novel an inextricable link between region and class. Combining the readings of both groups of students, I find that in their experience, as in the novel, an implied cultural class hierarchy exists among particular regions. Some regions have more cultural and actual capital than others, and the person who wants access to such capital inevitably goes to the place where access is to be had. In *The Great Gatsby*, that place is the East, particularly New York. To go east to college, as Nick does, is to go to the most prestigious place, the top of the class pyramid defined as much by geography as by anything else. By contrast, Gatsby is, at first, unable to leave his region and so remains cut off from the sort of prestige and capital that Nick clearly desires.

Drawing from my own experience with these cultural and geographical hierarchies, I encourage other teachers to do the same in whatever region they happen to be in when teaching this novel. Both schools where I have taught this novel appeal, by design, to a monocultural student population (and often faculty population as well). When I taught there in the 1990s, St. Olaf flew the Norwegian flag on its campus; today, it has one of only two Norwegian departments in the United States: its culture is that of the Norwegian American Lutheran. At the University of Southern Mississippi, although thirty percent of the students are African American, the overwhelming majority of all students, black and white, shares the Baptist, church-based, social milieu. Most students are working or lower middle class, and a significant percentage are first-generation college students.

As an urban Jewish northeasterner, I was an alien in both places and, with regard to the novel, in a strange position. My accent, my very being, stood for the one region—the East—that in the novel means to trump all the others both in terms of real and cultural capital. In the novel's terms, I embody the very region that challenges, usurps, overcomes, and denies the importance of all the others. The novel's principal characters see it as their mission to pick up and leave the provincial outpost in which they are stuck—whether in the South or in the Midwest, Nick, Jay, Tom, Jordan, and Daisy all go east.

My students, by contrast, had deliberately made every effort to stay away from the East: both St. Olaf College and the University of Southern Mississippi draw most of their students from the region, and few come from more than two hundred miles away. However they may have understood why Gatsby would leave his region, the idea of leaving theirs was as foreign to them as my own sense of inner exile was true to me. Only by being honest and willing to expose my experience as an easterner has it been possible for me to address the meaning of the East in this novel with my midwestern and southern students.

In teaching the novel, then, one needs to highlight rather than ignore the importance regionalism plays in it, particularly with regard to class. If one were teaching *Gatsby* in Germany, one might well begin by discussing the implicit cultural, class, and other differences between the former East and West German regions. Similarly, in California, one might discuss the differences between Northern and Southern California. Wherever one teaches, one can be sure that there exists an implicit cultural hierarchy in the local culture. It would therefore be helpful to any appreciation of the novel to raise those local issues first so that students can be more attuned to their value as both metaphor and analogy when discussing *Gatsby*. Highlighting the novel's connection between class and region, I believe, makes more sense if that same connection is revealed to exist in the students' own daily lives, whether the classroom is in Turkey or in Arizona.[1]

With the aim of facilitating such discussions, I offer three sets of questions to help bring this issue into the classroom: one on the Midwest, a second on the South, and a third more generally on the link between regionalism and class as an intellectual, literary problem. For reasons of space, I select only a few for commentary here, explaining the assumptions I have made and the purpose I see behind each question. I also use the questions as a means to introduce my own answers. The best discussion, however, depends on not having any particular answer in mind. These questions, then, are not meant to be Socratic, nor are their answers meant to be conclusive; I wish only to encourage more discussion on these issues in the classroom.

The Midwest

I start with a set of questions about Nick to begin a discussion about the culture of the Midwest, as well as about the novel's implicit view that the Midwest has less status than the East. At St. Olaf, these questions led to striking and illuminating discussion about the idea of the Midwest and about the particular culture of Minnesota, "Minnesota nice." They ask students to understand Nick's attitudes as class attitudes that are trumped or governed by a regional code of behavior. After all, Nick does go to college in the East, and, after spending some time after the war in the Midwest, he chooses to return to the East to make his fortune.

The first question, Why does Nick not stay in the East?, raises the issue of Nick's motivation and makes the novel's regional focus paramount. Nick's answer is wonderfully metaphoric: "I decided to go East and learn the bond business" (3). Cynical and lost, Nick hopes to restore his faith in people, in human bonds. But, as a bond man, he is also following the pattern of men in his class. To have power, one goes not only to the elite schools of the East (Yale) but also to the center of American financial power, Wall Street. For Nick, the East, and New York City in particular, proves to be the region with the most clout, power, and authority. At the outset, then, region and class connect in Nick's mind, revealing the cultural attitudes of the novel itself.

To my ear, however, Nick's claim that he came east to learn the bond business smacks of bitter irony. In "Reexamining Reality: The Multiple Functions of Nick Carraway," James Phelan has argued for a multilayered narrative voice, a voice with multiple functions. At times unreliable, at times omniscient, Nick's voice, according to Phelan, needs to be assessed contextually throughout. Other essays also focus on Nick's narrative style, and, like Phelan's, they have nothing to say about the specific midwestern regionalism of Nick as either a narrative voice or a character (see Coleman; Giltrow and Stouck, "Pastoral Mode"; Lehan, *"The Great Gatsby"*; and Preston).

Given the placement of Nick's admission (the very first chapter), I can only read it as ironic. He learned the bond business all right—not in the East but because of it. In answer to my own question, then, Nick goes east because he is trained, as a man of his class, to go where the power is. But once there, he discovers that his regional codes, not the class codes, matter more. Bonds may exist in Wall Street but his bonds, the midwestern bonds one sees in Gatsby's father at the pathetic funeral, are the only bonds of interest to Nick. After all, it is shortly after the funeral that Nick decides "to come back home" (176). I find it useful to raise this point in my classes since one usually does not find it in the scholarship. Even this theme, home, is more likely to be read in larger, more national terms than in a strictly regional sense (see Peek).

Specifically, Nick tells us:

> After Gatsby's death the East was haunted for me . . . distorted beyond my eyes' power of correction. So when the blue smoke of brittle leaves was in the air and the wind blew the wet laundry stiff on the line I decided to come back home. (176)

Only here, at the end of the novel, does the word "home" have a particular power. It is used not just after the description of Gatsby's funeral but after that funeral reveals to Nick that Gatsby is thoroughly of the West himself. Indeed, no sooner is Gatsby's true origin revealed through his father than Nick launches into an encomium to the Midwest (175–76). Nick's discovery that Gatsby comes from the same place he does explains, in other words, why Gatsby would value a bond of no monetary value. That the Midwest values the human relationship over and above all material or cash value leads to Nick's realization that his regional codes must trump the class code that sent him east in the first place.

Thus the Midwest is shown to have a nonmaterialistic social code that may explain why Nick claims his is "a story of the West" (176). Teachers, therefore, might consider asking students if similar distinctions apply to their own regional settings and if so how *Gatsby* might challenge or critique such distinctions. Alternatively, one might use such local regional or class distinctions to critique the novel's assessment of these issues.

The second question I pose to my students, What does Nick mean when he says that his is "a story of the West"?, raises the issues of the first one from a slightly different perspective. Here, too, one set of answers can be located at the end of the novel, when Nick praises "my Middle West" and affiliates himself with it by declaring, "I am part of that" (176).

I read Nick's statement "I see now that this has been a story of the West" as an epiphany. When I ask my classes to explain what they think he means, I mean to ask what they think this region, the West or the Middle West, means to Nick. What becomes quite clear is that this region exists in dialectic with the East. Considered as two mutually opposed value systems, the East becomes a place (Wall Street, East Egg and West Egg) where the bonds are monetary, whereas the West is a place where the bonds are, for lack of a better word, spiritual. Nick's epiphany depends on a hierarchy where the East posits itself as better than the West. Nick, in the end, realizes that the opposite is true. Two characters, Tom and Gatsby, both support this reading. Both characters chose to ignore, or willfully suppress, the values specific to their region in favor of a seemingly national, even international, ethical standard. What Fitzgerald's portrayal of both characters reveals, however, is that these seemingly national or international standards are actually specific only to the American East and to a specific social elite, a specific class in that region.

The power exerted by the East on one's identity can be understood as a principal reason for the change of Gatsby's name from Gatz. While ethnicity is often said to be central to this change, one can gain a great deal of insight by maintaining a focus on region and class as well. In the scholarship, the unspoken epithet Nick erases from Gatsby's door is now often understood to refer to Gatsby's presumed Jewish origin. For some scholars, it is precisely this ethnic mark that Nick means to erase (see Bender; Goldsmith).

With regard to region and class, however, the fact that Gatsby leaves behind not only his region but also his regional name is the most telling detail. One must consider the experience of region depends on more than mere geography; it is also a set of ethical codes of behavior that belong to a larger, cultural hierarchy of regions. These codes are meant to govern the class conflicts that emerge in various regions, but, as Fitzgerald demonstrates, they usually fail to govern and instead merely conflict with the class experiences they were supposed to smooth over.

Gatsby's name change indicates his desire to erase the entire problem: early in life, he adopts a standard of success based on material wealth, a goal he achieves thanks to his relationship with Dan Cody. Both his new name and the goal he commits himself to achieving align him with the East. But after meeting Daisy, Gatsby transforms himself again. This time he ignores the codes of each of the novel's principal regions and, in his pursuit of Daisy, seems to become his own unique antiregional, antinational figure; he is, as it were, a region and class of one. Or is he? Often my students read his character as tragic precisely because they believe he adopts too much of the eastern materialist sensibility even if he does so for noble reasons. Whether in Minnesota or Mississippi, they often find in Gatsby a man sucked into the vortex of the East, hardly unique but certainly tragic. Yet I am not convinced that this is the only way to understand his character, and so I encourage teachers to discuss the tension between region and class to understand better Gatsby's motivations as a character. Fitzgerald himself seems to make the issue all the more desperate and pressing when he not only brings Gatsby east but also puts him on the wrong side of the tracks. Even in the East, as a man of wealth and fame, he must live in the West (Egg); because, in fact, he is a man of the West—a man who does not value Wall Street's bonds.

Tom Buchanan, too, indicates the depth to which class is tied to regional affiliation. Tom, a man born to class privilege, easily crosses into all three regions of the novel. Equally at home in Lake Forest (Illinois), Louisville (Kentucky), and East Egg (Long Island, New York), his class standing proves to be the most mobile in the book. Despite his privilege and easy mobility, however, we might recall that Tom, the only character firmly ensconced in the upper-class milieu of the East, is also the character most afraid of losing his power: only he is obsessed with white supremacy. Walter Benn Michaels, in *Our America*, makes a great deal of this obsession as a particularly American one. But the novel suggests that such Americanness is actually a consequence of one character's failure to think regionally. Tom, perhaps even more than Gatsby, has forsaken the codes of his region, the codes we are taught to recognize through Nick's thoughts and actions. My own sense is that we are to believe that when Tom leaves the West behind, he also leaves behind his ethics. When Tom leaves the Midwest, he leaves behind a region that lacks a deep sense of heritage and history; but rather than affiliate himself with either Daisy's South or some patrician East, he turns to an even larger affiliation: race. That he marries Daisy, the southern ideal, even stereotype, of a pure white woman, neatly ties Tom to the South, but it does so for racist not regional reasons.

Tom and Gatsby, therefore, mark the two poles of a national rather than a regional sensibility. Gatsby denies his regional sense of self in favor of an individuality based entirely on his love for an other—a final, transcendent social bond. Tom, meanwhile, insists on his sense of self grounded in connection not to region, class, and heritage but to race, to an exclusion of all darker others.

In claiming his story for the West, then, Nick exposes the novel's oppositional subtext: the American West versus the American East. When he sides with the West, he is saying that the West is a more ethical, more moral, more humane place than the East. He both condemns Tom for his failure to recognize the values of the West and laments Gatsby for his inability to understand them.

The South

The questions about the South particularly resonate in Mississippi, "the hospitality state." As with the questions on the Midwest, these questions allow students to examine the intersection between region and class. They ask students to see the South not only in relation to the East but also, as the novel would have it, as part of the West. At the same time, the South is a place known particularly for hierarchy, tradition, manners, racism, and politesse. It is precisely these characteristics that one might set against the novel's view of the East. Unlike the Midwest, the South carries with it a heritage and an implicit cultural tradition that can and often does rival the similar heritage and tradition of the East. In fact, Gatsby is as much a foreigner in the traditional, cultural hierarchy of Daisy's South as he is in that of New York's East Egg. It is worth adding that, in Mississippi, my students often have a hard time imagining Louisville, so far to their north, as part of the South. Given the novel's point of view, and the recognition that a principal model for Daisy, Zelda, was from Alabama, the students are willing to suspend their disbelief.

The first question I ask students is, What, if anything, do Fitzgerald's portraits of Daisy and Jordan say about southern women? In line with that question, I once asked my students in Mississippi to write an essay on Fitzgerald's portrayal of the southern belle stereotype in *The Great Gatsby*. Their answers revealed just how important the stereotype of the southern belle is to the novel. Even this character, in the scholarship, is read more as a national than a regional type. According to Bryan R. Washington, Daisy is not a southerner, per se, but a national type, the American girl made familiar by Henry James. Similarly, Frances Kerr focuses on transatlantic artistic gender codes without offering much consideration of the specificity of southern gender codes. My students in Mississippi, by contrast, tend to respond best, even viscerally, to the regional identities of the characters. In their essays, no student denied the premise of the question, which they were free to do. They argued instead that both Jordan and Daisy did represent a stereotypical southern type. While their essays revealed many nuanced and complex reactions ranging from anger and bitter dismay to praise, one might well ask, What is the point of such an exercise? Why does it matter that such traits as submissiveness, hospitality, and concern with outward social appearance are associated with the southern belle? It matters, because this stereotype is, finally, at the center of Gatsby's story. His story's main interest lies in his attempt to transcend the particularity of regionalism in America. One needs to know that Daisy belongs to and is defined by the South to understand Gatsby's story as the attempt to forge a national, American man, a man who can exist outside and despite the limitations imposed by regions on one's identity—a man, moreover, who does not opt for Tom's racist solution to this question. To say that Gatsby's love of Daisy is his way of transcending the web of connections between region and class is particularly problematic given Nick's view that Gatsby's irrational behavior, his commitment to Daisy, is a result of his midwestern sensibility. To Nick, Gatsby is great precisely because he embodies the ethical sensibility of the West. Gatsby, by contrast, thinks otherwise; he means to forge a unique identity altogether.

Daisy's southernness matters because in the end it defeats Gatsby. He thinks he can overcome its requirements, but he cannot. An insight I have gained from my Mississippi students is the power and hold the southern ideals of family and heritage can have. If one reads Daisy as a southern belle, one must also read her as too invested in her cultural heritage to welcome Gatsby into her arms as a husband. What Daisy requires is certitude and security, and, no matter how racist and philandering Tom may be, he will always provide her with the lifestyle to which she has grown accustomed. Unless one accounts for the southernness of Daisy (and also of Jordan), Gatsby's story, as an attempt to escape from regionalism, makes no sense. Born in the Midwest, he tries to make it in the South and in the East. That he fails in both places carries its major thematic meaning, only if the distinctive characteristics, the distinctive ethical codes of each place, are understood. Gatsby wants to make his own universe, to remake the past in his own image. But he is, at every turn, defeated by the very terms of the region in which he lives. To Nick, however, such defeat is a victory. That Gatsby was never in it for the money is to Nick proof that his is a story of the West after all.

The Link between Regionalism and Class

The questions noted above reveal what I consider the central tension in *The Great Gatsby*—the conflict between region and class. Wherever this novel is taught such conflicts persist. Therefore, one might usefully extend the specific questions above into a deeper discussion concerning the relative importance of class and region as separate categories. One might introduce the current phenomenon of dividing the American republic into two camps, one red and one blue, to highlight the persistence of this issue into our own time. One might conclude a discussion of this novel with the question, Which triumphs in the novel, class identity or regionalism? The answer to this question remains ambiguous because at the end of the novel Gatsby is dead and Nick is back home in Saint Paul. Can the Midwest, the place that values human bonds, friendship, and other nonmaterial goals, be said to have won the day?

My sense is that Fitzgerald's great American novel is, ultimately, a defense of the American region over and against the modern commercial world's various attempts to universalize it out of existence. It would, however, be fascinating to see what conclusions students in other parts of the country and in other parts of the world make of the novel's conclusion: Nick's return home and Gatsby's death (not to mention Daisy's continuing her marriage with Tom). With these circumstances in mind, I close with the questions, Given that by the end of his tale, Nick has traveled from the East back home to Saint Paul, are we meant to see his journey home as a journey we, too, should follow? Is it one toward which we too should aspire or one from which we should retreat?

NOTE

[1] Regionalism in American literary study in the twentieth century has most often referred to a devalued literature of local, sentimental, often purely feminine interest. By contrast, a vigorous, masculine, nationally interested realism and modernism have often defined themselves artistically by arguing against the tepid localism of the regional. To invoke regionalism is to invoke this literary critical battle as well. A full discussion of that battle, and of the role of *The Great Gatsby* in it, however, is best left to a different essay. It is sufficient to say that Fitzgerald's artistry is all the more remarkable when one realizes that, in *Gatsby*, he sets regionalism and modernism against each other: a modernist style and a narrative voice manage to defend a regional sensibility (see Phelan, "Reexamining"). Recent scholarship is particularly interested in the larger national themes of *Gatsby*, often to the exclusion of any regional interest (see Baker; Breitwieser, "Jazz Fractures"; Callahan; Koster; Hilgart; Kerr; Pelzer; and Tyson, *Psychological Politics*).

Love, Loss, and Real Estate:
Teaching *The Great Gatsby* in the Suburban Age

Robert Beuka

As Fitzgerald closes *The Great Gatsby* with Nick Carraway's extended reflection on landscapes of the past, which moves from his recollections of the "Middle West" (176) of his youth to the final, lyrical passage in which he contemplates the once wondrous vision of the Long Island landscape—"the old island here that flowered once for Dutch sailors' eyes—a fresh, green breast of the new world" (180)—the first-time reader of the novel gains a retrospective understanding of something those who have been reading and teaching *The Great Gatsby* for years take as a given: that one of the primary concerns of the novel involves the characters' attempts to come to terms with the places they physically and psychologically inhabit. In teaching the novel, I stress the importance of place to the dynamics of the work, examining the ways in which Fitzgerald creates both a yearning remembrance of a vanishing pastoral terrain and a bustling, protosuburban narrative that chronicles the commodification of the natural landscape. In particular, I try to focus my students' attention on the embattled sense of place in the novel's exurban milieu, the towns of East and West Egg on Long Island's North Shore, or Gold Coast. It is here, in his treatment of the exurban setting, where Fitzgerald makes most clear the disparity between the major characters' relations to their present environment and the idealized visions they continue to hold of landscapes from their past. That all the major characters eventually fail in their quest to establish for themselves a comprehensible and fulfilling connection to this place suggests a central preoccupation of the novel—portraying the anxiety that inheres to place-bound experience in an increasingly metropolitan and rootless age.

For students coming of age in an era characterized by continued, relentless suburban development and sprawl, Fitzgerald's glamorous portrayals of New York City and the stately Gold Coast might seem, at best, a distant cultural memory. On the other hand, the connections between Jay Gatsby's gaudy West Egg estate and the architecturally outrageous "McMansions" that tower over today's cul-de-sac suburbia seem almost too obvious to miss. In fact, in many regards *The Great Gatsby* can be thought of (and taught) as a kind of presuburban novel. This approach allows many students to bring their own contemporary frame of reference to bear on the text while also exposing them to a less-discussed side of this classic work, its fascinating presentation of an American landscape in transition. To prepare students for this focus on houses and environment in the novel, instructors might first introduce a cluster of pre-*Gatsby* stories that demonstrate Fitzgerald's interest in depicting the emotional resonance of houses and landscapes from the past. The classic "Winter Dreams" (1922; *Short Stories* 217–36), as well as the lesser-known " 'The Sensible Thing'" (*Short Stories* 289–301) and "John Jackson's Arcady" (*Price* 143–61), both published in 1924, center on male protagonists fixated on loves and houses from their pasts. Fitzgerald wrote the latter two stories while living in Great Neck, the suburban Long Island town that would be the model for West Egg. Providing students with background on the author's period living in Great Neck, a town that featured both stately country living and a growing middle-class commuter set, helps set the stage for an examination of the physical and social environments in *The Great Gatsby*.

Fitzgerald's depiction in the novel of a rapidly evolving and often alienating landscape is a function of the specific historic and geographic setting of the novel, a central factor worth reviewing with students in some detail. In 1922, the time of the novel's action (and the year when Fitzgerald moved to Great Neck), Long Island's Gold Coast accommodated over five hundred estates similar to the Buchanan and Gatsby mansions (Randall 14). Built by millionaires and industry tycoons, these palatial homes both used and reshaped the natural geography of the North Shore, signifying social class through elaborate architecture and appropriation of the rural, seaside landscape. The creation of these homes, which the Gold Coast historian Monica Randall calls "an architectural phenomenon unparalleled both in excessiveness and originality" (11), began shortly after the turn of the century and continued into the 1920s. As Ronald Berman has argued, this phenomenon was most notable for its symbolic overtones, for the sense that "a new American history could be created in twenty-four hours, an illusion of ancestry long in the land" (Great Gatsby *and Modern Times* 41). Berman's observation is an apt one, for it is the very elusiveness of dreams of ancestry and of connection to the landscape that provides much of the dramatic tension and carries much of the thematic weight of *The Great Gatsby*.

Students needn't look far to find the deep and often conflicted connections between landscape and a sense of history and belonging in the novel. The paradigmatic connections between place and identity are set up in the opening pages, when Nick situates the Carraway family as "something of a clan," who have been anchored to the same "Middle Western city," a land of "wide lawns and friendly trees," for the past three generations (3). By contrast, Tom and Daisy Buchanan, whom we first meet a few pages later, are characterized by Nick as drifters; still, despite Nick's incredulity, Daisy has declared their move to East Egg a "permanent" one (6). And the carefully landscaped opulence of the Buchanan home suggests some sense of permanence, or in Berman's terms a feeling of "ancestry long in the land." Nevertheless, this sense of permanence and groundedness is manufactured and illusory, and as Tom stands on the porch showing Nick his estate, his proprietary ease seems to be undercut by a need to explain the orchestrated magnificence of the place:

> "I've got a nice place here," he said, his eyes flashing about restlessly.
> Turning me around by one arm, he moved a broad flat hand along the front vista, including in its sweep a sunken Italian garden, a half acre of

deep, pungent roses, and a snub-nosed motor-boat that bumped the tide offshore.

"It belonged to Demaine, the oil man." He turned me around again, politely and abruptly. "We'll go inside."   (7)

By deferring to the previous owner of the estate at the end of this speech, Tom reveals the anxiety that has accompanied his purchase of an unreadable symbolic landscape. As a homeowner thus once removed from his own landscape, Tom Buchanan quickly emerges as a character who is off-balance and literally out of place, one reason perhaps for his clinging to a reactionary and idealized vision of a lost civilization, a vision based on Manichaean racial attitudes and a larger sense of exclusionary paranoia.

Like Tom, Nick also finds himself out of place from the outset. As he confesses in the beginning of his narration, the "practical thing" on moving to New York would have been to "find rooms in the city"; instead, drawn by his longing for an environment at least superficially similar to that of his hometown, Nick settles in the "commuting town" of West Egg (3). Hence, though Nick and Tom have very different reasons for settling on the North Shore, they share a desire to create meaning and a sense of belonging through connection to the exurban landscape. While they both fail in this effort, they fail for different reasons, because they represent different historical moments in the evolution of their common landscape: Tom represents the vulnerable second generation of a Gold Coast elite whose time was already on the wane, whereas Nick—whether he recognizes it or not—stands as a member of the new commuter class, the growth of which was already in this era beginning to turn Long Island into the suburban mecca that it is today. If Tom cannot read the symbolic excess of his landscape because it is already a part of the past, Nick's dilemma is that the landscape to which he should belong—the soon-to-be-born Nassau County suburbia—has not yet arrived; the incongruity of his lone "cardboard bungalow" (3) sandwiched between West Egg mansions is an image that perfectly captures this novel's larger sense of a landscape in transition. It is perhaps the most visible manifestation of Fitzgerald's tendency to use landscape to look both forward and backward in time. As Richard Lehan argues, this is a novel that not only considers the lure of the past but also, at times, catches a "sense of the future" (Great Gatsby: The Limits 7).

Gatsby himself embodies this sense of being caught in an insupportable present—situated, as Lehan argues, "between a dead past and an implausible future" (Great Gatsby: The Limits 38). But Gatsby's temporal dilemma is a spatial one as well, since his romantic quest is consistently played out in terms of landscape. From the first appearance of Gatsby in the novel—as Nick spies him peering longingly across the sound, hands outstretched toward the green light on Daisy's dock (20–21)—to his last appearance, when Nick describes him just before the murder as being in "[a] new world, material without being real, where poor ghosts, breathing dreams like air, drifted fortuitously about" (161),

Gatsby's dream resides in landscapes. Nonetheless, Gatsby, whom Tom aptly refers to as "Mr. Nobody from Nowhere" (130), remains utterly disconnected from any sort of verifiable geographic background, a fact that poses a dilemma for those who, like Tom, are trying to read Gatsby. Nick eventually associates Gatsby with his West Egg home but does so in a way that effaces any real connections to place or landscape, insisting instead on the absolute autonomy of Gatsby's manufactured identity: "Jay Gatsby of West Egg, Long Island, sprang from his Platonic conception of himself. He was a son of God" (98).

If this observation confers on Gatsby a sort of idealized, Adamic status, at the same time it emphasizes the plasticity of Gatsby's identity, something he attempts to counter through the presentation of his West Egg landscape. Gatsby's manipulation of his own landscape draws attention to the malleable nature of the Gold Coast environment and thus emphasizes what Nick early in the novel refers to, somewhat mysteriously, as the "bizarre and not a little sinister contrast" between East Egg and West Egg (5). Gatsby's idea is to keep his home "always full of interesting people, night and day," to impress Daisy (90). This attempt to maintain a sort of perpetual *tableau vivant* for Daisy's sake necessitates a constant flow of partygoers, whom Gatsby shuttles in from the city in his Rolls Royce and from the train stations in his station wagon and whose "cars from New York are parked five deep in the drive" on a given Saturday night (40). Gatsby's need to populate his symbolic landscape—indeed, the guests are the principal symbol of this landscape—accentuates the sense of West Egg as a transitory landscape, a place quite literally filled with commuters.

Such a state is abhorrent to an East Egger like Tom Buchanan, a man who is attempting to shape exurban space in a different fashion, emphasizing an expansive rurality and the exclusive class identifications that go with it. Tom not only bristles at the insurgent, democratic impulse of Gatsby's parties—suggested by the ethnic family names on Nick's famous list of the partygoers—but also fears the push of urban progress itself, because he recognizes that urban progress involves expansion and intrusion, processes that are already imperiling his rural fantasy landscape. Daisy as well shares in this disdain for Gatsby's parties and what they represent; Nick's reading of her view of West Egg emphasizes her fear of the changing, increasingly mobile and urban landscape:

> She was appalled by West Egg, this unprecedented "place" that Broadway had begotten upon a Long Island fishing village—appalled by its raw vigor . . . and by the too obtrusive fate that herded its inhabitants along a short-cut from nothing to nothing.   (107)

The irony of Daisy's reaction to Gatsby's parties and what they represent lies in the fact that Gatsby is not trying to create a landscape of the future; instead he is seeking rather desperately, through the manipulation of landscape, to return to the past. The Gatsby mansion and all that comes with it are mere symbolic devices meant to lure Daisy away from East Egg and back to a relationship that is psychologically situated in the Louisville landscape of 1917. As Nick's narration so clearly emphasizes, Gatsby's dream-vision of Daisy is inextricably bound up with his memories of Louisville, specifically of Daisy's girlhood home: "He went to her house, at first with other officers from Camp Taylor, then alone. It amazed him—he had never been in such a beautiful house before" (148). Remarkable for the way that it links romance and real estate, this passage goes a long way toward explaining the motivations behind Gatsby's creation of what Nick calls "that huge incoherent failure of a house" (179). And yet it is no coincidence that Gatsby's stories of Louisville produce in Nick a sympathetic reaction, one in which he too is on the verge of remembering "something—an elusive rhythm, a fragment of lost words"—from his own past (111). Gatsby is not the only character in the novel who is in some sense trapped in landscapes of the past. If, as Berman suggests, the "ur-dream" of this novel is "the memory of Eden" (Great Gatsby *and Modern Times* 102), it seems that all the major characters maintain visions of their own personal Edens—Nick's "Middle West" (176), Daisy's beautiful "white girlhood" (19), Gatsby's Louisville of five years past, Tom's "civilization" (13)—places that are idealized, for the most part imaginary, and ultimately inaccessible.

The disparity between such idealized images of past environments and the realities of the contemporary landscape is a recurring motif in the novel, nowhere more carefully portrayed or infused with the force of history than in the scene of Gatsby and Daisy's first reunion. In a telling passage from this reunion scene in Gatsby's house, Nick describes the onset of night in West Egg:

> Outside the wind was loud and there was a faint flow of thunder along the Sound. All the lights were going on in West Egg now; the electric trains, men-carrying, were plunging home through the rain from New York. It was the hour of a profound human change, and excitement was generating on the air.   (95)

Fitzgerald's language here is significant; his synesthetic pairing of the "flow of thunder along the Sound" with the "plunging home" of the commuter trains reminds us of the machine in Gatsby's garden; this is not Louisville, 1917, but Long Island, 1922—a bustling suburb in the making, a lapsed Eden characterized by a merely illusory sense of rootedness and a stark contrast to the transcendant Louisville landscape that exists forever fixed in Gatsby's mind. It is not very surprising when Nick observes, immediately following this moment, that "the expression of bewilderment had come back into Gatsby's face" (95); thrust into the present time and place, Gatsby at this moment realizes the incongruity between his dreams and reality. It is indeed the hour of a profound human change.

This is not the novel's only specific mention of commuting. With its near constant motion between New York and East and West Egg, the narrative is literally shaped by the act of commutation, and what the various commutes reveal is the sharp contrast between ways of living in urban and exurban spaces. New York itself comes to be associated with violence, as in Tom and Gatsby's show-down at the Plaza Hotel (126–36) and, more explicitly, in Tom's breaking of Myrtle's nose in the 158th Street apartment (37). East and West Egg, by contrast, are represented at least early in the novel as havens, fantasy worlds seemingly protected from violence and decay by their very distance from the urban center. The third term in this equation is the "valley of ashes," the industrial Queens landscape that is traversed in the various commutes between the city and the exurbs. The valley is presided over by the infamous billboard eyes of Doctor T. J. Eckleburg, which underscore the notion of the Queens landscape as a primarily visual phenomenon, a visible record of the outward progress of urban blight. Indeed, this site/sight cannot be avoided; while the commuters' motor road and railroad run beside each other temporarily in an attempt to "shrink away" from this landscape (23), the effort is futile, for we are told that "passengers on waiting trains can stare at the dismal scene for as long as half an hour" (24).

Hence the very visibility of this landscape gives the lie to the myth of commutation—that one can be a "city person" while at the same time maintaining a rural identity. Instead, the surreal inversion of rurality in the valley's landscape, which is likened to a "fantastic farm where ashes grow like wheat into ridges and hills and grotesque gardens" (23), emphasizes the corruptibility of landscape. Fitzgerald situates the killing of Myrtle in the valley and uses the setting to underscore the fear of urban violence and decay spreading outside the bounds of the city center. Fittingly, Myrtle's death occurs during—indeed, is caused by—another commute out of the city. In subsequently making his final commute east to Gatsby's home, George Wilson completes the movement of urban violence eastward into the exurban landscape.

After the death of Gatsby and the disappearance of Tom and Daisy, actions that in their own right reveal the changing nature of the Gold Coast environment, two other moments transpire near the end of the novel that serve as reminders of the extent to which *The Great Gatsby* can be read as an examination of a landscape in transition. The first involves Gatsby's father, who excitedly shows Nick a prized possession:

> It was a photograph of the house, cracked in the corners and dirty with many hands. He pointed out every detail to me eagerly. "Look there!" and then sought admiration from my eyes. He had shown it so often that I think it was more real to him now than the house itself.   (172)

While the irony of Mr. Gatz's action—being fixated on an old photograph of his son's house even as he stands inside it—borders on the pathetic, he is really doing nothing more than others have done throughout the novel: confusing idealized representations of place for the real thing, searching for place-bound connections to the past in the face of an alienating and unreadable present moment. Indeed, one of Nick's final actions carries the same symbolic message. In what may be, from the perspective of landscape and place, the most telling moment of the novel, Nick describes his final effort to preserve the idealized memory of Gatsby's landscape:

> On the last night, with my trunk packed and my car sold to the grocer, I went over and looked at that huge incoherent failure of a house once more. On the white steps an obscene word, scrawled by some boy with a piece of brick, stood out clearly in the moonlight, and I erased it, drawing my shoe raspingly along the stone. Then I wandered down to the beach and sprawled out on the sand.   (179–80)

This action—which immediately precedes Nick's expansive, lyrical close to the narration—underscores the inevitability of the decay of this exurban landscape. But perhaps more significantly, Nick's erasure stands as a last effort to maintain an idealized vision of place, to freeze a living, evolving landscape into a fixed and permanent symbol. That such an effort is doomed to failure is one of the principal insights of the novel.

Teaching *The Great Gatsby* with an eye on landscape and place may offer both students and instructors an alternative to more well-worn approaches to the novel. Moreover, for students who have grown up in an age of suburban sprawl, Fitzgerald's depiction in the novel of a landscape in transition might well hold a particular resonance. Like many contemporary students, Fitzgerald himself, during his time on Long Island, lived in a bustling environment undergoing rapid changes. And like many of his characters, he repeatedly looked back in time, invoking in his fiction architectural and environmental symbols from the past, rich with emotional resonance, as counterweights to the uncertainty of the present. While a sense of longing for beloved environments of the past would become a standard theme in suburban fiction and popular culture of the postwar years and onward, when suburban sprawl would rapidly remake and homogenize the American landscape, students may well be interested to see this theme anchoring a great American novel from the 1920s. Focusing on landscape in teaching *The Great Gatsby* will not guarantee that students will be appropriately heartbroken by the magical last line of the novel and carry it with them always, as we do, but it may provide a nudge in the right direction.

"Among the Ash-Heaps and Millionaires": Teaching *The Great Gatsby* through the Lens of Class

Veronica Makowsky

When I begin a discussion of *The Great Gatsby* in a graduate or undergraduate survey of American literature, I put on the blackboard the phrase "Among the Ash-Heaps and Millionaires" to emphasize one of Fitzgerald's greatest contributions to American literature: his sensitive, remarkably calibrated depiction of America's troubled relation with social class. "Among the Ash-Heaps and Millionaires" was one of Fitzgerald's working titles for *The Great Gatsby*, and it raises queries typically evoked by Fitzgerald's works. In a society that espouses equality, why are some living in ash heaps while others are millionaires? Fitzgerald's intriguing use of the preposition "among" suggests further questions. One might wonder what comes between ash heaps and millionaires—perhaps an ordered continuum, but perhaps not. By making available to students the quotations and situations from Fitzgerald's other works that relate to class, instructors can set the stage for a complex exploration of class in *The Great Gatsby*. The quotations from his other works can be used as prompts for writing assignments or discussions that, through close reading and contextual comparisons, challenge students to grapple with this slippery issue as it appears in *The Great Gatsby*, American literature, and their own lives in the twenty-first century.

The concept of class provokes discomfort, and students are initially unwilling to discuss it. After all, the very notion seems un-American. Americans have, however, derived their own peculiar definitions of class. In some other societies, class is assigned by birth and is fixed there by the occupations available to that class. In America, though, we tend to think of class as mobile, as a reward for merit or as punishment for lack of merit. Or is class mobile because of money, not merit or birth? or because of money and birth? These searching and difficult questions, all relating to the theme of the American dream, are commonly discussed in American literature surveys and unsparingly explored in the works of F. Scott Fitzgerald. If, as Fitzgerald said, "[t]he test of a first-rate intelligence is the ability to hold two opposite ideas in the mind at the same time, and still retain the ability to function" ("Crack-Up" 69), Fitzgerald's intelligence is certainly beyond question—his literary corpus features a plethora of contradictory ideas about class, which we should explore with our students as we discuss *The Great Gatsby*.

Rereading Fitzgerald's works, I am struck by how very little he has to say about the middle class. The lengthiest and most detailed passage I can find is in his second novel, *The Beautiful and Damned*. It describes a cabaret called the Marathon, where the privileged Anthony and Gloria Patch go "slumming" in an unsuccessful attempt to titillate their jaded palates. The floating and weighting down of these men and women can be profitably contrasted in class discussion with the scene in *Gatsby* in which Daisy and Jordan are anchored to the sofa in the Buchanans' airy drawing room and brought to earth by Tom's peremptory and weighty entrance (8).

> There on Sunday nights gather the credulous, sentimental, underpaid, overworked people with hyphenated occupations: book-keepers, ticket-sellers, office-managers, salesmen, and, most of all, clerks—clerks of the express, of the mail, of the grocery, of the brokerage, of the bank. With them are their giggling, overgestured, pathetically pretentious women, who grow fat with them, bear them too many babies, and float helpless and uncontent in a sea of drudgery and broken hopes.
>
> (Fitzgerald, *Novels* 491–92)

This passage distressingly yokes together relentless realities and enduring dreams. The realities are the objects to which the men and women are joined—the men to account books, tickets, offices, sales, the express, the mail, the grocery, the brokerage, the bank; the women to their babies and to their overburdened men. The dreams are expressed in the words "credulous," "sentimental," "overgestured," and "pretentious." The distress in this passage comes not from the failure of the American dreams of upward mobility to become realities but from the way men and women ceaselessly and hopelessly keep striving despite their repeated failures, much like the lower-middle-class Gatsby in his futile pursuit of upper-class Daisy. They are indeed "overworked" since, as the name of the cabaret indicates, they are engaged in a marathon, very much like one of those 1920s dance marathons that could end only in exhaustion or death.

The hopelessness of this stalemate between dreams and realities, this Sisyphean labor, repels Fitzgerald and causes him to avoid the middle class in his works. Students could compare the breadwinners in the Marathon to the scanty description of George Wilson in *The Great Gatsby*. George Wilson lives between, or in the middle of, the ash heaps and the millionaires' mansions of East and West Egg:

> He was a blond, spiritless man, anæmic, and faintly handsome. When he saw us [Nick Carraway and Tom Buchanan] a damp gleam of hope sprang into his light blue eyes. . . . A white ashen dust veiled his dark suit and his pale hair as it veiled everything in the vicinity.   (25, 26)

Like the habitués of the Marathon, George Wilson dreams the American dream of prosperity and mobility; if only he can buy that car from Tom Buchanan, if only he can, like the pioneers of the frontier, get out West with his wife, Myrtle. But like the couples in the Marathon, chained to the harsh realities of drudgery, Wilson and Myrtle are doomed, ashes to ashes, dust to dust, as indicated by the shroud-like veil of "ashen dust" that links them to the ash heaps of the poor, not to the millionaires to whom they aspire.

What, then, are the people like who dwell in the ash heaps of poverty? Students can analyze the title "Among the Ash-Heaps and Millionaires" and discover that the millionaires are identified as people, millionaires, but the poor are only evoked by their environment, ash heaps. In Fitzgerald's works, their individuality is largely erased because they do not speak for themselves but are mediated through the perceptions of upper-class characters. Many of these encounters are on trains or streetcars or subways, and students could compare the examples cited here with the train rides in *The Great Gatsby* and find that such means of mass transportation could be symbols of the journey of life or of the mobility of the American dream. Fitzgerald's protagonists, however, plainly shun such democratic proximity on their journeys through American life. Here is Amory Blaine, the main character of Fitzgerald's first novel, *This Side of Paradise*, on a train during World War I:

> When Amory went to Washington the next week-end he caught some of the spirit of crisis which changed to repulsion in the Pullman car coming back, for the berths across from him were occupied by stinking aliens— Greeks, he guessed, or Russians. He thought how much easier patriotism had been to a homogeneous race, how much easier it would have been to fight as the Colonies fought, or as the Confederacy fought. And he did no sleeping that night, but listened to the aliens guffaw and snore while they filled the car with the heavy scent of latest America.
>
> (Fitzgerald, *Novels* 132)

Russians, Greeks—the "stinking aliens"—all look alike to Amory. He seems to forget that these aliens are citizens who would fight for America in World War I, just as the "homogeneous races" did for the thirteen states or for the Confederacy. Despite his largely olfactory repulsion, by the end of the passage he does grudgingly recognize that they are here to stay and are Americans just as much as he is. Their scent may be "heavy," but it is the freshest or "latest," unlike Amory's, and suggests the possibility of renewal. Students can compare this passage with Tom Buchanan's eugenicist obsession with keeping America for the "white race" in *The Great Gatsby* (12–13).

When the poor are not on the train with the protagonist but are viewed from the train by one of Fitzgerald's privileged observers, they seem a bit different, as in this description from Anthony Patch in *The Beautiful and Damned*:

> The train moved in through the deepening twilight, above and past half a hundred cheerful sweating streets of the upper East Side, each one passing the car-window like the space between the spokes of a gigantic wheel, each one with its vigorous colorful revelation of poor children swarming

in feverish activity like vivid ants in alleys of red sand. From the tenement windows leaned rotund, moon-shaped mothers, as constellations of this sordid heaven; women like dark imperfect jewels, women like vegetables, women like great bags of abominably dirty laundry.

(Fitzgerald, Novels 663)

Because Anthony can view the Upper East Side from "above," his perception is more positive than that of Amory Blaine, who is sharing the car with the "aliens." The children are at least "colorful," "cheerful," and "vivid"; their mothers are compared to jewels, stars, and the moon. Yet these attractive terms are always linked to the animalistic or inanimate. The children are "swarming" like "ants." Their mothers are compared to "vegetables" and "great bags of abominably dirty laundry."

Although we may flinch at these seemingly callous characterizations, it is important that students learn to distinguish Fitzgerald's point of view from that of his characters. Amory Blaine is a callow, arrogant youth who has a lot to learn "this side of paradise." Fitzgerald signals Anthony Patch's egotism in the sentences that immediately follow the women as "great bags of abominably dirty laundry":

> "I like these streets," observed Anthony aloud. "I always feel as though it's a performance being staged for me; as though the second I've passed they'll all stop leaping and laughing and, instead, grow very sad, remembering how poor they are, and retreat with bowed heads into their houses."
>
> (Fitzgerald, Novels 663)

Fitzgerald is clearly mocking Anthony Patch, who thinks the world revolves around him; the residents of the Upper East Side exist solely to entertain those "above." He even has the arrogance to believe that they view poverty as a personal failing so shameful that "they retreat with bowed heads into their houses." He is incapable of perceiving the cause as class and ethnic prejudice. Instructors can use passages like these to motivate their students to examine Nick Carraway's prejudices as the first-person narrator of *The Great Gatsby*.

But even in an early short story like "The Four Fists," which appeared in *Scribner's Magazine* in June 1920 and was later collected in *Flappers and Philosophers*, Fitzgerald clearly distinguishes his point of view from that of the protagonist. Once again the encounter takes place on mass transportation and troubles the protagonist's delicate olfactory nerves. While on a crowded urban horse-car, Samuel Meredith is seated next to "a heavy-eyed laboring man . . . who smelt objectionably of garlic" and "sagged slightly against Samuel and, spreading a little as a tired man will, took up quite too much room" (420). When four giggling teenage girls enter, Samuel relinquishes his seat. The laborer, despite Samuel's admonitions, refuses to do so, "quietly" replying, "I pay my fare." When they get off the streetcar, "[s]eeing his chance, Samuel no longer resisted his aristocratic inclination. He turned around and, launching a full-featured, dime-novel sneer, made a loud remark about the right of the lower animals to ride with human beings." The laborer turns on him, knocks him to the ground with his fist, and cries, "Don't laugh at me! . . . I been workin' all day. I'm tired as hell!" Samuel knows "intuitively that he had been wrong again. This man's strength, his rest, was the protection of his family. He had more use for his seat in the street-car than any young girl" (421). Students can compare this story with a scene in *The Great Gatsby* in which Nick Carraway displays a similar sense of mingled repulsion and shame when he crosses to the other side of the train to avoid the sight of the ash heaps after Myrtle's death (156).

Although I am making a case for Fitzgerald's consciousness of the monstrousness of some of his protagonists' attitudes toward the poor, particularly immigrants, students should also learn to see how Fitzgerald to some degree shares his characters' repulsion. It is largely based on aesthetics and on Fitzgerald's fear of bodies, bodies that are not so easily disguised and glamorized by clothing, bodies that may not have frequent opportunities to bathe and so draw attention to their physicality by an odor. Consider this description of wealthy children clad in their Easter finery in Fitzgerald's short story of 1920, " 'O Russet Witch!' ":

> Around them delightedly danced the two thousand miraculously groomed children of the very rich, correctly cute and curled, shining like sparkling little jewels upon their mothers' fingers. Speaks the sentimentalist for the children of the poor? Ah, but the children of the rich, laundered, sweet-smelling, complexioned of the country, and, *above-all*, with soft, in-door voices.   (1005; emphasis added)

Note that these children are their mothers' jewels without qualification, unlike those of the Upper East Side mothers, whom Anthony Patch perceives as "dark, imperfect jewels." These children are so clean and sweet-smelling and their voices so "soft" that they are ethereal, almost as free of the body as angels. Students can compare these two sets of children with little Pam Buchanan, Tom and Daisy's daughter, and also consider the way a poor but ambitious young man viewed the wealthy young Daisy: "Gatsby was overwhelmingly aware of the youth and mystery that wealth imprisons and preserves, of the freshness of many clothes, and of Daisy, gleaming like silver, safe and proud above the hot struggles of the poor" (150). Daisy, another rich man's child, is also "above-all" unlike the "gray, scrawny Italian child . . . setting torpedoes in a row along the railroad track" whom Nick sees near the ash heaps "a few days before the Fourth of July" (26). Students could compare Nick with Amory Blaine and Anthony Patch in their inability to see beneath the ashes of class and ethnicity, and the revolutionary holiday the "Italian child" is celebrating with potentially menacing torpedoes.

Fitzgerald's consideration of the poor, seen only from the perspective of the rich, indicates his perception of the rich. Students should explore the question of how the rich are, in the words of the narrator of Fitzgerald's short story "The Rich Boy," "different from you and me" (318). One reason is that wealth so shields them from the exigencies of the body that they become almost inhuman. Daisy may gleam, but she is hard and cold "like silver." Because of their seemingly limitless wealth, Tom and Daisy Buchanan, in Nick Carraway's words, "smashed up things and creatures and then retreated back into their money or their vast carelessness, or whatever it was that kept them together, and let other people clean up the mess they had made" (179). Nick, like Fitzgerald, may be conveying Tom and Daisy's point of view; but, like them, he finds it easier to distance himself from wrecked "things and creatures" than from acknowledged human beings. Fitzgerald, unlike the Buchanans, recognizes the cost of that "safe and proud" inhumanity to "other people," as he indicates in this description of the fabulously wealthy Nicole Diver in Fitzgerald's fourth novel, *Tender Is the Night*:

> Nicole was the product of much ingenuity and toil. For her sake trains began their run at Chicago and traversed the round belly of the continent to California; chicle factories fumed and link belts grew link by link in factories; men mixed toothpaste in vats and drew mouthwash out of copper hogsheads; girls canned tomatoes quickly in August or worked rudely at the Five-and-Tens on Christmas Eve; half-breed Indians toiled on Brazilian coffee plantations and dreamers were muscled out of patent rights to new tractors—these were some of the people who gave a tithe to Nicole. . . .   (71–72)

Students should compare this description with those of Daisy. Like Daisy, Nicole is an artifact like silver, "the product of much ingenuity and toil," whose "safe and proud" beauty is purchased at the cost of the labors and lives of the working class and American "dreamers," who were "muscled out" as a "tithe" to the goddess Nicole.

Students can also compare the vampirelike qualities of these fabulously wealthy characters, who, though well protected from the exigencies of the body, cannot fully escape its desires, which they attempt to satisfy through draining the lifeblood of the lower classes. Daisy is responsible for the deaths of Gatsby and Myrtle, and Nicole more slowly destroys her husband, Dr. Dick Diver, by feeding on his strength and vitality. In particular, instructors can draw their students' attention to Fitzgerald's upper-class men, who seek warmth through "the hot struggles of the poor" but fail in their attempts to humanize themselves, instead only humiliating those they exploit. In *The Beautiful and Damned*, Anthony Patch uses and leaves two lower-class women, Geraldine and Dot, after raising false hopes in them. Dick Diver in *Tender Is the Night* attempts to divert himself from Nicole's dangerous allure by an affair with a "telephone girl" who was "red-lipped like a poster, and known obscenely in the messes as 'The Switchboard' " (164). Tom Buchanan breaks the arm of a chambermaid in an automobile accident in Santa Barbara before he breaks Myrtle's nose in New York. And Nick Carraway, often considered a sympathetic character, tells us, "I even had a short affair with a girl who lived in Jersey City and worked in the accounting department, but her brother began throwing mean looks in my direction, so when she went on her vacation in July I let it blow quietly away" (56).

These upper-class characters are seeking what they have lost: vitality and hope. Students can compare them with those who have physical vitality and its spiritual manifestation in hope and are not yet fixed in a class; they are the aspirants, the liminal, the classless class, who are some of the most interesting of Fitzgerald's characters. Take Myrtle Wilson in *The Great Gatsby*, who wants to marry Tom Buchanan. Nick comments that he "had a glimpse of Mrs. Wilson straining at the garage pump with panting vitality as we went by" (68). Like the dancers in the Marathon, Myrtle strains and pants; her efforts to pump herself out of the gas station are indefatigable. Even in death, Nick remarks, she looks "as though she had choked a little in giving up the tremendous vitality she had stored so long" (137). Myrtle's physical vitality is translated into what Nick calls "an extraordinary gift for hope" (2) in American literature's most prominent aspirant, Gatsby, who keeps hoping until the moment of his death for the phone call from Daisy that will raise him to her level.

Instructors could here ask their students what could raise these aspirants to Daisy and Tom's level and what is that level besides economic? They could examine the opening passages of *The Great Gatsby* in which Nick Carraway provides two seemingly contradictory answers. He quotes his father's advice: "Whenever you feel like criticizing anyone . . . just remember that all the people in this world haven't had the advantages that you've had" (1). Daisy, Tom, and Nick's status arises from external circumstances, "advantages," not from something innate or hereditary. But, at the end of the passage, Nick restates his father's advice: "as my father snobbishly suggested, and I snobbishly repeat, a sense of the fundamental decencies is parcelled out unequally at birth" (2). This "parcell[ing] out . . . at birth" is, of course, the opposite of environmental "advantages." Or is it? What Nick may really be discussing here is the relation of morality to manners: a "sense of the fundamental decencies," morality, would make you exercise good manners and refrain from "criticizing anyone." The essential question for Nick, for Fitzgerald throughout his works, and for our students is, Are good manners also a reliable indicator of good character? Another way the question could be asked is, Are the rich simply different from you and me because, as Ernest Hemingway stated in his short story "The Snows of Kilimanjaro," they have more money or because their "advantages" make them better people? Or do they just have a more attractive facade?

Students can consider the relation of these facades to the American dream because, as his works demonstrate, to Fitzgerald the rich are merely attractive facades that would tumble over if moved since there is nothing behind them and they have no foundations. Here are two passages that students might read closely and compare. In *This Side of Paradise*, Amory Blaine, Fitzgerald's alter ego, "resented social barriers as artificial distinctions made by the strong to bolster up their weak retainers and keep out the almost strong" (Fitzgerald, *Novels* 40). Amory's observation is abundantly illustrated in a famous passage from *The Great Gatsby*. Tom and Nick enter a room at the Buchanan mansion where Daisy and Jordan are already seated. Nick recalls:

> The only completely stationary object in the room was an enormous couch on which two young women were buoyed up as though upon an anchored balloon. They were both in white, and their dresses were rippling and fluttering as if they had just been blown back in after a short flight around the house. I must have stood for a few moments listening to the whip and snap of the curtains and the groan of a picture on the wall. There was a boom as Tom Buchanan shut the rear windows and the caught wind died out about the room, and the curtains and rugs and the two young women ballooned slowly to the floor.   (8)

Tom is strong and stops the "flight" of his "weak retainers" with the "whip," "boom," and "snap" of his power. He ends their subjection to the winds of time, change, and life, but he also removes the beauty that is an intrinsic part of their vulnerability, the "rippling" and "fluttering" of their flight. When Daisy tells Nick, "I'm p-paralyzed with happiness" (8), and both women state, "We can't move" (115), they are acknowledging the static death-in-life concealed by the facade of happiness provided by money.

These facades are deceptive, and students can compare the unhappiness of the deceived with that of the deceivers. Myrtle Wilson tells Nick that she married George because she "thought he was a gentleman" (34); but, she discovers, to her great chagrin, that George borrowed the suit in which he was married, his gentlemanly facade. Myrtle, however, does not learn from her mistakes. She tells Nick of her first sight of Tom Buchanan (on a train, of course): "He had on a dress suit and patent leather shoes, and I couldn't keep my eyes off him" (36). Tom may be rich, but he's no gentleman: he breaks Myrtle's nose when she mentions Daisy's name, mistakenly believing that a gentleman would defend his wife's honor by striking his lower-class mistress.

In a sense, we are taking our students down the path of that classic literary theme of appearance versus reality, but Fitzgerald takes it to a deeper level when he explores the way appearances manifest themselves in behavior—in manners. Students can compare Nick Carraway's recollection of his father's advice at the beginning of *The Great Gatsby* with Dick Diver's memory of his father in *Tender Is the Night*:

From his father Dick had learned the somewhat conscious good manners of the young Southerner coming north after the Civil War. Often he used them and just as often he despised them because they were not a protest against how unpleasant selfishness was but against how unpleasant it looked.   (214–15)

Dick believes that manners too often refer only to the level of superficial aesthetics, "how unpleasant it looked," instead of the level of the moral, "how unpleasant selfishness was." He later tells his wife's sister:

Good manners are an admission that everybody is so tender that they have to be handled with gloves. Now, human respect—you don't call a man a coward or a liar lightly, but if you spend your life sparing people's feelings and feeding their vanity, you get so you can't distinguish what *should* be respected in them.   (233)

For Fitzgerald, then, the endless maintenance of facades in oneself and others leads to life as a funhouse mirror that is not really any fun because it reflects a fundamental emptiness. Millionaires can be ash heaps beneath their pleasant facades.

Through an exploration of Fitzgerald's vexed and vexing representations of class in America throughout his works, we can help our students avoid a binary, simplistic approach to Fitzgerald and his characters and to respect the ambiguity that pervades all his works, including *The Great Gatsby*. The seemingly promiscuous jumbling among rather than between ash heaps and millionaires is the way that Fitzgerald sees American life. Class is essentially meaningless and empty, a facade, because it is composed of arbitrary categories that inhibit life, change, and motion. And for Fitzgerald, life cannot be static. Beauty, grace, and character are alive, changing, and evanescent: vital. Ultimately, life is a process, not a status or a class. If Fitzgerald cherished a privileged class, it would not be found in socioeconomic reports and surveys; it would be the freemasonry of artists like himself. In *Tender Is the Night*, Dick Diver contemplates his upper-class, fabulously wealthy wife, Nicole:

The frontiers that artists must explore were not for her, ever. She was fine-spun, inbred—eventually she might find rest in some quiet mysticism. Exploration was for those with a measure of peasant blood, those with big thighs and thick ankles who could take punishment as they took bread and salt, on every inch of flesh and spirit.   (242)

"Explorations" and "frontiers": those are the border areas, the liminal states, the seams of the class system in which the artist works. For Fitzgerald, the master class and the master of class is the artist spinning his American dreams from chaos among the ash heaps and millionaires.

What Makes Him Great? Teaching *The Great Gatsby* and the New Historicism

Stephen Brauer

My students tend to think in easy oppositions. When they read *The Great Gatsby*, they understand Gatsby to be the protagonist and Tom Buchanan to be his foil, based on the rivalry for Daisy's heart and affections. They also readily recognize other criteria that Gatsby and Tom have in opposition, including the geographical distinctions between West Egg and East Egg and the fact that Tom's family was "enormously wealthy" (6), whereas Gatsby grew up the son of "shiftless and unsuccessful farm people" (98). But my students' propensity for interpreting narratives through the lens of dualities leads them to translate this opposition into a formulation that Gatsby, as one student put it, is the good guy and Tom is the bad guy. While at first blush we might understand how students would conceive of Tom as a bad sort—he cheats on his wife, treats his mistress and her cuckolded husband rather shabbily, and willingly allows Gatsby to play the gallant in taking responsibility for the hit-and-run accident that kills Myrtle Wilson—it is a stretch to imagine Jay Gatsby as the good guy in the novel. Such a conception negates the complexities of his character and the narrative. After all, while Tom is a married man having an affair with another woman, Gatsby is pursuing an affair with a married woman.

Inevitably, though, each time that I teach the novel to my undergraduate students, one of them insists that we need to acknowledge that Gatsby is the hero of the novel. This assertion is almost always met with a chorus of approval. Some students defend Gatsby by claiming that he followed his heart; others try to aim higher in suggesting that he believed in the "green light," the American dream; finally, one student will declare with a triumphant air, "He was loyal to his dream, to be with the woman he loved, and he worked like hell to make it happen. What's so wrong with that?" All these statements resonate with me; the consistency with which they appear suggests that this character touches something deep inside many readers. Of course, I say to my students, there's nothing wrong with wanting to be with the one we love, but what does it entail to shift the wanting to having? What is it about Gatsby, I ask them, that is great? Is it his desire for Daisy or his doggedness in pursuing her? The difference, it seems to me, is crucial in that it dramatizes the distinction between our dreams and how we go about achieving them.

What makes Gatsby the good guy, or the hero, of the novel? His charm? His ability to throw the best parties of the summer? His sense of color in stockpiling dress shirts? Or perhaps, more seriously, is it his willingness to shoulder the blame for the death of Myrtle Wilson? Not to my students. What they tend to celebrate is his love for Daisy—his steadfastness and its intensity, his loyalty to his conception of her, and his desire to will their moment together in Louisville back into existence. My students admire this trait, projecting a bit of the Romantic hero onto his doomed project, lauding him as a man with faith in his own agency and power to such a degree that he believes he can do anything, including repeat the past.

In these discussions with my students, I am forced to consider how I can help them grapple with the complexity of the novel. Rather than merely dismiss their feelings of association with Gatsby and his love for Daisy, I try to help them complicate their reading of Gatsby the man. Although they tend to want to see him only as a hero, I want them to reconcile this image with what he is when we meet him in the novel—the front man for Meyer Wolfsheim's criminal syndicate. There is nothing terribly heroic in that role. But there is something in Gatsby's past that is—or should be—compelling to us as readers, his story of success. His evolution from James Gatz to Jay Gatsby—and his consequent rise from clam digger on the shore of Lake Superior to lord of the manor on the Long Island Sound—on one level follows the inspirational model of self-making in America through self-improvement. At the same time, the means through which he achieves wealth represents a dynamic of success at any cost that is much more attuned to the 1920s than to that of the eighteenth or nineteenth centuries. In my experience, grounding students' reading of the novel in the context of the 1920s and the cultural currents of the time in which Fitzgerald produced the text is the most useful way to help them arrive at a more textured reading of Gatsby. While I hesitate to call him the good guy in the novel, I am not fully opposed to their perception of Gatsby as a hero; I just want them to recognize the nuances and even the messiness of what that might mean in the text and in the culture of the time.

Since 1994, critics have offered valuable examples of scholarship that situates the novel in its cultural moment. In Kirk Curnutt's edited volume *A Historical Guide to F. Scott Fitzgerald*, scholars provide different types of historical and cultural contexts from the first decades of the twentieth century for Fitzgerald's work, including the literary marketplace of the 1920s, the rise of film and the representation of women, and the aftereffects of World War I. A contributor to this volume, Ronald Berman, has produced three books—The Great Gatsby *and Modern Times*, The Great Gatsby *and Fitzgerald's World of Ideas*, and *Fitzgerald, Hemingway, and the Twenties*—in which he considers how the novel reflects contemporaneous currents of thought. All these works have been influenced by the rise of the new historicism, a methodological approach that interrogates what Stephen Greenblatt has called "the half-hidden cultural transactions through which great works of art are empowered" (4). Staking a critical claim outside the purview of New Criticism, Catherine Gallagher argues in *Practicing New Historicism*—written in collaboration with Greenblatt—that "the writers we love did not spring up from nowhere and . . . their achievements must draw upon a whole life-world" (12). New historicists investigate the relation between the work of art and the culture of the time period in which it was produced. Such a critical methodology, Gallagher and

Greenblatt argue, does not diminish the writer or the accomplishment of the writer's work by placing it in the context of the broader culture. The new historicist project, they say,

> is not about "demoting" art or discrediting aesthetic pleasure; rather it is concerned with finding the creative power that shapes literary works *outside* the narrow boundaries in which it had hitherto been located, as well as *within* those boundaries. (12)

As cultural critics, new historicists treat "all of the written and visual traces of a particular culture as a mutually intelligible network of signs." Their goal is to decode those signs and that network, enabling them to recognize "particular historically embedded social and psychological formations" and to understand better how the work of art is informed by these formations (Gallagher and Greenblatt 7). This "circulation of social energy," in Greenblatt's formulation, can help readers pose questions that go beyond authorial intention and extend to how the representation of ideas, images, and concepts in the text have broad cultural and historical implications. In terms of *The Great Gatsby*, the new historicism serves as an especially valuable methodological approach to consider such issues as how the repeated references to advertisements in the novel bespeak the evolving social and economic power of advertising in 1920s culture or how Tom Buchanan's interest in " 'The Rise of the Colored Empires' by . . . Goddard" evokes contemporaneous debates surrounding immigration and nativism during the first decades of the century (12).[1]

To demonstrate further how the new historicism serves as a useful methodology in teaching the novel, I like to consider the concept of the self-made man and how Fitzgerald's use of this deeply American trope was contingent on contemporaneous shifts in definitions of self-making. At seventeen, James Gatz, a college dropout and wanderer, took the name Jay Gatsby and set out on a new path by rowing out to Dan Cody's yacht to inform him that the yacht was in danger on the lake flat. James Gatz would never return. Fitzgerald writes that "he invented just the sort of Jay Gatsby that a seventeen-year-old boy would be likely to invent, and to this conception he was faithful to the end" (98). James Gatz made himself anew, figuratively shedding his skin and emerging with a new name and a new potential destiny for greatness.

As I explain to my students, to understand best what makes Gatsby so compelling to readers, indeed what makes Gatsby great, we must interrogate what "great" might have meant to people at the time Fitzgerald wrote the novel. Readers get some insight into this term when Gatsby's father comes to help bury his son and discusses his lost future with Nick Carraway:

> "He had a big future before him, you know. He was only a young man, but he had a lot of brain power here."
>
> He touched his head impressively, and I nodded.

"If he'd of lived, he'd of been a great man. A man like James J. Hill.
He'd of helped build up the country." (168)

Mr. Gatz's allusion to James J. Hill, an American railroad tycoon of the late
nineteenth and early twentieth century, suggests an equivalency between
Gatsby and the major industrialist robber barons such as Hill, Jay Gould, and
Andrew Carnegie. Considering Gatsby's—and Fitzgerald's—Minnesota roots,
it comes as no real surprise that Hill serves in the novel as a role model for a
"great man." At fourteen, following his father's death, Hill began working to
support his family. After years of working in the shipping and railway business,
he recognized the evolving importance of efficiently transporting goods across
and through the Midwest to the West. In pursuit of the vast economic opportunity present at the time, he forged a series of sagacious economic alliances
and partnerships that established him as the leading figure in the exploding
railroad industry in the Northwest, as the owner of the Great Northern Railway, which extended from Minnesota to the Pacific Ocean. Hill was, as the saying goes, a capital success.[2]

Success is important to Gatsby, and not merely as a means of recapturing
Daisy's heart.[3] Fitzgerald alludes to the tradition of the self-making narrative
with the daily schedule that Mr. Gatz shows to Nick, along with the list of "General Resolves" that Gatsby wrote as a young boy in his "ragged old copy of a
book called *Hopalong Cassidy*" (173). The list for improving himself and his
station—with such items as "Bath every other day" and "Read one improving
book or magazine per week"—evokes the tenets set out by Benjamin Franklin
in his *Autobiography*. In his text, Franklin details how he set out to make his
fortune as a young man in Philadelphia while improving his character. He
draws a strong correlation between his socioeconomic rise and his deep commitment to virtuous behavior, and he suggests that others can follow his example if they too want to improve their status. American self-making mythology,
with its roots in Puritan notions of hard work and virtue, had its first authoritative articulation in Franklin's *Autobiography*.[4]

Critics have long had a sense of Fitzgerald's allusions to the self-making tradition in the novel, but the new historicists' emphasis on what Gallagher and
Greenblatt identify as "the singular, the specific, and the individual" has complicated the critical response to the novel's representation of that tradition (6).
Mr. Gatz's allusion to Hill as the model for greatness that his son was destined
to achieve is especially revealing of the shift in the conception of self-making
(for more on this subject, see Brauer). This shift had roots decades before the
1920s, in the late nineteenth and early twentieth century, when the robber
barons of that time helped transform the concept of success from its close connection to virtue to one that privileged the exploitation of economic opportunity. The outgrowth of the rhetoric of uninhibited socioeconomic mobility that
had been implicit in Franklin was that robber barons such as J. P. Morgan,
Carnegie, Gould, and others came to embody self-making. Joseph G. Pyle's

authorized biography of Hill, published only eight years before *The Great Gastby*, offered an intriguing example, with its themes of struggle, perspicacity, and success.

But the stories of the robber barons were not the equivalent of Franklin's. The robber barons asserted their place among the highest of the American social and economic elite through their exploitation of opportunity and circumstances. They fulfilled the demands of a changing marketplace in a rapidly evolving industrial economy, combining luck and good timing with fierce competitiveness, discipline, and business acumen. Unlike Franklin, the robber barons were not overly concerned with virtuous conduct, nor were they always lionized for their achievements; historians and critics, even by the 1920s and 1930s, had long critiqued their ruthlessness and selfishness in business matters, as when Hill and Morgan battled E. H. Harriman for control of the common stock of the Northern Pacific Railroad in 1901, instigating a Wall Street panic and crushing a series of speculators and investors (F. L. Allen 65).

By the beginning of the 1920s, the age of the robber barons was over, and those who believed in the possibility of socioeconomic mobility needed to look elsewhere for their models. Although his father proclaims Hill as someone to emulate, Gatsby turns to other types of figures for his mentors. His first one is Dan Cody, the man with whom he apprenticed for five years, serving as "steward, mate, skipper, secretary, and even jailor" (100). From Cody, Fitzgerald writes, Gatsby received a "singularly appropriate education" (101); but students may wonder, Appropriate for what? Cody made his fortune in the West by remaining persistent and faithful to his belief that he could strike it rich in the competitive field of mining natural resources. Eventually making his millions in Montana copper, he was "a product of the Nevada silver fields, of the Yukon, of every rush for metal since seventy-five" (99). The persistence and perseverance of the traditional self-making narrative are present in this description. Fitzgerald, however, also describes Cody as "the pioneer debauchee, who during one phase of American life brought back to the Eastern seaboard the savage violence of the frontier brothel and saloon" (100). With this description, I point out to my students, Fitzgerald signals a shift in the traditional success narrative. Cody represents a lowering of Franklin's standards that the young James Gatz had sought to emulate as a boy. While Franklin emphasized moral character and virtue as fundamental to the self-making project, Fitzgerald portrays Cody as wholly deficient in these qualities. In fact, the "appropriate" education that Gatsby receives seems to be a preparation for succeeding in a culture in which ethics and morality take a backseat to the acquisition of money and the conspicuous display of consumption.

Gatsby's alliance with the gangster Meyer Wolfsheim as his mentor takes him even further away from Franklin's privileging of self-improvement as the foundation for success. Following the end of the era of the robber barons and the institution of Prohibition and its concomitant illegal markets, gangsters came to serve as new emblems of self-made men. In the 1920s, the American economy climbed to newfound heights, as the gross national product rose nearly 40% (Henretta et al. 728). This rapid growth was stimulated by the demand for consumer products, particularly the automobile—at the start of the decade, nine million vehicles were on the road, and by 1930 there were twenty-seven million (Roark et al. 897–98). Inspired by the increased emphasis on consumption, manufacturing output expanded 64%, and the demand for goods and services kept unemployment around 3% or 4% for much of the decade (Henretta et al. 728). With an economy driven by the public's desire for consumer products, there were a variety of new opportunities for those who were able to take advantage of the emerging markets for goods and services. The new markets included those created by the National Prohibition Act; the Prohibition years saw an upsurge in crime directly resulting from the need to supply the continuing demand for alcohol. In *The Great Gatsby*, the services that Gatsby and Meyer Wolfsheim provide their clients are never made explicit, but they seem to include bootlegging, gambling, and loan sharking. Gatsby's wealth and Wolfsheim's notoriety demonstrate that they are highly successful in their business.

Fitzgerald repeatedly places his narrative in the milieu of crime, and his fictionalization of the gangster type mirrored actual criminals of the era.[5] Wolfsheim tells Nick of his involvement in the Herman Rosenthal murder (70), a reference to a notorious crime in 1912. Moreover, critics have argued that Fitzgerald based his characterization of Wolfsheim on Arnold Rothstein, a well-known criminal figure in the 1920s, who was a gambler, bootlegger, pawnbroker, dealer of narcotics, and participant in numerous other criminal schemes. At one point, Gatsby says to Nick that Wolfsheim was responsible for fixing the 1919 World Series (73), a crime widely attributed to Rothstein. The 1920s saw the mythologizing of men such as Rothstein, Al Capone, and Lucky Luciano, who rose to prominence in the popular culture of the Roaring Twenties. Indeed, crime took on a romanticized allure highlighted in the tabloids and later represented in such films as *Little Caesar*, *Public Enemy*, and *Scarface*.

Wolfsheim says of Gatsby, his protégé, "I raised him up out of nothing, right out of the gutter. I saw right away he was a fine-appearing, gentlemanly young man, and when he told me he was an Oggsford I knew I could use him good" (171). I explain to my students that this conflation of rags-to-riches imagery with the language of the gangster nicely encapsulates the cultural shift in conceptions of success by the 1920s. That conflation was evident in an even more obvious way in Fred Pasley's *Al Capone: Biography of a Self-Made Man*, in which Pasley recounted Capone's rise from a thug in Five Points in New York to the top of the rackets in Chicago. To a new historicist, Fitzgerald's representation of Gatsby, in the context of the gangster films of the late 1920s and early 1930s and in the context of Pasley's imagining of a gangster as a self-made man, tells us a great deal about how people in the culture conceived of achieving success. Defining what self-making meant in the culture in which Fitzgerald produced his novel, through a tracking of what Gallagher and Greenblatt call the "particular historically embedded social and psychological formations" (7), allows students to recognize a moral decay in the culture.

That moral decay, I also like to mention to my students, is present in a number of other novels published in 1925, the same year Fitzgerald published *The Great Gatsby*. John Dos Passos, in *Manhattan Transfer*, tells the story of Congo Jake, who, like Gatsby, chooses crime as his means of socioeconomic ascent. Another character, Ellen Thatcher, sleeps with a succession of men who will benefit her career and social position. In *Gentlemen Prefer Blondes*, Anita Loos offers a different version of this type of figure with her portrayal of Lorelei Lee, a beautiful and sexy woman who manipulates a series of men to underwrite her expenses and desires. Lorelei subtly and not so subtly uses her physical charms to convince these men to buy her jewelry, to pay for her travel abroad, and to finance her film career. Theodore Dreiser, in *An American Tragedy*, dramatizes most fully the corruption of the self-making narrative. Clyde Griffiths, who begins the novel as the son of street preachers, uses family connections and hard work to reach a secure socioeconomic standing. Yet his ambition to establish a romantic relationship with the wealthy Sondra Finchley leads him first to abandon Roberta Alden, a factory worker he has impregnated, and then to be complicit in her death by drowning. I use Dreiser's dramatization of ambition and the desire for success even in the face of moral bankruptcy as a powerful echo of Fitzgerald's story of what Jay Gatsby wants and what he is willing to do to achieve it.

The new historicist methodology, in which readers situate the novel in its cultural moment and decode "the written and visual signs of particular culture" (Gallagher and Greenblatt 7), complicates how we read literary texts beyond our immediate response to what is on the page. The interrogation of the singular and particular reference to James J. Hill in the text, a hallmark of new historicism, helps students untangle Fitzgerald's portrayal of a shift in the conception of the American dream. The representation of self-making in the novel derives from the distinct allusions to an established American tradition that harkens back to Franklin, as captured in the language and rhetoric in James Gatz's notations in the back of *Hopalong Cassidy*. Fitzgerald contrasts that tradition with two other models in the novel—Dan Cody and Meyer Wolfsheim—both of whom are updates of the tradition and who are willing to use savage violence to further their aims.

Having adopted Cody and Wolfsheim as his models of how to achieve success, Gatsby defines his social status through very public displays of his material possessions (for discussions of possessions and consumption in *Gatsby*, see Donaldson, "Possessions"; Posnock; and Curnutt, "Fitzgerald's Consumer World"). His house is opulent in its size and its furnishings, exemplified by the many books in his large library, which are authentic but remain uncut and unread. These books are mere commodities that exist for exhibition, not for edification. The myriad shirts in his wardrobe that he shows to Nick and Daisy are further examples of his belief in the importance of appearances. Gatsby flaunts his wealth through the accumulation of shirts—"shirts of sheer linen and thick silk and fine flannel, which lost their folds as they fell and covered the table in many-colored disarray" (92). Throughout the novel Fitzgerald notes, as with the books and the shirts, the rampant commodity fetishization of the time. He deliberately eroticizes possessions and even goes so far as to picture Gatsby's car as a phallic symbol: "It was a rich cream color, bright with nickel, swollen here and there in its monstrous length with triumphant hat-boxes and supper-boxes and tool-boxes, and terraced with a labyrinth of wind-shields that mirrored a dozen suns" (64).

While we might excuse Gatsby's displays as his attempt to capture Daisy's notice and to bring her back into his life, his belief that this is a viable strategy illustrates something fundamental about the culture of the time. Gatsby's possessions—the house, the property, the books, the shirts, and the car—all signify his wealth, but students need to see that they do not efface the reality of how he went about making his fortune. Rather, his moral corruption is merely hidden underneath his adherence to the social and economic tenets of a consumer culture, much like Loos's representation of Lorelei Lee in *Gentlemen Prefer Blondes*. When Tom Buchanan makes public those services that Gatsby and Wolfsheim provide, Daisy rejects Gatsby, signaling a dismissal not of wealth—she remains married to Tom, after all—but of the methods he used to attain wealth.

Hoping to provoke students into thinking further about what is at play in the novel, I like to suggest that maybe Daisy was right to turn away from Gatsby. The Buchanans are not people we root for, to be sure, but is Daisy wrong to throw Gatsby aside? When we read Gatsby as only a hero, the novel flattens into a mere tragedy of lost love and failed dreams, and we miss out on a richer engagement with what Fitzgerald is lamenting in the novel. I want my students to understand that Fitzgerald is doing more than dramatizing the difficulty of realizing or maintaining an ideal love and more than bemoaning the difficulty of following the green light and what this evokes about achieving the American dream. I want them to deal with the murkiness of Gatsby as a character, which means dealing with his flaws and his moral vacuity. If they recognize the title as a Romantic celebration of a man who rises to new heights, they also need to acknowledge that the title is certainly overreaching in how it imagines Meyer Wolfsheim's protégé. There is tragedy in this novel, but there is also plenty of irony and a correlating critique of the culture of the 1920s. In *The Great Gatsby*, Fitzgerald offers a damning portrait of success and the desire to achieve one's dreams regardless of the costs. Again, I wonder aloud to my students, what makes Gatsby so heroic, so great? Is he really the good guy? If so, what are our standards?

NOTES

[1] Two well-known advertising references in the novel are the description of the billboard for the services of Doctor T. J. Eckleburg (23–24) and Daisy's remark to Gatsby, "You resemble the advertisement of the man" (119). There is a great deal of material to use in considering the role of advertising in the 1920s, and many critics like to begin with Bruce Barton. With Tom's reference to Goddard, Fitzgerald seems to be alluding to the similarly titled *The Rising Tide of Color*, by Lothrop Stoddard. For more on nativism, see Michaels, *Our America.*

[2] To have a broad understanding of Hill and his place in the culture, readers should contrast Pyle's authorized biography with the more current versions of Malone and A. Martin.

[3] As an example of how new historicists might take different approaches to the same text, and even to the same concept, contrast Brauer and Berman (Great Gatsby *and Modern Times* 166–76) on success.

[4] The description of *Hopalong Cassidy* as "ragged" seems purposefully evocative of Horatio Alger's *Ragged Dick*. Alger, in his many fictional rags-to-riches narratives in the mid-nineteenth century, further popularized Franklin's self-making ideology.

[5] There is an array of scholarship on the multifaceted ways in which Fitzgerald may have derived his characterizations from both well-known gangsters and lesser-known criminals. See Bruccoli, *Some Sort*; Castille; D. Gross; Kruse, "Real Jay Gatsby"; Pauly; and Piper, "Fuller-McGee Case."

Teaching Gatsby as American Culture Hero

Kim Moreland

What makes Gatsby great? This question, implicitly raised by the novel's title, will generate hours of productive class discussion, whether in the usual context of an American literature course or in the context of courses in American studies or American history, where Fitzgerald's novel is sometimes taught, typically from a sociological or historical perspective. A modernist novel that is simultaneously romantic and realistic, it represents both the spirit and the material reality of Jazz Age America. Technically brilliant, this short and readable novel appeals to students and instructors alike, whether it serves as the primary focus or as a supplement to sociological studies or histories of the 1920s.

Certainly some students will respond that Gatsby is not great, that he is a gangster and a con man, or even that he is a fool for loving Daisy, whose bad driving reveals her moral carelessness and that of the class and time to which she belongs. But other students will come to his rescue, will insist that he is great, that despite their discomfort with some of his actions there is something about him—as Nick describes it, "something gorgeous . . . some heightened sensitivity to the promises of life" (2)—that separates him from the "rotten crowd" (154).

It may prove useful at this point to ask students if they know who Robert Redford and Sam Waterston are. Almost all will know Redford, and some will know Waterston. It is easy to make the point that Redford is a certifiable star and celebrity (with his own film festival and catalog company), and Waterston is a journeyman actor whose starring roles (in Joseph Papp's 1972–73 Broadway production of *Much Ado about Nothing*, in the 1984 film *The Killing Fields*, and in television's 1990s–2000s ensemble series *Law and Order*) have brought critical acclaim but comparatively limited fame. I ask students why Redford was cast as Gatsby and Waterston as Nick Carraway in the 1974 film of *The Great Gatsby*. Students attuned to America's celebrity culture will recognize that Redford's star power is of an order of magnitude different from Waterston's fame and that this difference reflects that between Gatsby and Nick (just as their names do—in the novel or in the critical literature Gatsby is seldom referred to as Jay, and Nick is almost never called Carraway).

Gatsby lives on the plane of celebrity, his "notoriety . . . increas[ing] all summer" to the point that "an ambitious young reporter from New York" tracks him down for a random "statement" (97); Gatsby dies on that plane too, his murder fodder for the "photographers and newspaper men" whose tabloid-like "reports were a nightmare—grotesque, circumstantial, eager, and untrue" (163). Like the instructor and the students, Nick lives on the plane of quotidiar. reality, and his romance with ⁓n (played in the 1974 film by the actress Lois Chiles) provides a cⁿ ⸱ counterpart to that of the glamorous Gatsby and Daisy (playeⁿ rity Mia Farrow). It is Gatsby and Daisy's romance, not Nick and Jordan's, that elicits the music of the spheres: "So he waited, listening for a moment longer to the tuning-fork that had been struck upon a star. Then he kissed her" (110–11). Appropriately, stars are often associated with Gatsby and Daisy.

Once Gatsby has been identified as a star, students may be invited to analyze his character through the lens of the American cult of celebrity. What is the stuff of his fame? How is his fame spread? How do the other characters respond to his fame? What is its price? Is there a typical arc to the celebrity biography, and does Gatsby's story conform to that arc? Why are Americans drawn to such biographies? What needs do they fill? Is there a relationship between the cult of celebrity and the burgeoning movie industry of the 1920s? What is the significance of the scene at Gatsby's party between the "moving-picture director and his Star" (106–07)? Here it might be useful to point out that Fitzgerald himself became a celebrity at twenty-three with the publication of his first novel, *This Side of Paradise,* and to note Fitzgerald's own personal and professional encounters with the early film colony on Long Island; his later Hollywood experiences as a screenwriter; his brief romance with the Hollywood starlet Lois Moran; his starlet-character Rosemary Hoyt (based on Moran), who provides the occasion for scenes set on movie lots in *Tender Is the Night;* and the Hollywood focus of his last, uncompleted novel, *The Last Tycoon,* in which the resonantly named protagonist Monroe Stahr is based on the legendary Hollywood producer Irving Thalberg.

If Gatsby's star power aligns him with the movie industry, it also suggests his identity as one of the figures from Greek mythology who live on in the starry constellations of the sky. Gatsby in his "silver shirt" and his "gold-colored tie" (84), driving his yellow car "with a labyrinth of wind-shields that mirrored a dozen suns" (64), with "fenders spread like wings . . . scatter[ing] light" (68), is a modern Apollo, the sun god who drives his golden chariot across the sky, dazzling those who behold him. And just as another sun god, Helios, allows Phaëthon to drive his chariot, so Gatsby allows Daisy to drive his phaeton—and both drives end in crashing destruction and death.

In the popular culture and the mythological sense, then, Gatsby is a star who attracts attention, exerting a gravitational pull not only on other characters but also on generations of readers. He is great in part because he is larger than life, and he is larger than life because he incorporates multiple iconic identities. As a repository of these identities, Gatsby appeals to readers at both the conscious and unconscious levels.

Mere mention that Gatsby "had committed himself to the following of a grail" is likely to elicit from students the observation that he is like one of King Arthur's knights (149). While courtly love and chivalry may be unfamiliar or shadowy concepts, the popular conception of the knight in armor who battles for his lady love will be familiar from contemporary renditions of medieval romances and chansons de geste. As I have argued in *The Medievalist Impulse in American Literature,* Gatsby's dedication to a married woman of a higher social station and his quest to win her by deeds of valor may be linked to the medieval ideal of courtly love, where ennobling love and even sexual passion is celebrated over the social contract of marriage (136–45). But if Daisy "gleam[s] like silver" (150), what should one make of the fact that her voice is "full of money" (120)? The spiritual idealism of the Middle Ages has been transformed in modern America into materialism. If Daisy is a tarnished grail, then is Gatsby a fool for committing himself to her? Or does his love for her, however misguided, nonetheless ennoble him, enabling him to be a better man, as the medieval knights were ennobled by love for their ladies? In this regard, a useful contrast can be drawn between Gatsby and Tom Buchanan, who also engages in an affair with a married woman, yet whose relationship with Myrtle Wilson is rendered quite differently from Gatsby's relationship with Daisy. What are these differences, and how do they affect the reader's judgment of the relationships and of the men?

Having drawn a comparison between the Middle Ages and modern America, the instructor might ask the students to identify the American analogue of the knight, after noting that *chivalry* derives from *chevalier* (literally, "horseman"). The quintessential American man on horseback is of course the cowboy, the hero of the American West whose individualism and courage are celebrated in countless dime novels of the nineteenth and twentieth centuries. Young James Gatz repeatedly read at least one such novel, "a ragged old copy of a book called *Hopalong Cassidy*" (173). What values might such a novel have taught James Gatz, and what dreams might it have encouraged? How might it have contributed to his creation of the identity of Jay Gatsby? In what ways is Gatsby like a cowboy? Does he have a frontier in which to adventure? What happens to cowboys when they run out of frontier? How might that loss relate to Gatsby's migration from the Midwest to the East—the reverse of the nineteenth-century western migration epitomized in Horace Greeley's famous command, "Go West, young man"?

In the margins of *Hopalong Cassidy*, young James Gatz constructed a list of "RESOLVES" that subtextually inscribes another American figure, a historical man around whom a myth quickly grew. Even students unfamiliar with Benjamin Franklin's *Autobiography* will associate Franklin with the listed plans to "study electricity" and "study needed inventions" (173)—two important associations that Floyd C. Watkins explores in his seminal essay "Fitzgerald's Jay Gatsby and Young Ben Franklin." The instructor might provide some salient details from the *Autobiography*—first among them that Franklin there consciously transforms his life into myth, rendering himself, in this text addressed to his own son, one of the founding fathers of America, transforming himself from literal father to mythic father. Representing himself as decidedly nonaristocratic—in contrast to Virginia cavaliers like the plantation owners George Washington and Thomas Jefferson and Boston Brahmins like John Adams—Franklin introduces himself in an early scene as a young man walking into Philadelphia (and manhood) with a loaf of bread under each arm. Franklin recounts his own adoption of a new identity, Poor Richard, under whose guise he issues practical maxims designed not so much to make man good as to make him successful. Franklin posits that he practiced what he preached in the maxims he published, the result of which, he would have us believe, was to transform a country bumpkin into the first American success story.

This eighteenth-century success story is incarnated in the nineteenth century most popularly in the boy-protagonists of Horatio Alger's dime novels. Alger presents a series of poor young American boys who by pluck (their own intrinsic talents) and luck (typically embodied by a rich older man who serves as mentor) manage to gain material and social success. Surely seventeen-year-old James Gatz of North Dakota, clam digger and salmon fisherman, demonstrates pluck when he borrows a rowboat to warn the yacht owner Dan Cody that his anchorage "over the most insidious flat on Lake Superior" is dangerous (98). This baptismal journey results in a name change—James Gatz becomes Jay Gatsby. But it also results in a lucky career change, and Gatsby is "employed in a vague personal capacity" as steward and general factotum to fifty-year-old Dan Cody for five years, during which he travels widely and learns the ways of the world (100). Though his $25,000 inheritance (a sum James Gatz could not have imagined) is swindled from him after Cody's death, Gatsby gains considerable polish from his time with the tycoon of the Nevada silver fields, and he puts the lessons he has learned to good use when later opportunities appear.

Lionel Trilling, in his chapter on Fitzgerald in *The Liberal Imagination*, reminds us that the archetype of the young man from the provinces derives from figures of European legend and was adopted by nineteenth-century novelists, notably writers of bildungsromans such as Honoré de Balzac in his *Comédie humaine*. Richard Chase, in his *American Novel and Its Tradition*, explores the ways in which Gatsby resembles this legendary figure: his obscure origins, his intrinsic talents coupled with a certain unscrupulousness, his will to conquer the social world (in the form of the big city) that would reject him. But the young man from the provinces values the social and material triumph in itself, whereas Gatsby, as Chase reminds us, values it only insofar as it enables his attainment of Daisy.

Gatsby originally gains access to Daisy Fay's Louisville house because "the invisible cloak of his uniform" opens doors (149); World War I dressed men in military uniforms and thereby blurred distinctions of wealth and social privilege that would otherwise obtain. But these doors remain open to Lieutenant Gatsby because he has learned the social lessons provided by his mentor, Dan Cody. Taking Daisy "under false pretenses" (149), Gatsby sets about making them real. Doing "extraordinarily well in the war" (150), he becomes first a captain and then a major in command of divisional machine guns. This war of attrition offered an opportunity for particularly rapid promotion to officer rank—the province of the aristocrat in peacetime and in the early days of World War I. A commoner war hero like Sergeant Alvin York, Gatsby earns medals "For Valour Extraordinary" in the battle of the Argonne Forest (67). Gatsby's five-month postwar tenure at Oxford—an opportunity offered to "some of the officers after the Armistice" as a means of managing the demobilization process—provides a patina beyond the polish that this "young roughneck" (129, 48) first gained from his five years with Dan Cody. His affected Oxbridge vocabulary, notably "old sport," signifies the social transformation, as does the photograph he carries of himself in Trinity Quad holding a cricket bat, "the man on [his] left . . . now the Earl of Doncaster" (67).

Like his social transformation, Gatsby's material transformation requires the sponsorship of a mentor who admires his pluck. Meyer Wolfsheim claims not merely to have "start[ed Gatsby] in business" after the war but also to have "made him, . . . rais[ing] him up out of nothing" because he saw great possibilities in this "fine-appearing, gentlemanly young man" (171). Gatsby describes Wolfsheim as "the man who fixed the World's Series back in 1919," a "gambler" too smart to be caught (73). Whether Gatsby participated in the fixing of the World Series, a seminal cultural event, remains murky; but he certainly works with Wolfsheim in the criminal underworld of gangland murders, fixed traffic tickets, bootleg liquor, gambling, and illegal bond trading. Gatsby's extraordinary wealth, accumulated in only three years, derives from these activities.

Gangland activities provide the matter for much "romantic speculation" among the hundreds of guests at his parties (44). Gossip swirls around Gatsby, creating an excited speculation not unlike that in the 1920s stock market. While shocked, Gatsby's guests are also intrigued, elaborating "[c]ontemporary legends" about his underworld activities, which paradoxically provide him access to high society (97). What is the appeal of the gangster for law-abiding American citizens? How is this appeal related to the Prohibition era, when alcohol was outlawed in America yet the law was routinely flouted, so that having one's own bootlegger became a mark of status? To what degree has the appeal of the gangster outlived Prohibition (enacted in 1919 and repealed in 1933)? Why do Americans continue to be fascinated by the figure of the gangster, as represented in popular culture by the 1972, 1974, and 1990 *Godfather* films (based on Mario Puzo's best-selling 1969 novel and directed by Francis Ford Coppola, who also wrote the screenplay for the 1974 film of *The Great Gatsby*), by Martin Scorsese's 1990 film *GoodFellas*, by Quentin Tarantino's 1994 film *Pulp Fiction*, and by the wildly popular HBO television series *The Sopranos* (1999–2007)? What qualities does the gangster have that Americans admire—indeed, regard as fundamentally American?

The essential America is revealed to Nick in the famous conclusion of *The Great Gastby*, when "the inessential houses began to melt away until gradually [he] became aware of the old island here that flowered once for Dutch sailors' eyes—a fresh, green breast of the new world" (180). And so Gatsby, at last, is linked to the proto-Americans who purchased Manhattan from the Indians for a handful of trinkets and settled New York. Yet Nick thinks not of the purchase or of the settlement but of the Dutch sailors' "æsthetic contemplation" of this new world before landfall on the continent. This "last and greatest of all human dreams" inevitably becomes complicated and messy once the dream is realized on landfall. Yet "for a transitory enchanted moment" man is "face to face for the last time in history with something commensurate to his capacity for wonder" (180). How is the Dutch sailors' dream of the New World like Gatsby's dream of Daisy, who is associated with the "green card" (104) that she jokingly indicates is the price of a kiss and more famously with the "green light" at the end of her dock (21)? To what degree is Gatsby like the Dutch sailors before landfall and after landfall? Does this final iconic identity suggest that Gatsby is the archetypal American? What does it suggest about the fate of the American, and America itself, in the modern world?

James Gatz is transformed into Jay Gatsby who is transformed into the Great Gatsby. By asking what makes Gatsby great, the instructor will elicit an unpacking of Gatsby's identity. The ensuing discussion will enable students not only to understand better the appeal of Fitzgerald's classic novel but also to identify and to analyze critically those culture heroes that Americans honor and emulate.

Rhetoric and Ethics in *The Great Gatsby*; or, Fabula, Progression, and the Functions of Nick Carraway

James Phelan

How does F. Scott Fitzgerald persuade his audience that Jay Gatsby, a deluded and corrupt social climber, deserves Nick Carraway's admiration, and why is it that most readers feel a sense of genuine loss at Gatsby's death? What do we make of Fitzgerald's acts of persuasion today? What are the ethical dimensions of being persuaded or resisting his efforts to persuade, and on what grounds would we do one or the other? These questions are central to my teaching of *The Great Gatsby*, because, from the perspective of the rhetorical theory of narrative that I typically want my students to learn, they capture the key interpretive and evaluative issues of the novel. By using this theoretical perspective to help students identify and answer these questions—or, more accurately, recognize various ways of answering them—I hope to illuminate both the workings of the novel and some important elements of the theory. In this essay, I trace one path toward that mutual illumination, a path that follows the transformation of the basic elements of the narrative into Fitzgerald's novel and that leads to questions about the novel's ethics. Let me begin, then, by describing briefly the concerns of a rhetorical theory of narrative.

This theory views narrative as a communication from author to reader that engages the reader's cognition, psyche, emotions, and values. It is concerned with the specifics of the communication—the techniques and structures of the text, the conventions it draws on—as they reveal the author's multilayered invitation to the audience. This concern with audience and effects helps make the approach appealing to students because it invites them to use their reading experiences as the starting points for our discussions. At the same time, the concern with the specifics of the communication encourages students to seek the causes of their experiences in the details of the text, a seeking that may lead them to revise their understanding. The approach also views the act of reading as having two main parts, what I call reconstruction and response.

Analyzing the transformation of the events of Gatsby's life into the finished novel is one productive way of reconstructing its rhetorical power, and in the classroom I conduct that analysis through a focus on two matters of Fitzgerald's technique. The first is the complicated relation among the events of the narrative in their chronological order (what the Russian formalists called a narrative's *fabula*) and the specific narrative progression of the novel. By narrative progression I mean the dynamics of the novel's movement from beginning to end and the way those dynamics affect readers' developing interests. The second matter is Fitzgerald's use of Nick Carraway, particularly the way Nick functions as character and as narrator. The process of reconstruction will, in turn, identify key issues that are worth discussing during the class sessions (or writing assignments) devoted to evaluation.

The concept of progression subsumes the concept that the Russian formalists paired with *fabula*, *sjuzhet*, the rendering of the *fabula* in the narrative text. Where the Russian formalists' focus on *fabula* and *sjuzhet* calls attention to differences between the order of events in the *fabula* and the order of events in the *sjuzhet*, the concept of progression goes further by calling attention to the effect of that difference on the audience. More specifically, progression refers to narrative as a doubly dynamic mode of discourse, a mode that involves time and change both in its represented action and in the experience of reading it. The progression of any narrative develops through the introduction and complication of instabilities, unstable relations between and among characters or between one character and his or her particular situation, or tensions, differences in beliefs, opinions, knowledge, or values between an author and the intended audience or between a narrator and the authorial audience (for more on progression see Phelan, *Reading* and *Experiencing*).

Fabula *and Progression in* The Great Gatsby

Once students understand the distinction between *fabula* and progression, they can set to work reconstructing the *fabula* of Fitzgerald's novel, focusing especially on Gatsby and on Nick, though it can also be profitable to see how many events in the lives of Daisy, Tom, Jordan, and Myrtle and George Wilson the narrative includes. Here I offer possible reconstructions of the *fabulas* of the stories of Nick, Daisy, and Gatsby. Of course, readers may reconstruct the *fabula* in different ways, since they may interpret elements of the *sjuzhet* differently; in the classroom, these differences can be used to identify interpretive cruxes in the narrative.[1] If one wants to look more closely at Fitzgerald's handling of a specific part of the *fabula*, Matthew J. Bruccoli's appendix "Note on Chronology" (215–16), in his 1991 Cambridge University Press edition of *Gatsby*, offers a helpful discussion of the chronology of events in the summer of 1922—including a demonstration that Fitzgerald has crowded too much into the final weeks of August. For the sake of clarity in this essay, I offer only one sketch of each *fabula* and indicate the kinds of questions that these sketches open up.

Nick Carraway

Event in Chronological Time		*Location in Nick's Narration*
1892	Born in Saint Paul	Date in chapter 7; place identified in chapter 9
1915	Graduates from Yale	chapter 1
1916–18	Fights in World War I	chapter 1
1918–22	Lives restlessly in Midwest	chapter 1
1922	Moves to New York	chapter 1
1922	Meets Jordan Baker at Daisy's	chapter 2
1922	Sees Gatsby standing on the dock; later meets him at one of his parties	chapter 2
1922	Invites Daisy and Gatsby to lunch	chapter 5
1922	Witnesses progress of Daisy and Gatsby's romance and its outcome	chapters 5–9
1922	Breaks up with Jordan; returns to Midwest	chapters 8, 9
1924	Tells his story	chapters 1–9

Daisy Fay Buchanan

Event in Chronological Time		*Location in Nick's Narration*
1899	Born in Louisville	chapter 4; implied in Jordan's account
1917	Meets Gatsby; falls in love	chapter 4, from Jordan
1918	Marries Tom Buchanan	chapter 4, from Jordan
1919	Gives birth to Pamela; moves to France	chapter 4, from Jordan
1920	Returns with Tom and Pamela to Chicago	chapter 4, from Jordan
1922	(Summer) Reunites with Gatsby at Nick's house	chapter 5
1922	(Late summer) Chooses Tom over Gatsby; kills Myrtle Wilson while driving Gatsby's car	chapter 8
1922	Complicit in murder of Gatsby; continues life with Tom	chapters 8–9

Jay Gatsby

Event in Chronological Time		*Location in Nick's Narration*
c. 1890	Born in the Midwest	Date indicated in chapter 3; place named by Gatsby in chapter 4
1906 (12 Sept.)	Writes schedule for self-improvement	chapter 9, revealed by Henry Gatz
1912–17	Works for Dan Cody	chapter 6; narrated by Nick; revealed by Gatsby
1917	Meets and falls in love with Daisy Fay	chapter 4, narrated by Jordan to Nick; chapter 6, from Gatsby; chapter 8, from Nick
1917–18	Does "extraordinarily well" in World War I	chapter 8, from Nick
1918	Learns that Daisy has married Tom	chapter 8, from Nick
1918–22	Illegally accumulates wealth in quest to win Daisy	Implied several places; asserted by Tom, chapter 7
1922	Buys house in West Egg	chapter 4, from Jordan
1922	Gives parties to impress Daisy	chapters 3, 6
1922	(Summer) Reunites with Daisy at Nick's house	chapter 5
1922	(Late summer) Loses Daisy in confrontation with Tom; is killed by George Wilson	chapter 8

The *fabulas* in and of themselves underline an important feature of the novel: although Fitzgerald has titled the story *The Great Gatsby*, he has told two stories that twice intersect and diverge—those of Gatsby and Daisy—plus the story of the witness-narrator, Nick. The differences among the relations of the three stories are striking. Clearly, the events of Daisy's story and those of Gatsby's are inextricably connected: if Gatsby had not gone to Louisville in 1917 and New York in 1922 and if Daisy had chosen differently at either point, their stories would be radically different. But, with the exception of Nick's role as host for their lunch, the events of Nick's story have no significant consequences for Daisy's and for Gatsby's stories—and it is easy to imagine Fitzgerald finding another way for Daisy and Gatsby to meet again. By contrast, significant events in Nick's story, especially his breaking up with Jordan, his returning to the Midwest, and his telling this tale, are the result of events in the other two stories.

Recognizing these varied relations among the stories raises the questions of why Fitzgerald elaborates a story for Nick at all and why he makes that story depend on, but not significantly influence, the other two stories. These questions can best be answered after a look at the relation between *fabula* and progression in Daisy's and in Gatsby's stories. Because of space limitations, I discuss only Gatsby's story here, but I hope the discussion can provide a model for how students could themselves address the relation between *fabula* and progression in Daisy's story.

The Gatsby *fabula* is well-suited for a melodramatic soap opera: Gatsby breaks the law to become rich, single-mindedly pursues another man's wife, and then is rejected by that woman, who becomes complicit in his murder. But Fitzgerald uses numerous techniques to give us a progression with a much different effect. What is most striking about the progression is that the major instability, Gatsby's pursuit of Daisy, is introduced so late, complicated so little, and resolved so efficiently. Fitzgerald does not tell us about the events of 1917 until the end of chapter 4. Furthermore, Daisy and Gatsby do not meet again until chapter 5, almost halfway through the narrative, and the only other scene between them until the climax and resolution is in chapter 6, when Daisy and Tom attend what turns out to be Gatsby's last party. The scene at the Plaza Hotel in chapter 7 provides the climax, when Gatsby's quest is defeated by Tom with Daisy's acquiescence, and then the rest of the resolution is quickly brought about through the agency of, first, Myrtle and, then, George Wilson—with an important assist from Tom.

Fitzgerald arranges the progression of the first four chapters to accomplish four main purposes: to influence our view of Gatsby so that we see him, despite the serious ethical deficiencies of his character, as a larger-than-life figure who is fundamentally sympathetic; to introduce thematic issues that provide a larger context for our understanding of the major instability and its complication and resolution; to introduce instabilities between Tom and Daisy that seem to move the progression toward their separation but turn out not to be powerful enough to produce that outcome; and to introduce instabilities and tensions surrounding Nick's story. All four effects are crucial for the effective resolution of the novel.

Nick's well-known opening address to his audience (his narratee) contributes to the first and fourth of these purposes, especially through its introduction of Nick as a guide to Gatsby and its careful introduction of tensions of unequal knowledge between Nick and the narratee and, thus, between Nick and Fitzgerald's audience:

> When I came back from the East last autumn I felt that I wanted the world to be in uniform and at a sort of moral attention forever; I wanted no more riotous excursions with privileged glimpses into the human heart. Only Gatsby, the man who gives his name to this book, was exempt from my reaction—Gatsby, who represented everything for which I have an unaffected scorn. . . . [He had] an extraordinary gift for hope, a romantic readiness such as I have never found in any other person and which it is not likely that I shall ever find again. No—Gatsby turned out all right at the end; it is what preyed on Gatsby, what foul dust floated in the wake of his dreams that temporarily closed out my interest in the abortive sorrows and short-winded elations of men.   (2)

What Nick knows that we do not are the answers to the following puzzles: why he returned from the East; why he has such a strong reaction to his experience there; how Gatsby represents everything he scorns; what "foul dust" preyed on Gatsby; and what it means to say that he turned out all right in the end. What is not in question is Nick's positive view of Gatsby, a view that has great authority for several reasons. First, it is part of the very beginning of the book, and, as Peter J. Rabinowitz has shown, beginnings are privileged positions in narrative (58–65). Second, at this point in the progression we tentatively regard Nick's view as endorsed by Fitzgerald, since the convention for reading character narration is that we regard it as reliable until we have evidence of unreliability. Third, Nick is offering his perspective from the time of the narration after he has had time to reflect on and learn from his experiences. Thus we can conclude that Nick's obvious romanticism is shared by Fitzgerald.

These effects give us an interpretive lens through which to regard Gatsby for the rest of the narrative. Even as our knowledge of Gatsby's character and his past increases, we continue to see at least the potential for the separation between Gatsby's romantic readiness and heightened sensitivity, on the one hand, and his selfish and deluded ambitions, on the other. To be sure, many students find that the more they learn about Gatsby the more they are inclined to question Nick's view of him—and thus to question one of the bases of Fitzgerald's narrative. I encourage these questions and point out how they indicate that the step from rhetorical reconstruction to ethical response is a short one, and I promise to address them more fully after we do more reconstruction.

From chapter 1 until chapter 4, when Jordan tells Nick that Gatsby wants him to invite Daisy to lunch, the progression proceeds by piling up further tensions about Gatsby—particularly about his mysterious past—and by introducing instabilities involving Tom and Daisy (Tom's affair with Myrtle Wilson, Daisy's apparent unhappiness) and Nick himself (his adjustment to New York, the development of his relationship with Jordan).[2] In addition, Fitzgerald develops the thematic component of the narrative through Nick's description of the symbolic landscape in which the action unfolds: East Egg and West Egg, sites of suburban affluence, and the ash heaps lying between the suburbs and New York City, a wasteland brooded over by the eyes of Doctor T. J. Eckleburg.

The further tensions about Gatsby combine with those in the first chapter to make him a larger-than-life figure, and consequently his later pursuit of Daisy takes on a larger-than-life quality. But the symbolic landscape also invites us to contemplate the extent to which the worlds of East Egg and West Egg, worlds built on money and dedicated to consumption and entertainment, are actually built on foundations of ash. The instabilities about Tom and Daisy form part of a larger, intriguing progression that students can be invited to trace, a progression in which the instabilities get increasingly complicated and then swiftly resolved as Daisy and Tom end up back together—not happy but stable and comfortable behind their money—even as Myrtle, Gatsby, and George are eliminated from their lives.

By chapter 4, Fitzgerald has established several tensions and instabilities that guide our developing interest in Nick. There is the question of why he returned from the East and why he is telling the story. In addition, he has embarked, somewhat tentatively, on a relationship with Jordan Baker. The instabilities of this relationship are tied in direct and indirect ways to the instabilities surrounding Gatsby, but the more crucial issue is why Fitzgerald develops this strand of the narrative at all. In raising this question with students, I reiterate that Fitzgerald's chief challenge involves the transformation of the raw material of Gatsby's story into an effective narrative. As the revelations about Gatsby's character and his past mount, as the specifics of his dream increasingly lead us to question whether the "great" in the title is intended ironically, Fitzgerald needs a convincing means to persuade his audience of Gatsby's worth. The means he chooses is Nick—not just as retrospective witness but also as a character whose life changes as a result of knowing Gatsby.

Fitzgerald invites us to see the similarities between Gatsby's relationship with Daisy and Nick's with Jordan. Jordan Baker is Daisy's close friend, and she moves in the same circles as the Buchanans. Like Tom and Daisy, she is self-absorbed and, when it suits her purposes, dishonest. Nick is attracted to her beauty and glamour and money. Nick's breaking up with Jordan the day after Daisy kills Myrtle while driving Gatsby's car is precipitated by Jordan's pique at his not wanting to enter the Buchanans' house the previous night, but Fitzgerald asks us to infer a deeper cause: Nick is recoiling from the world that he had previously been attracted to because of what he has seen it do to Gatsby.

In Nick's final scene with Jordan, after he has decided to return to the Midwest, Fitzgerald reinforces the inference. When Jordan tells Nick that she is engaged, Nick does not quite believe her, but his attraction to her resurfaces, and he wavers briefly—"For just a minute I wondered if I wasn't making a mistake"—but only briefly: "then I thought it all over again quickly and got up to say good-by" (177). The "it" is the question of which world he wants to inhabit—that of Jordan and the Buchanans or that of the Midwest. Though Nick's decision is clear, his attraction to Jordan and what she represents remains. The scene ends with Nick's description of his exit: "Angry, and half in love with her, and tremendously sorry, I turned away" (177). If Nick had not witnessed what happened to Gatsby, he would have remained in the East and continued his pursuit of Jordan and the world she represents, an outcome that Fitzgerald asks us to see as inferior to Nick's return to the Midwest. In this sense, Gatsby's life and death have made a significant difference for Nick, and because we see that difference we can feel that something valuable went from the world when Gatsby was murdered by George Wilson.

Character Narrators and the Multiple Functions of Nick Carraway

Once students have worked through the progression, they have laid the groundwork for analyzing Fitzgerald's complex uses of Nick as character and as narrator. Given the importance of Nick in both roles for Fitzgerald's challenging task of transformation, students will not be surprised to learn that a major debate about the novel is whether Nick is a reliable narrator. Indeed, since Wayne C. Booth's statement in *The Rhetoric of Fiction* that Nick is a "thoroughly reliable" guide to the action of the novel (176), the critical tide has been flowing in the opposite direction, toward the shore of unreliability.[3]

I invite a debate about Nick's reliability after a brief discussion of the different kinds of unreliability. Narrators may be unreliable on the axis of facts and events and so be unreliable reporters; they may be unreliable on the axis of perceiving and understanding and so be unreliable readers; or they may be unreliable on the axis of ethics and values and so be unreliable regarders or judges (for a fuller discussion of these points, see Phelan, *Living*). I use the evidence brought forth in the debate about Nick to suggest that here we have a case of both/and rather than either/or. That is, Nick is sometimes reliable, sometimes not, and the fluctuations are related to his dual role as character and as narrator. I also make the general point that although the dual roles of most character-narrators, including Nick, will intersect at some points, those roles may at other points run along parallel tracks.

One dramatic way to show that this parallelism sometimes operates in Nick's narration is to cite passages where Nick functions as an authoritative third-person narrator. The most prominent passage is his account in chapter 8 of what happened at Wilson's garage "after we left there the night before" (156). Nick the character essentially drops out of the narrative, as Fitzgerald uses Nick the narrator to report authoritatively things that he did not witness, everything from the exact dialogue between Michaelis and Wilson to Michaelis's internal thoughts. The passage is crucial because it shows us Wilson's mistaken but deeply held convictions that the driver of the car deliberately ran over Myrtle and that the driver was the man with whom she had been having an affair—and these convictions lead to the final resolution of instabilities.

Another intriguing example occurs earlier in chapter 8 when Nick reports what Daisy was feeling in 1917–18, while she was in Louisville and Gatsby was overseas in the war: "And all the time something within her was crying for a decision. She wanted her life shaped now, immediately—and the decision must be made by some force—of love, of money, of unquestionable practicality—that was close at hand" (151). Again, Nick narrates information that he has not had any way to acquire, but the narration is authoritative and important, since it resolves the tension of why Daisy married Tom when she was in love with Gatsby. To keep these instances of authoritative narration from being undermined, Fitzgerald is careful to have Nick be consistently reliable in his reporting of the facts and events.

There are also places in the narrative where Nick's function as narrator becomes largely irrelevant to his function as character. In these passages, Nick reports dialogue and action but does not show much awareness of what his report reveals, especially about himself. Perhaps the best example occurs when Nick unsuccessfully urges Wolfsheim to attend Gatsby's funeral, a scene rendered almost entirely in dialogue except for Nick's two descriptions of actions, one by each character: "The hair in his nostrils quivered slightly, and as he shook his head his eyes filled with tears" (171). And "I saw that for some reason of his own he was determined not to come, so I stood up" (172). It seems unlikely that Nick as either character or narrator recognizes that Wolfsheim's tears are insincere; it also seems unlikely that Nick as character or narrator realizes the depth of his own investment in having people at Gatsby's funeral, an investment that has him pay this visit to a man whom he otherwise shuns. Yet Fitzgerald's audience sees these things clearly because the technique almost effaces Nick in his role as narrator and leads us to focus on his role as character.

Because Fitzgerald needs the story of Nick's change to help make Gatsby's story more effective, he does sometimes show the deficiencies of Nick the character without also showing Nick the narrator's awareness of those deficiencies. In these instances, Nick is an unreliable reader and evaluator of himself. A good example is Nick's claim that he is "one of the few honest people that I have ever known" (59). The context of the statement clearly calls attention to its unreliability: it follows shortly after Nick's claim that Jordan's dishonesty "made no difference" to him because "[d]ishonesty in a woman is a thing you never blame deeply" and just after his statement that he had been sending weekly letters to a woman back home and signing them "Love, Nick," when he was not thinking of her with love at all. The larger context is also important: Nick is explaining why he does not respond more fully to Jordan's effort to shift their relationship by openly declaring her attraction to him; Nick says that he needs to get out of "that tangle" with the woman back home first (58). The unreliability of both statements points to Nick the character's lack of self-knowledge, a lack that extends to his role as narrator. Nick is not able to see—even after the events of the novel—that the reason he dismisses Jordan's dishonesty is his attraction to her wealth and beauty and glamour. Nick is also not able to see that he has not been as honest as he claims. As a result, we see that Gatsby's effect on Nick is subtler than Nick himself comes to realize. Nick leaves Jordan and leaves the East in part because, after witnessing what happened to Gatsby, dishonesty in a woman is something that does make a difference to him (for a related but somewhat different analysis of this part of Nick's narration, see Preston).

Finally, Fitzgerald occasionally uses Nick as a mask through which to speak almost directly to his audience. The best example of this technique is the novel's famous conclusion, Nick's reflections on Gatsby's dream:

> And as I sat there brooding on the old, unknown world, I thought of Gatsby's wonder when he first picked out the green light at the end of Daisy's dock. He had come a long way to this blue lawn, and his dream must have seemed so close that he could hardly fail to grasp it. He did not

know that it was already behind him, somewhere back in that vast obscurity beyond the city, where the dark fields of the republic rolled on under the night.

Gatsby believed in the green light, the orgastic future that year by year recedes before us. It eluded us then, but that's no matter—to-morrow we will run faster, stretch out our arms farther. . . . And one fine morning—

So we beat on, boats against the current, borne back ceaselessly into the past.   (180)

Although Nick the narrator is very much present here, Nick is now such a reliable spokesperson for Fitzgerald that we have the sense of being almost directly addressed by the author. The advantage of this technique is obvious. It allows Fitzgerald simultaneously to show Nick's more mature understanding of Gatsby and of the significance of his quest and its failure and to articulate for his audience both what is admirable and futile not just in Gatsby's dream but in all our dreams.

Ethical Response

As I noted earlier, it is a short step from rhetorical reconstruction to ethical response because the reconstruction involves understanding the ethical values on which the novel is built and the way that the narrative guides the authorial audience's response to that value structure. To capture the acts of ethical understanding and ethical response, the way that the narrative seeks to place its audience ethically and the way that we respond from our own ethical locations, I have coined the term "ethical position." At any given point in a narrative, our ethical position results from the dynamic interaction of four ethical situations:

1. the characters within the story world;
2. the narrator in relation to the telling, the told, and to both the narratee and the authorial audience (unreliable narration, for example, constitutes a different ethical position from reliable narration);
3. the author in relation to the authorial audience (the implied author's choices to adopt one narrative strategy rather than another affects the audience's ethical response to the characters; each choice also conveys the author's attitudes toward the audience);
4. the flesh-and-blood reader in relation to the set of values, beliefs, and locations indicated by the first three situations.

Students can draw on the previous discussions to identify features of the first three situations. Fitzgerald has designed much of the novel so that we recognize Gatsby's ethical deficiencies and the reasons not to condemn him, even as we recognize the deficiencies of Tom, Daisy, and Jordan. At the same time, Fitzgerald asks us to recognize Nick's evolution toward—though not full attainment of—the value structure underlying the novel. That structure includes, most prominently, both the affirmation of romanticism and a condemnation of the particular forms that romanticism can take in the American 1920s. Indeed, the poignancy of the novel—and of Nick's closing narration—arises in large part from this value structure.

But there is another feature of Fitzgerald's relation to us that deserves new discussion. What kind of ethical relation does he establish with us through his use of Nick as our guide to the narrative? By adopting Nick as guide and by deploying him in such a variety of roles, Fitzgerald has made things difficult for himself, since his communication to us is mediated in multiple ways. In that sense, the technique conveys a high degree of trust in both himself and us, a trust that we will be able to cooperate successfully in this complex narrative communication.

Furthermore, given the value structure of the novel and Nick's role in communicating it, Fitzgerald also leaves both Nick and himself open to many searching questions from individual readers. I invite students to share their questions, and typically they raise good ones: Is there something deficient in an ethical system that places a higher value on one's capacity to dream than on what one actually does? What are the ethics of structuring the novel so that we are asked to view one woman as the corruption of the male protagonist's dream and another woman as the temptation for the character-narrator? Does Fitzgerald's representation of the glamour associated with the wealth of Gatsby and of the Buchanans work at cross-purposes with its representation of the dangers of such wealth? Does Nick's role in that representation show that he remains more susceptible to that glamour than he—and perhaps Fitzgerald—would like us to think? What kind of assumptions does Fitzgerald make about race and class when he implicitly presents Gatsby's story as a version of the American dream?[4]

Even more than the questions about *fabula* and progression, these questions about ethics and politics generate varied responses. Some students find the book reprehensible, others find it inspiring, and still others find it both. Because students' answers to the evaluative questions are tied to their individual ethical and political beliefs, I am interested in generating variety and inviting students to try on one another's positions as a way of challenging and perhaps revising their own. At this point in my teaching, then, I shift from the communal reconstruction of the author's invitations to a general recognition of the multiple kinds of productive responses we can make to those invitations. Recognizing that multiplicity becomes a way of enriching the experience each of us has—and an appropriate reward for reading and discussing the novel together.

NOTES

[1] The criticism of the novel offers radically divergent views about the actual events of the novel, views that clearly imply *fabulas* different from the ones I identify here. See Wasiolek, who contends that both Gatsby and Nick are gay and so reinterprets the events significantly (e.g., Nick's arranging the reunion with Daisy is arguably a different event in Wasiolek's account of the novel than it is in most others). For another example, see Lockridge, "F. Scott Fitzgerald's *Trompe l'Oeil*," who makes Wolfsheim a much larger actor in the *fabula* of Gatsby's life. For a clear and useful guide to different approaches to the novel based in contemporary theory, see Tyson, *Critical Theory*.

[2] One of the more puzzling scenes in the narrative occurs at the end of chapter 2, when Nick leaves Tom's party with Mr. McKee. Wasiolek uses the scene as the basis for his reading of Nick as gay. But it also can be read—and I would suggest read more plausibly—not as the key to the novel but as a thread that Fitzgerald introduces but never weaves into the rest of the narrative.

[3] For a tour de force essay on Nick's unreliability, see Lockridge, "F. Scott Fitzgerald's *Trompe l'Oeil*." Among many other fine essays on Nick as narrator, see especially Donaldson, "Trouble"; Cartwright; Coleman; Hilgart; and Preston. What I say in this section of the essay draws on my discussion of Nick's dual roles in chapter 5 of *Narrative as Rhetoric*, "Reexaming Reality."

[4] For good discussions of these questions, see Fetterley; Tyson, *Psychological Politics*; Hilgart; and Preston.

Using a Heraclitean Approach in Teaching *The Great Gatsby*

Mark Shipman

Both in style and content, *The Great Gatsby* is a novel of profound intricacy and texture. It is common for students to be familiar with the basics of the novel, but this basic knowledge can, unfortunately, be an impediment to them as they seek to engage the novel. Rather than undertake the close reading and critical analysis needed for an appreciation of the depth and scope of Fitzgerald's work, students can be attracted to a quick, superficial view of *The Great Gatsby*.[1]

Many students remain idealistic and romantic. These traits, coupled with what David Geoffrey Smith calls "an incredible pressure to perform" in the university classroom (105), can result in students' settling for a reading of *The Great Gatsby* that suits their necessity and ideology, the notion that it is simply an indictment of the crassness, solipsism, and futility of ostentatious wealth garnered through the excesses of unregulated capitalism.[2] They take this view at the expense of looking at Fitzgerald's choices with respect to the structure and content of the novel. Scott Donaldson contends that it is on "the most banal level" that "*The Great Gatsby* documents the truism that money can't buy you love" ("Possessions" 195).

Jay Gatsby's doomed attempt to win back Daisy, and to "[wipe] out forever" the years they spent apart (132), requires of Gatsby a highly idealized perception of the role that the passage of time plays on the human condition. The importance of time in *The Great Gatsby* led me to contemplate how Gatsby's desire to repeat the past evokes the philosophical implications of the passage of time in the elegant admonition that the Greek philosopher Heracleitus (c. 535–c. 475 BC) presents in his twenty-first fragment: "One cannot step twice into the same river, for the water into which you first stepped has flowed on" (14). I have been using Heracleitus successfully in my classes as a way of presenting to students Gatsby's attempt to recapture the past, an idea that Fitzgerald reinforces throughout the course of his novel.

While Gatsby's quest is doomed in its execution, it may well have been equally doomed in its conception. Further reading and analyses of the Heraclitean fragments can reveal a framework of other philosophical ideas that provides students with insight into how the narration of the novel itself exposes the fallacy on which Gatsby bases his quest. Donald Phillip Verene notes in *The Art of Humane Education* that ideas can be captured through metaphors that stimulate the student's imagination and that ordinary statements can substantiate the student's common-sense experience and appeal to the student's desire for structural understanding (43). When presented as comments germane to the content of the narrative in *The Great Gatsby*, Heracleitus's epigrammatic fragments give students opportunities to think about the novel using this metaphoric venue through which Verene suggests ideas can be captured.

In his preface to the 1992 Scribner's paperback edition of *Gatsby*, Matthew J. Bruccoli describes Nick Carraway as "a trustworthy reporter and [reluctant] . . . judge" (xii). This view of Nick's character and the legitimacy of his narration is, however, by no means monolithic. As early as 1961, R. W. Stallman refers to Nick as "a perplexed narrator writing backwards a disassociated chronology, confused and embittered by his own failure" and "a prig with holier-than-thou airs" (*Houses* 134, 137; see also Cartwright; Scrimgeour; and Hays, "Hemingway"). In an attempt to reconcile Stallman's commentary on the novel with the more generous assessments Nick receives from proponents of formalist criticism, Richard Foster suggests that the "neoclassical" components of Nick Carraway's character and narration have allowed critics to find it both "right and natural to identify their own style of moral intelligence with that of neoclassical Nick" (95).

As a narrator, Nick invites critical scrutiny of his credibility by acting in ways and engaging in commentary that belie his self-described objectivity and reliability. Nick says he is "inclined to reserve all judgments" (1), yet he repeatedly and often stridently expresses judgments regarding the people, situations, and behaviors in the novel. He claims to be "one of the few honest people that [he has] ever known" (59), yet he readily engages in deception and subterfuge to facilitate the relationship that develops between Gatsby and Daisy. The various interpretations of Nick's character and the attendant issue of his reliability therefore are reasonable critical responses to the contradictory elements in his narration. It is not surprising, then, that Nick's own comments regarding his reliability as a narrator are viewed by some students as a sort of overcompensation, an attempt to verify through direct comment situations that do not make themselves manifest in his actual presentation of events, or even as the sanctimonious assertions of a narrator possessing "holier-than-thou airs."

The existence and nature of contradiction is a venerable philosophical issue, but few philosophers are as readily identified with it as Heracleitus. Contradiction, as Heracleitus recognizes it, is inevitable in a universe that exists in a state of constant change: "the beautifullest harmonies," he believes, "come from opposition" (28). Drew A. Hyland uses terminology in his description of Heracleitus that is quite similar to what some critics have used regarding Nick Carraway, referring to him as "a rather arrogant and aristocratic person," with a writing style "replete with apparent contradictions" (160).

From a Heraclitean perspective, the contradictions that exist in Nick's assertions of both his capabilities as a narrator and his understanding of Gatsby's situation would support, rather than undermine, the idea that Nick possesses the capabilities that he asserts. As a first-person narrator, Nick is something of a rarity, because over the course of the narration he often eschews objectivity and presents the story from a perspective (particularly in his descriptions of Gatsby's character) of limited omniscience. This practice indicates that Nick is acting in a manner consistent with the behavior Heracleitus believes to be appropriate for a person who possesses an understanding of what he calls the Logos, a person's understanding of "an all-important truth about the constitution of the world of which men are a part . . . valid for all things and accessible for all men if only they use their observation and their understanding" (Kirk and Raven 188). In his second fragment, Heracleitus gives a negative definition for the Logos: "Let us therefore notice that understanding is common to all men. Understanding is common to all, yet each man acts as if his intelligence were private and all his own" (11). When a person acts on personal as opposed to common understanding, that action confirms that person's disassociation from the Logos.

Students often react negatively to Nick Carraway because they can see arrogance, laced with cynicism and irony, in his narration. They are therefore often quick to see blatant hypocrisy in his contradictions. Rather than indicate a weakness in the narrator's character, however, Nick's self-assured tone and contradictory pronouncements might establish him as a person who possesses an understanding of the Logos; and, in fact, some of Nick's narration is similar to the Heraclitean fragments. Nick's call to Gatsby as he leaves him the final time—"They're a rotten crowd. . . . You're worth the whole damn bunch put together" (154)—is reminiscent of Heracleitus's statement, "One man, to my way of thinking, is worth ten thousand, if he is the best of his kind" (25). Nick's comments about his restlessness after his return from the war in Europe (3) evoke the sentiment Heracleitus puts forth in his twenty-fifth fragment: "War is the father of all of us and our king. War discloses who is godlike and who is but a man, who is a slave and who is a freeman" (15). The last lines of the novel, "So we beat on, boats against the current, borne back ceaselessly into the past" (180), contain an echo of the twentieth fragment: "Everything flows; nothing remains. Everything moves; nothing is still. Everything passes away; nothing lasts" (14).

I use basic Heraclitean philosophical tenets with my students to establish the legitimacy of Nick Carraway's narrative capabilities; this approach is particularly appropriate to the structural and thematic elements of *The Great Gatsby*. Ronald Berman describes Gatsby as a man who "not only becomes more of an individual, he becomes more of an individual than anyone in the book" (Great Gatsby *and Fitzgerald's World* 16). The process of becoming is an integral part of Heracleitus's belief in the constantly changing nature of the universe, so much so that Hyland refers to Heracleitus as "the spokesman for becoming" (160). In searching for one's self, in seeking the Logos, the soul goes beyond the self (Kirk and Raven 214), becoming something greater as it comes to possess understanding.

In a foreshadowing of how his experiences with Gatsby will affect him, Nick indicates the importance that the issue of change will have in the novel:

> No—Gatsby turned out all right at the end; it is what preyed on Gatsby, what foul dust floated in the wake of his dreams that temporarily

closed out my interest in the abortive sorrows and short-winded elations
of men.   (2)

In this often cited passage, Nick puts in place the caveat for his narration of the
novel—that Gatsby will undergo an affirmation and that he will turn out "all
right." Some students see this reference to Gatsby's fate (with no hint of inten-
tional irony) as the first overt contradiction in the narration, because they see
Gatsby's failure and death as an indication that he did not turn out well at all.
I like to show students that this contradiction is apparent rather than actual,
however, because from Nick's perspective, Gatsby's "turn[ing] out all right" results from Nick's eventual acquisition of understanding and knowledge of the
Logos.

Nick's descriptions of Gatsby's behavior and circumstances are not without
Heraclitean contradictions; Nick expresses an obvious admiration for Gatsby
the man, but that admiration is tempered by his observation that Gatsby's perception is a function of personal illusion, an example of Heracleitus's description of a person without the Logos, "[acting] as if his intelligence were private
and all his own" (11). Nick describes Gatsby not as a hopeless romantic or a
doomed idealist but as an entity with intrinsic philosophical and theological
connection to his environment, one who springs "from his Platonic conception
of himself. . . . a son of God—a phrase which, if it means anything, means just
that—and he must be about His Father's business, the service of a vast, vulgar,
and meretricious beauty" (98). Daisy Buchanan is the motivation for Gatsby's
"Platonic" creation of himself, so it is not surprising that the disconnect between the perceptions of reality held by the two men, Nick's Logos-centered
rationality and Gatsby's private intelligence, is most obvious in Nick's description of what he believes Gatsby's reactions are to her. Nick surmises that
Gatsby's unrealistic expectations prevent his reunion with Daisy from providing
the level of gratification that he has anticipated, when he comments regarding
that reunion that she must have often "tumbled short of his dreams—not
through her own fault, but because of the colossal vitality of his illusion" (95).

One of the most frequently quoted exchanges of dialogue between Nick and
Gatsby occurs in the aftermath of Tom and Daisy's departure from Gatsby's
party. Nick believes he understands Gatsby's hope for himself and Daisy:

> He wanted nothing less of Daisy than that she should go to Tom and say:
> "I never loved you." After she had obliterated four years with that sen-
> tence they could decide upon the more practical measures to be taken.
> One of them was that, after she was free, they were to go back to
> Louisville and be married from her house—just as if it were five years
> ago.   (109)

In an attempt to temper Gatsby's desire with some element of reality, Nick
makes the seemingly innocuous comment, "You can't repeat the past" (110).

Few students view Gatsby's incredulous response, "Can't repeat the past? . . . Why of course you can!" (110), as an expression of a literal belief, but they may see it as the intrinsic flaw in Gatsby's pursuit of Daisy. Gatsby is clear about his intention to reestablish his relationship with Daisy by surrounding himself with the sort of conspicuous wealth that will both catch her attention and prove his ability to provide her now with the life he was unable to provide her with in the past. Gatsby's idea that true love can effectively be achieved by such "vast, vulgar, and meretricious" materialistic means runs contrary to conventional wisdom, in much the same way that the idea that the past can be repeated runs contrary to natural law.

Even though this exchange between Nick and Gatsby occurs well into their acquaintanceship, I point out to my students that it serves as a watershed moment in the narration from a Heraclitean perspective; it is an overt statement of Nick's understanding of the Logos countered by a response from Gatsby that reveals private intelligence as his motivation. Gatsby's statements regarding the obliteration of time and repeating the past are metaphoric as opposed to literal, but even in their most nonliteral sense they reveal a perception of reality on his part that is predicated on his own illusion, and this individual basis for understanding runs contrary to Heraclitean philosophy.

I find the Heraclitean metaphor of the impossibility of stepping twice into the same river useful in establishing the inevitably of change. The water in the river is fluid in both form and time. Even though the environment through which it flows appears to remain rather static, time elapses between the first step into the river and the second, and in that time the river moves onward in response to the physical requirements of natural law. From a more philosophical perspective, this metaphor for the understandable natural order of things, the Logos, applies to human endeavor as well. Nick's speculation that Gatsby wants to have Daisy obliterate the time she has been married to Tom by denying that she has ever loved him indicates that Gatsby seeks not the physical impossibility of the obliteration of actual time but the obliteration of the changes in Daisy resulting from the time she has spent with Tom and away from Gatsby. He is ignoring the Heraclitean concept of the natural, necessary, and relentless nature of change. Irrespective of Gatsby's conspicuous, suspicious, and corrupting wealth and of the materialistic excesses that will be the mechanism of his destruction, it is the metaphor of change that highlights the folly of his intentions.

I like to show that at this point in the novel Nick's Logos-centered narration and Gatsby's personal intelligence align; Gatsby's apparent disengagement from the Logos, his inability to understand the nature of change, begins to transform his character. After the party at his house, he tells Nick that he feels "far away from [Daisy]" and that "it's hard to make her understand" (109). Even though Gatsby has realized his own reinvention and a reunion with Daisy, he still perceives a distance between them. Even though she was the person on whom the whole activity was centered, she cannot share in Gatsby's illusion.

In the pages subsequent to this exchange, Nick describes a radical change in Gatsby—the end of "his career as Trimalchio" (113). Ironically, since Daisy cannot be a part of his illusion, the relationship itself becomes detrimental to its vitality, and the external elements that Gatsby once viewed as crucial to his re-created past become a sacrifice to, rather than a necessary component of, his relationship with Daisy. The "colossal vitality of his illusion" becomes increasingly moribund (95), and the grandiosity of his vision of a recaptured past gives way to the pedestrian necessities of their relationship. His extravagant parties end, and his expansive lifestyle contracts to the point that Nick fears that Gatsby is ill. Gatsby's servants are released, and they are replaced by "some people Wolfsheim wanted to do something for," whose main qualification, according to Gatsby, is that they "wouldn't gossip" (114). The man whom Nick has described as being capable of Platonic self-creation begins to behave in the manner of one who personifies Heracleitus's observation in his fifty-first fragment, "It is hard to withstand the heart's desire, and it gets what it wants at the psyche's expense" (19).

Gatsby's affirmation, his change, his becoming, occurs in conjunction with the ultimate destruction of his illusory perception of reality. During the afternoon before the climactic confrontation at the Plaza Hotel, Daisy introduces her daughter to Nick and Gatsby. Nick describes Gatsby as noticeably nonplussed: "Afterward he kept looking at the child with surprise. I don't think he had ever really believed in its existence before" (117). Given her crucial role in the change that Gatsby will undergo, the objectification of the child, the use of the pronoun "its" as opposed to "her" in Nick's narration, is both striking and appropriate. The dehumanizing reference places the child in the role of an objective metaphor; her existence undermines Gatsby's preconceptions regarding his ability to recapture the past. As long as he was able to keep the child in the context of his illusion, he could think about her as an abstract component of the past that he hoped to obliterate. After he has met her, however, his awareness of her existence equates with his awareness of the relentless and constant nature of change. Thus Daisy's comment that "[s]he doesn't look like her father" is immaterial (117). In terms of Gatsby's developing awareness, Daisy's daughter is not a biological manifestation of an intimacy that Tom and Daisy once shared; she is a physical representation of the irrevocable change that the passage of time has wrought. As such, the girl becomes the force that initiates Gatsby's acquisition of the Logos. Heracleitus, in the final three lines of his first and longest fragment, bemoans the perception of persons who function without the Logos: "Men have talked about the world without paying attention to the world or to their own minds, as if they were asleep or absent-minded" (11). At this point in the novel, I tell my students, Gatsby can no longer proceed without paying attention.

Gatsby's becoming, however, is not yet complete. Heracleitus states in his eightieth fragment that "everything comes about by way of strife and necessity" (Hyland 167), and the climactic conflict of the novel occurs during the short, yet intense scene in the Plaza Hotel. It is there that Gatsby makes one last impassioned plea for Daisy to "[wipe] out forever" her life with Tom, to "tell him the truth—that [she] never loved him" (132). When Daisy proves incapable of definitively affirming that she has never loved Tom and accuses Gatsby of "[wanting] too much" (132), Gatsby's illusion is so thoroughly destroyed that even the otherwise benighted Tom is capable of making the observation that Gatsby "realizes that his presumptuous little flirtation is over" (135).

Gatsby's understanding, his alignment with the Logos, comes not in an epiphany but by degrees. After the automobile accident that claims Myrtle Wilson's life, Nick finds Gatsby lurking outside the Buchanan house. In a sad, belated reach for the nobility that he believed once fueled his quest, he informs Nick that even though Daisy was driving the car when it ran down Myrtle, that "of course" he would say that he had been (143). Nick leaves Gatsby outside the house, and, in a comment reminiscent of the one Tom had made at the Plaza, Nick perceives that Gatsby is "watching over nothing" (145).

The next morning, Gatsby suggests to Nick that perhaps Daisy loved Tom "just for a minute, when they were first married—and loved me more even then" (152). That attempted rationalization runs contrary to the essential necessity of Gatsby's illusion. It is followed immediately by what Nick calls Gatsby's "curious" admission, "In any case . . . it was just personal" (152). Admitting that his pursuit of Daisy was personal indicates that he has seen the fallacy of what Heracleitus calls "personal intelligence."

Nick's penultimate comment to Gatsby, "You're worth the whole damn bunch put together," is an expression of admiration, but Nick delivers it in a contradictory context: "I've always been glad I said that. It was the only compliment I ever gave him, because I disapproved of him from beginning to end" (154). If Nick is indeed the possessor of a Logos-type understanding, students see that he can simultaneously disapprove of Gatsby's illusion while expressing admiration for the man, affirming that because of Gatsby's changed perspective, he has "turned out all right" (2). Gatsby's response seems to support this affirmation: he breaks "into that radiant and understanding smile, as if [he and Nick had] been in ecstatic cahoots on that fact all the time" (154).

Current trends in the cultural, social, economic, and political forces to which students are exposed have inclined them toward results-oriented expectations in their course work. They are increasingly more focused on the end result—being told that something happened to the exclusion of thinking about why something happened. As students engage *The Great Gatsby*, providing them with a philosophical framework that helps explain why the novel works the way it does and why it continues to affect readers can give them the opportunity to examine the texture of Fitzgerald's work. Students are also, as Verene has noted, receptive to the use of metaphor as a tool for accessing ideas. For these reasons I have found Heraclitean philosophy a workable venue through which students can effectively examine and analyze the complexity and depth of *The Great Gatsby*.

NOTES

¹ Current editions of university-level anthologies frequently describe *The Great Gatsby* as socioeconomic commentary. McMichael and his coeditors' *Anthology of American Literature* calls it a novel that depicts "the stridency of an age of glittering innocence" and portrays "the hollowness of the American worship of riches" (1318). Cain's *American Literature* sees it as an "evocative study of the American dream of success" (600), and Perkins and Perkins's *The American Tradition in Literature* describes it as "the most striking fictional analysis of the age of gang barons and the social conditions that produced them" (1138).

² My point here is not that analyses of *The Great Gatsby* based on observations of the socioeconomic conditions presented in the novel are in any way inappropriate or lacking in rigor. Much insightful and incisive scholarship has been done in the analysis of socioeconomic factors in *The Great Gatsby*. As Scott Donaldson observes, Fitzgerald "tells a cautionary tale about the debilitating effects of money and social class on American society and those who seek fulfillment within its confines" ("Possessions" 210). Donaldson correctly identifies the literary, cultural, social, and political scope of *Gatsby* and suggests fertile and wide-ranging opportunities for examination of the socioeconomic foundations for the theme and content of the novel. I have, however, occasionally had students who saw the novel as just another commentary on love and wealth and were reticent to engage the texture of the novel's construction.

Symmetry versus Asymmetry: Structuring *The Great Gatsby*

Heidi M. Kunz

When we teach poetry to undergraduates, we customarily include versification, prosody, and other specific analyses of form. By identifying patterns and correspondences of sound and their relative placements in a poem, we discern emphases and juxtapositions, points and counterpoints presumably arranged by the poet to enhance the meanings of his or her art. Similarly, when we teach drama, we are likely to acknowledge the importance of the playwright's design: What effect does Shakespeare promote by dividing his tragedies into five acts? What does O'Neill accomplish by keeping the Tyrones indoors for the whole of *Long Day's Journey into Night*? When we teach prose fiction, we easily address aspects of organization—plot and narrative structures, for example—for which we have ready technical descriptions but less easily discuss aspects of form for which extant terminology is more diffuse.

Cleanth Brooks and Robert Penn Warren undertake to improve the classroom discussion of form in their classic pedagogical text *Understanding Fiction*. The study of form, they write, can be subdivided into studies of structure and style, where *structure* is "the ordering of the larger elements such as statements, episodes, scenes, and details" and *style* is "the arrangement of words." But then Brooks and Warren add, "[I]n the fullest sense, both the terms become synonymous with form"; they leave us with a tautology instead of a taxonomy (605). More recently, J. A. Cuddon explains literary form as "shape and structure" (327) and structure as "the sum of the relationships of the parts to each other" (871). While Cuddon does not attempt to specify "shape" or genre and stops short of naming specific "parts," his definition, involving correspondences within a work of literature, suggests welcome possibilities for the teaching of structure in prose fiction. To demonstrate the integral role of form to the achievement of a great novel, we can teach our students first to identify balances and other patterns of arrangement within the work and then to understand how the writer's design adds essential dimension and significance to his or her art.

Although now and again some critic agrees with H. L. Mencken that F. Scott Fitzgerald's *The Great Gatsby* is no more than "a glorified anecdote" ("As H. L. M. Sees It" 156), Linda W. Wagner summarizes the consensus of scholarly opinion: "In 1923 William Carlos Williams wrote what he called *The Great American Novel*. The book that deserves that title, *The Great Gatsby*, appeared in 1925" (882). *The Great Gatsby* is a particularly apt choice for teaching form because it is accessible, it is familiar, and it is a profoundly effective work of modernism. One reason for its appeal and accessibility is Nick Carraway, who narrates from a postcollegiate point of view in vernacular yet evocative English.

Although he is older than most undergraduates, Nick maintains important attitudes from his university days—his perception of Tom Buchanan, for one—and draws from his Yale reputation when he introduces himself, so that he almost seems to be students' peer. Students are likely to have read *The Great Gatsby* before entering our classrooms, but even if they have not, they are likely to know something about it. Their familiarity supports their confidence with the text and prepares them to approach it in fresh, more challenging ways. Learning to appreciate the organic form of *The Great Gatsby* helps the student understand its critical stature and cultural pervasiveness. It is a great as well as popular novel because Fitzgerald uses form to facilitate meaning, arranging symmetry against asymmetry to create structural tension that conveys modernist anxiety to the reader.

To supply specific criteria for Cuddon's definition, we can begin by asking our students to consider fundamental parts of the novel and how these might be understood to relate to other parts. If we make the basic choice to consider the opening and the ending, chapters 1 and 9, we find that Fitzgerald balances them in several ways. The first and final sections frame the text like bookends, carefully wrought to reflect each other. Fitzgerald's handling of Nick shows this correspondence. Chapter 1 presents Nick as uniquely prepared to tell Gatsby's story, as the one character in the cast with exactly the experience, temperament, and manner that will win the principal characters' confidence (as well as the reader's). In college, he says by way of introducing himself, he "was privy to the secret griefs of wild, unknown men," although "[m]ost of the confidences were unsought" (1). He surmises that his classmates wanted his ear because he is "inclined to reserve all judgments," but his dispassion is only an inclination; he freely acknowledges his own snobbery a few sentences later by admitting his agreement with his father's suggestion that "a sense of the fundamental decencies is parcelled out unequally at birth" (2).

Nick may be the best possible narrator for *The Great Gatsby*, but he warns the reader that he is a complicated and even a calculating one (see Donaldson, "Trouble"): he knows that "the intimate revelations of young men, or at least the terms in which they express them, are usually plagiaristic and marred by obvious suppressions" (1–2). Accordingly, while chapter 1 introduces the four other principal characters, Nick seems more occupied with himself than with his putative subject. Once he describes his attitude, he elaborates his identity by working outward in successively broader frames of reference, noting briefly his family background, explaining his domestic arrangements, placing himself socioeconomically, and attributing his decision to relocate to a national trend. Finally, he surrounds his individual circumstances with cultural authority. When a stranger "helplessly" asks him for directions, Nick recalls, "I told him. And as I walked on I was lonely no longer. I was a guide, a pathfinder, an original settler" (4). Nick refers to Gatsby several times in the chapter, but Gatsby appears only once, briefly, as a mysterious shadow-figure in the dark distance, slipping wordlessly in and out of view (20–21).

Fitzgerald crafts chapter 9 in direct and figurative relation to chapter 1. We can encourage students to note that here Nick confirms the experiential and temperamental credentials he claims in the first chapter. The reader finds that, to a remarkable extent, Nick is indeed "privy to the secret griefs of wild, unknown men." Nick alone witnesses self-indulgent, immoral Tom Buchanan grieving for the mistress Tom dares not acknowledge in public. Nick is the only person on hand to welcome the inscrutably banal Henry Gatz to the funeral of the son who was at once a notorious bootlegger and "Mr. Nobody from Nowhere" (130). (Meyer Wolfsheim, a man wild and unknown in other senses, also confides his grief to Nick.) And the confidences are indeed unsought; Nick happens upon Tom in a busy New York street, and he receives Mr. Gatz with uncertain surprise since Gatsby had "never told [him] definitely that his parents were dead" (165). If Nick does not quite "reserve all judgments," he achieves a similar result by neutralizing his own opinions, as when he accepts Tom's handshake because "it seemed silly not to," just after declaring, "I couldn't forgive him or like him" (179).

We can direct students toward a more figurative understanding of correspondence by guiding them to build interpretively from their observations about all the main characters. In chapter 1, Nick encounters the four principals; in chapter 9, he leaves them. Gatsby, in the first chapter distanced by reticence, is by the last chapter removed by death. Jordan Baker, who treats Nick disdainfully at their first meeting, dismisses him from their final one. Tom, who Nick "always" feels "wanted me to like him with some harsh, defiant wistfulness of his own" (7), speaks harshly, defiantly, and wistfully in their farewell conversation. Daisy Buchanan, initially "p-paralyzed with happiness" (8), is ultimately fixed for life with her husband and not actively present.

If we ask students to reread only chapters 1 and 9, they may notice repeated patterns of information. Like the introductory chapter, the concluding chapter is primarily about Nick and by the same tokens. He remembers his childhood and youth, conceptually returning to the personal and socioeconomic identifiers of family and home, and he once again provides the reader with fussy domestic details. We can lead our students to recognize that the conclusion of the novel, with its Dutch sailors exploring "a fresh, green breast of the new world" (180), elevates Nick's experience into the archetypical American experience, for, like the "original settler[s]" (4), he turns west in the hope of finding "something commensurate to his capacity for wonder" (180). Then we may teach them to appreciate how Fitzgerald's form supports meaning and operates to extend a correspondence beyond the system of the text, securing relation with the reader (assuming he or she is an American reader).

Such close correspondence between the opening and closing parts constitutes a structural balance or symmetry. Since devising symmetry requires forethought, we can present Fitzgerald to our students as an artist who designs his work with meticulous care. We can encourage them to look beyond Fitzgerald's handling of Nick to discover more balances of situation and detail elsewhere in the novel. Working in from the bookends, chapters 2 and 8 depict the novel's adulterous relationships (Tom and Myrtle Wilson in chapter 2, Daisy and Gatsby in chapter 8). Chapter 3 is about the party at Gatsby's house that ends with automobile emergencies and Jordan's observation that "[i]t takes two to make an accident" (58); chapter 7 is about the gathering at the Plaza Hotel that ends in a fatal automobile accident caused by two reckless people. Working in further, the reader finds that chapters 4 and 6 contain notorious gossip (about, respectively, Gatsby's guests and Gatsby's reputation), accounts (first Gatsby's, then Gatz's) of the title character's family, details of his mysterious relationships with underworld mentors (Wolfsheim in chapter 4, Cody in chapter 6), and recollections (earlier from Jordan, later from Gatsby) of the Gatsby-Daisy courtship and then end in a kiss (in chapter 4, between Jordan and Nick, and in chapter 6, between Daisy and Gatsby). The pivotal event of the novel—the reunion of Daisy and Gatsby—occurs in its center part. Significant patterns of figure and symbol also reverse at chapter 5. Dan Seiters points out, "Through the first half of the novel water promises life, a rebirth every spring; through the second half it symbolizes disaster and death" (78), and he observes similar halving in the connotations of transportation, communication, and other image systems. James E. Miller, Jr., calls chapter 5 the "fulcrum" of *The Great Gatsby* (*F. Scott Fitzgerald* 115). Appropriate to its many symmetries, the novel turns on the episode that most prominently features the title character.

But in the modern world, to paraphrase Yeats, the center does not hold. Why, then, does Fitzgerald choose symmetry as an organizing principle for a work of modernism? Balance connotes justice, and justice implies positive resolution, or, at least, satisfaction—and the end of *The Great Gatsby* gives neither of these. We can help our students see the modernism of the novel through further structural analysis. Gatsby may be at the literal core of the novel, but he is not the literary force that keeps it together. Instead, Fitzgerald uses Nick to regulate the narrative. Nick dominates our first and final impressions; moreover, as he says, he is the author of "this book" (2) and has the first and the final words. In Fitzgerald's conceit, Gatsby appears in the middle because the author Nick has decided to locate him there. Occasionally, Nick reminds us of his dual role, as in chapter 3, where he muses, "Reading over what I have written so far"; and he evinces a sense of presentation as he continues, "I see I have given the impression . . ." (55).

If Nick is aware of an author's power to shape a reader's perception of a story, why then, we must ask our students, does he choose to write a novel about Gatsby by beginning and ending with himself? Nick's strategic priority in his own narrative suggests that he writes not to memorialize Gatsby but to sort through his own confusing experience and to present his result to the reader. As a younger man he prided himself on his extraordinary perspicacity, his ability to validate wild, unknown logics without judgment; he confesses that he has come to recognize ruefully that "life is much more successfully looked at from a single window, after all" (4). Nick applies his "single window" theory when he organizes his verbal scrapbook into elegant patterns of relation. He exercises writerly prerogatives of selection and arrangement on his written memory in an effort to bring the chaotic summer of 1922 to "a sort of moral attention forever" (2). Inevitably, his tone at the end of the novel is deeply, ruefully fatalistic. As an intelligent citizen of the modern world, he apprehends that framing a single window exacts the high price of deliberate limitation—his own "obvious suppressions"—and artificial imposition of order.

If we remind our students that Nick is a well-educated bonds salesman rather than a trained artist, we open them to the powerful imperfections in his carefully wrought symmetry. Extending Cuddon's notion of parts into longer units of structure, we should point out that chapters 1–3 build rising action around Nick's recollection of three social gatherings. Many scholars, including W. T. Lhamon, Jr., Robert Emmet Long (*Achieving*), and Sergio Perosa (119–29), accord these chapters particular significance, praising the use of setting to differentiate "the three distinctly separate social spheres to which [the main characters] belong" (Long, *Achieving* 119). The first, at the Buchanans' home in East Egg, involves family and a close friend, Jordan; the second, in Tom and Myrtle's apartment in New York, includes paramours and acquaintances; the third, at Gatsby's house in West Egg, attracts virtually anyone "with a simplicity of heart that was its own ticket of admission" (41).

Chapters 7–9, however, present no corresponding falling action of contained social episodes. Instead, the last trio of chapters splinters into numerous fragments: chapter 7 collects images from Nick's surreal daydreams on the commuter train, from Tom's confrontation of Gatsby at the Plaza, and from the fatal accident and its immediate aftermath. A series of unsuccessful or incomplete communications that range in result from interruption to disappointment to murder comprise chapters 8 and 9. In one section of chapter 8, Nick jettisons his memory altogether and relies on secondhand sources and a police report to construe George Wilson's behavior after the death of Myrtle (156–61). Nick seems unable here to subordinate his crowded and painful memory to his authorial control. The pattern of episode established in the first three chapters is neither repeated nor completed in the final three. Wittingly or unwittingly, Nick writes a structural imbalance that undermines the primary symmetrical scheme of his book.

The first three chapters of the novel mount still another structural challenge to Nick's symmetrical design: he calls his book a "history of the summer" (5) and incorporates the view from a third "window." Students readily understand that time does not align people and events in well-matched pairs and that situations rarely end in neat reflections of their beginnings. Thus they can detect that Nick writes against his own organization by approximating the method of a historian. He declares his biases in the exposition, documents his sources—nearly always citing the firsthand experience or the informant from which he derives his data—and seems to progress through the season from June to October. He embellishes his account with anecdotes from his youth and from the youths of the other major characters, however, and so makes the unhistorian-like choice to depart from strict chronology. He frequently interpolates flash-backs and eventually unbalances the book by disproportionately freighting the last chapters with the past (see Miller, *F. Scott Fitzgerald* 114). Thomas A. Pendleton contends that Nick skews the linear sequence of events to develop effects (31–32); but even if Nick does so, he writes still another asymmetry that competes with and detracts from his symmetry. By adding modes of organization that destabilize his structure, Nick fails to confine himself—despite his conscious effort—to a single order that might eventuate in an emotionally satisfying, or at least "more successful," conclusion.

Nick's narrative ends in unresolved structural discord. His history of the summer seems to end with the onset of autumn, and the last paragraphs resonate with the first chapter, but he knows he has not tidied or ended the messiness of memory. He has found himself inadequate to the task of making sense of his Gatsby episode. The structures of the novel show us how he sabotages his own modernist search for an order sufficient to his experience. On the last page, he tries to conclude by offsetting the chaotic past with "the orgastic future" (180), apparently straining for an ultimate correspondence that might finally assuage the anxiety compelling him to write a book. When the reader sees that Nick writes no more pages, he or she understands that Nick has abandoned the effort. We may need to remind our students that Nick can abandon the effort because Fitzgerald causes his character to abandon the effort. When Nick quits the page, the ruse of his authorship necessarily quits with him. The reader is left not with Nick's narrative but with Fitzgerald's novel.

We should note that the reader is also left with the implications of the novel, for Fitzgerald has not dismissed him or her as he has Nick. In fact, it is part of Fitzgerald's design to retain the reader. The final paragraphs show the integration of form and meaning in *The Great Gatsby*. If we pursue the structurally supported suggestion that Nick's experience is archetypal, we interpret him as a template for ourselves. His experience figuratively becomes our experience, his task becomes our task, his anxiety becomes our anxiety. Fitzgerald uses form to capture us for his artistic purposes. We cannot escape the structural mechanism for involving us in Nick's predicament any more than we can escape the corroborating language. In just that part of the text that establishes a correspondence to the reader, Fitzgerald has Nick write inclusively by slipping out of his usual grammatical first person singular and into the plural. The universal coherence that Nick hopes will reconcile all meanings "elude[s] us," but "we" nevertheless "beat on" (180). By means of his masterful handling of structure and what Brooks and Warren would term his style, Fitzgerald demonstrates Nick's modernist anxiety in the text of *The Great Gatsby* and effectively assigns it to us. When we consider the book, we revisit Nick's revisitation of his memory, and his troubling, unresolved past—our troubling, unresolved past—flows unobstructedly through the present tense of the narrative's concluding sentence, directly into our extratextual present.

By examining the correspondences between parts and units in *The Great Gatsby*, we can encourage our students to attend to a text with the care and sensitivity essential to literary criticism. A study of symmetries and asymmetries in the novel illuminates one way that Fitzgerald elicits the emotional attachment many of us profess for *Gatsby*. As they learn to discern the patterns that structure the narrative, we may help them recognize the role of form in supporting, enhancing, and activating the meanings of a great work of prose fiction. When they can articulate elements of structure and appreciate Fitzgerald's genius, they will have achieved a more sophisticated understanding of the experience of reading, the craft of writing, and a work of art.

"If I Couldn't Be Perfect I Wouldn't Be Anything": Teaching Becoming and Being in *The Great Gatsby*

Jonathan P. Fegley

In "*Remembrance of Things Past* Remembered," John Updike writes, "For a book to be great in a reader's life it is not enough for the book to be great; the reader must be ready" (162). After nearly three-quarters of a century, the status of *The Great Gatsby* as a great book—if not *the* great American novel—seems to have been forever solidified. Certainly few novels of the twentieth century have so fully satisfied Fitzgerald's own definition of literary greatness: "The wise writer, I think, writes for the youth of his own generation, the critics of the next, and the schoolmasters of ever afterward" (*Letters* 459). To that list we can add fellow writers. But no matter what the status of *The Great Gatsby* among scholars, teachers, and writers, it remains less clear how we can make sure that our students—the youth of the present generation—can realize and appreciate its greatness.

The complication of failing to recognize the validity of Updike's caveat regarding great books was illustrated to me in my first year of teaching as a graduate assistant. At that time a student in one of my introductory literature classes contended that Fitzgerald's greatest novel was not *The Great Gatsby* but his first novel, *This Side of Paradise*. I was momentarily stunned by the sheer naïveté of such a claim, but I recovered quickly. Armed with the smugness of the burgeoning academic, I easily and disdainfully dismissed her argument, quoting first the *New Republic* review that labeled *This Side of Paradise* "the collected works of F. Scott Fitzgerald" (R. V. A. S. 49), then paraphrasing the arguments of everyone from H. L. Mencken and Carl Van Doren to Jackson R. Bryer and Matthew J. Bruccoli.

I went home that night assured that I had not only proved the worth of my education but also justified the faith of my university in placing me in front of a roomful of freshmen students. As time has passed, though, I remain troubled by my response to that student's assertion and by my failure to appreciate—or even to understand—what lay behind her assertion. And I have come to modify how I regard Updike's message and to believe that as teachers we must not only make certain that our students are ready to appreciate great books but also be ready to approach those books in ways that facilitate their appreciation.

While the principal characters of *The Great Gatsby* are older than Amory Blaine, the principal character of *This Side of Paradise*, their worldview arguably might be no more mature. In "Afterthoughts on the Twenties," John W. Aldridge contends that the limiting vision inherent in that adolescent worldview is the damning flaw in almost all the American modernists:

They were a group of highly talented but narrow writers, and their narrowness was most dramatically revealed in the fact that they had one abiding interest—themselves when young, an interest that, in the case of some of them, became the literary preoccupation of a lifetime. Their books . . . told over and over again the story of self-discovery through the first conquest of experience. (73)

Even if we accept Aldridge's judgment that the modernist vision limited the universality of American literature, we should remember that it is a vision shared by the students we teach: persons whose principal subject is themselves and whose primary interest lies in their own process of becoming. Furthermore, the means of expression that Aldridge finds so limiting might be the only means by which one can convey the experience of America, the subject of most of American modernism. After all, as Michael Vincent Miller writes, the beauty of the American dream

is the beauty of adolescence, enchanting to behold, poetic and meretricious at the same time in how far it will go, in what sublime, almost insane risks it will endure, to realize its stubborn belief that pure wanting can make the fantastic happen. (153)

I try to keep these ideas in mind when I teach *The Great Gatsby*. I also try to keep in mind the words of that student from long ago. As a general philosophy, I believe success in teaching and in keeping either a course or a particular novel fresh, interesting, and relevant lies in looking for what I don't know as opposed to what I do know. I learn much by reading and listening to other scholars or speaking with colleagues about ideas, approaches, or problems either in general pedagogy or in specific subject matter. I also try to listen closely for the same from my students, attempting to filter out the typical student grumbling without dismissing students' legitimate issues and concerns, whether related to the approach or to the substance of the course. How does that philosophy help shape my approach to teaching *The Great Gatsby*?

Because I usually teach *Gatsby* in introductory or survey courses to college freshmen and sophomores, I develop discussions along a broad spectrum of subject matter. My study guides include topics ranging from *The Great Gatsby* as the great American novel to the effectiveness of the title to the role of Nick as narrator—all important to a general understanding of the novel. While I address these and other topics, I focus discussions on questions that in my experience have generated the greatest connection to the novel for my students—that is, the strongest sense of awareness and insight from my students. Those questions center on the novel's exploration of the duality of becoming and being.

I think I understand the words of that student much better now because I understand that duality much better. Armed only with her own (limited) life and reading experience, she made the claim of greatness because *This Side of*

Paradise spoke to her in ways that *The Great Gatsby* did not. Was the claim valid? Assuredly, it was to her. I remember her argument well enough to believe that she had been attracted to Fitzgerald's earlier novel's exploration of the duality between becoming and being—an exploration that seemed a closer parallel to her own emergence into adult consciousness, her own process of becoming. If I was teaching that student today, I would not deny her assertion; instead, I would show her how what she might have been connecting to in *This Side of Paradise* appears even more powerfully, more evocatively, and more eloquently in *The Great Gatsby*.

I try to show my students that the essential power of Fitzgerald lies in the interface between becoming and being. Early in *This Side of Paradise*, Fitzgerald says of Amory Blaine, "It was always the becoming he dreamed of, never the being" (*Novels* 24). The importance Fitzgerald attached to the process of becoming predates even his published work. In an entry in his ledger dated February 1915, he had written, "If I couldn't be perfect I wouldn't be anything" (*F. Scott Fitzgerald's Ledger* 169). Although such unflinching belief in one's potential might be expected in a sheltered, ingenuous child, in 1915 Fitzgerald was a Princeton University undergraduate who had experienced disappointment in his home life, his love life, his athletic aspirations, and his academic career.

While at Princeton, Fitzgerald reiterated his belief in unlimited potential regarding his hypothesized future as a writer. In perfect candor, he told Edmund Wilson, "I want to be one of the greatest writers who ever lived, don't you?" (qtd. in Bruccoli, *Some Sort* 68). Though Wilson was already both widely read and realistic enough to understand the foolhardy notion of such a statement, he also appreciated its sincerity, its capacity for boundless hope:

> I had not myself really quite entertained this fantasy because I had been reading Plato and Dante. Scott had been reading Booth Tarkington, Compton Mackenzie, H. G. Wells and Swinburne; but when he later got to better writers, his standards and his achievement went sharply up, and he would always have pitted himself against the best in his own line that he knew. I thought this remark rather foolish at the time, yet it was one of the things that made me respect him.   (qtd. in Bruccoli, *Some Sort* 70)

Wilson's simultaneously dismissive and laudatory assessment echoes throughout *The Great Gatsby* in Nick Carraway's contradictory judgments of Gatsby. It seems appropriate that Wilson mentions Plato first among his own reading, for the arrogant innocence manifested in Fitzgerald's aspirations to be a writer and in Gatsby's aspirations to realize his all-consuming dream might well derive from the aspiration toward the ideal inherent in Plato. Wilson, Fitzgerald's acknowledged "intellectual conscience" ("Crack-Up" 79), might have been able to discuss the concepts of Plato on a level far beyond the intellectual capacity of Fitzgerald, but only Fitzgerald, with his remarkable ability and belief, could create Jay Gatsby.

Certainly it required a person with a vision of unlimited potential to epitomize the Platonic duality between becoming and being in a character as vividly
imagined as Jay Gatsby, who "sprang from his Platonic conception of himself"
(98). Gatsby seems to reflect Fitzgerald's own Platonic distinction between being and manifestations of being. Indeed, one way of explaining Fitzgerald's insistent use of the terms "personage" and "personality" in *This Side of Paradise*
(see esp. Fitzgerald, *Novels* 94) is seeing those terms as an attempt to clarify or
at least to reinforce that distinction between being and manifestations of being.
The realization of success for Gatsby might be the degree to which he achieves
the status of personage, whether his manifestations of personality are really
steps in a process of becoming or little more than affectations.

To underscore the distinction between the states of becoming and of being, I
begin my classroom discussion with an examination of the character who least
represents the idealized sense of becoming: Tom Buchanan. Tom is not in the
process of becoming anything, and Fitzgerald's expressive presentation fully
reinforces that fact. In a letter to Maxwell E. Perkins, Fitzgerald called Tom
Buchanan the "best character I've ever done . . . [one of] the three best characters in American fiction in the last twenty years" (Kuehl and Bryer 90). In a
novel in which our understanding of the title character comes to us only in
a pastiche of color, light, and innuendo, Tom is certainly the most detailed and
definitively drawn character.

Beginning with Tom's first appearance, Fitzgerald draws a sharp distinction
between Tom and Gatsby and a more subtle distinction between Tom and the
rest of the novel's characters:

> [H]e was a sturdy straw-haired man of thirty with a rather hard mouth
> and a supercilious manner. Two shining arrogant eyes had established
> dominance over his face and gave him the appearance of always leaning
> aggressively forward. Not even the effeminate swank of his riding clothes
> could hide the enormous power of that body—he seemed to fill those
> glistening boots until he strained the top lacing, and you could see a great
> pack of muscle shifting when his shoulder moved under his thin coat. It
> was a body capable of enormous leverage—a cruel body.   (7)

Tom's athleticism is characteristic of the Romantic heroes of Fitzgerald's childhood: "among various physical accomplishments, [Tom] had been one of the
most powerful ends that ever played football at New Haven—a national figure
in a way" (6). But in Tom Buchanan this trait suggests nothing of Romantic
ideals. Instead, it suggests simply the brute force and the cold, unfeeling power
(as well as the dissipation of potential that frequently characterizes the rich in
Fitzgerald's work) that mark Tom throughout the novel.

The description also suggests that Tom is nothing more and nothing less than
what we see he is. Mockingly called by Daisy a "brute of a man, a great, big,
hulking physical specimen" (12), Tom expresses no ideals or even ideas, simply

aping the bigotry of "this man Goddard" and stumbling to attach some "scientific stuff" to his vague mutterings about the dissolution of civilization (12, 13). Even in the shadows of his life, he exhibits neither idealism nor a particularly acute need to shield what he is. Indeed, he quickly draws Nick Carraway into his not-so-secret life with no apology for his adultery or for involving Nick as a coconspirator against Nick's cousin Daisy. And while Gatsby likewise will draw Nick into his adulterous affair, the relationship between Gatsby and Daisy stands in dramatic opposition to the relationship between Tom Buchanan and Myrtle Wilson because of its idealistic foundation.

Tom's relationship with Myrtle tells us everything we need to know about him. He uses it to satisfy his immediate needs, with no idealized expectation—indeed, no desire for an idealized expectation—of the future (though Myrtle harbors such an ideal). On the train to New York, Tom can invoke for Nick a wondrous image of Myrtle and then break her nose before the evening is finished. More Machiavellian than Platonic, Tom regards himself as the last standard-bearer of both Western civilization and the American family even as he engages in an adulterous affair with the wife of a garage mechanic he sees as being beneath any regard. Then, after the death of Gatsby, he can defend himself to Nick and even seek Nick's absolution by confessing not his complicity in Gatsby's murder but his sentimental reaction (amid the wholly pragmatic action of canceling the lease on the New York apartment) to finding the biscuits for the dog he had bought for Myrtle (178–79). Tom is what he is and forever will be—the setting of his various affairs and betrayals might change, but he will not.

Throughout the novel, Gatsby stands in dramatic opposition to Tom Buchanan. Fitzgerald begins making the distinction between Gatsby and Tom Buchanan through his depiction of Gatsby. We meet Gatsby, as we meet Tom, through Nick's filtering lens but not, as with Tom, through a full physical description. Indeed, the first time he meets Gatsby, Nick fails to recognize the man as his rich, eccentric neighbor, who he expected "would be a florid and corpulent person in his middle years" (48). And when he actually describes Gatsby, Nick does so in terms not of physical appearance but of the impression Gatsby makes:

> He smiled understandingly—much more than understandingly. It was one of those rare smiles with a quality of eternal reassurance in it, that you may come across four or five times in life. It faced—or seemed to face—the whole external world for an instant, and then concentrated on *you* with an irresistible prejudice in your favor. It understood you just as far as you wanted to be understood, believed in you as you would like to believe in yourself, and assured you that it had precisely the impression of you that, at your best, you hoped to convey.   (48)

Elsewhere, Gatsby is conveyed in the impressionistic nuances of color and light. When Nick leaves Gatsby on the night of Myrtle's death, he turns back to gather his last physical impression: "His gorgeous pink rag of a suit made a bright spot of color against the white steps" (154). The impressionistic use of color and light complements the initial means by which Nick—and we—come to understand Gatsby: the generally malicious gossip that innumerable revelers contribute about their elusive host, ranging from Gatsby's being an "Oxford man" (49) to his being a killer or a spy (44).

Although the poor sales of the novel during his lifetime caused Fitzgerald to question its character development, his assertion to Perkins that "Gatsby sticks in my heart" anticipated the enduring response to the novel (Kuehl and Bryer 90). At the very least, Fitzgerald's technique serves a practical purpose. Gatsby's historical models, the Long Island bootlegger Max Gerlach and the New York stock swindler Edward M. Fuller, suggest little of the Platonic idealist. The fictional Jay Gatsby rises above such a genesis as a composite who, despite his unsavory background, his excesses, and his ingenuousness, compels not only acceptance but even admiration.

Stung by those poor sales, Fitzgerald judged that his portrayal of Gatsby was a problem, especially in the romance with Daisy. He admitted:

> I gave no account (and had no feeling about or knowledge of) the emotional relations between Gatsby and Daisy from the time of their reunion to the catastrophe. . . . I felt that what [*Gatsby*] really missed was the lack of any emotional backbone at the very height of it.
>
> (*F. Scott Fitzgerald: A Life* 109)

But a too realistic portrayal of a Long Island bootlegger–stock swindler would have made Gatsby so unsavory as to deny him our vicarious hopes and sorrows, as well as belie Nick's parting judgment: "You're worth the whole damn bunch put together" (154).

Demonstrating for students the relation of form and function, I stress that a detailed, expressionistic, physically oriented characterization of Gatsby would also contradict the novel's thematic direction. Fitzgerald has rendered Gatsby through the only means possible; Gatsby is in the process of becoming, not in a state of being, and thus exists in an ephemeral state. Standing in the rain at Gatsby's funeral, Nick "trie[s] to think of Gatsby then for a moment, but he [is] already too far away" (174).

Gatsby never achieves what he hopes to achieve. Despite the characterization of Gatsby's quest as an attempt to "repeat the past" (110), Gatsby never achieved his goal in Daisy's Louisville in 1917, though he approached it. Although he briefly possesses Daisy in a physical sense, at the time of his death on Long Island five years later he remains incomplete, still seeking to become (or, as Nick supposes, having relinquished the ideal of becoming) that which he had hoped to be, to "recover something, some idea of himself" (110). Everything that moves him toward the fateful day of the confrontation at the Plaza Hotel, which triggers both the death of his dream and his physical death, is simply a step toward recovering the idea of that past moment to create a future ideal. Gatsby's attempt to recover that idea and to achieve the state of being he desires, to fulfill the ideal reality of his Platonic conception of himself, is related only peripherally to his rise to wealth or even to his seduction of Daisy Buchanan. The wealth he has amassed serves only as a means of attracting Daisy, and attracting Daisy serves only as the means of becoming that which he once envisioned himself to be:

> some idea of himself perhaps, that had gone into loving Daisy. His life had been confused and disordered since then, but if he could once return to a certain starting place and go over it all slowly, he could find out what that thing was. . . .   (110)

Daisy complements Gatsby and offers him the means of making an incomplete self whole.[1] In addition, she operates in the role of other in signifying Gatsby's being. The novel's title simultaneously suggests magnificence and illusion, and Daisy functions in the novel in the same capacity of ambivalent suggestion. From Gatsby's perspective, if Daisy fulfills the role that he wants her to fulfill, then Jay Gatsby becomes fully realized and attains a level of magnificence. If she does not, Jay Gatsby becomes not merely an illusionist but a delusionist. As such, he stands in the line of descent from the greatest delusionist in literature; Carroll B. Johnson's remarks regarding Don Quixote ring true of Gatsby:

> By naming himself, Don Quixote literally wills himself into existence. . . . Naming is a process that moves in two directions. Projected from inside the individual, the name announces to the world who he thinks he is, or wants to be. Imposed from without, the name designates what or who the world thinks the person is or wants him to be. . . . Nobody can really believe he is who he thinks he is unless the world, the Other, validates his identity by reflecting it back on him, crystallized in the name he calls himself.   (40–41)

Don Quixote never confronts or absorbs his idealized other, Dulcinea, and eventually Sancho Panza assumes the role of other in validating the identity of Don Quixote (inasmuch as that identity can be validated). But Gatsby cannot transfer the role of other onto Nick Carraway or anyone else, so his fate remains forever entwined with his Dulcinea, Daisy Fay Buchanan.

Gatsby's attempt to become the idealized vision of himself is doomed to failure by the impossibility of "repeat[ing] the past" (110), no matter how much Gatsby believes in such green lights, and by the limitations of Daisy as the vehicle for attaining that idealized embodiment in the present. I ask my students to consider Daisy the novel's pivotal character, because she almost transcends the opposing states of being and becoming. Though she is rendered in terms far different from Tom, she, too, opens the novel as a character who fully is, much to her chagrin. The image of the "frosted wedding-cake of the ceiling" fore-shadows the limitation inherent in Daisy (8); her marriage to Tom has immersed her in a life of being, devoid of any belief in the imagined possibility of becoming (though she still seems to long for such belief). In the novel's opening scene, Daisy says, "Do you always watch for the longest day of the year and then miss it? I always watch for the longest day in the year and then miss it." Then, in response to Jordan Baker's suggestion that they should "plan something," Daisy "*helplessly*" replies, "What'll we plan? . . . What do people plan?" (11; emphasis added).

I encourage my students to focus on the image of the wedding-cake ceiling and to connect it to other images or words in the scene. One of the first suggestions of whiteness, the image precipitates Fitzgerald's use of color in the passage. His repeated allusions to the color white (or, more properly here, the absence of color) serve not to heighten a sense of purity or innocence but instead to intensify the sense of the static and the empty. Complementing this use of color imagery, Fitzgerald blends such words as "stationary," "anchored," and "motionless" (8) with the general ennui of the evening (and the lives of the Buchanans) to create a sense of the stultification that Daisy endures in her marriage. The first words to emerge from Daisy's mouth as she greets Nick reinforce that sense of the static: "I'm p-paralyzed with happiness" (8). And the confession to which she subjects Nick when he asks about her daughter conveys the confinement inherent not only in the role of mother but in being female at that time and in that place: "the best thing a girl can be in this world [is] a beautiful little fool" (17). The sense of ennui and static confinement that defines Daisy's life as Mrs. Tom Buchanan culminates on the same day that she abdicates the role of objective correlative to Gatsby's Platonic ideal—and with it the possibility of transcending that ennui and static confinement. Her nervous musing echoes T. S. Eliot's *The Waste Land*: " 'What'll we do with ourselves this afternoon?' cried Daisy, 'and the day after that, and the next thirty years?' " (118).

For all her sense of disillusionment and entrapment, Daisy tantalizes with a promise that functions as the transcendent element in the novel. Fitzgerald renders that promise, as well as her character, as he does Gatsby's character, in tone; the tone in Daisy's case is one not of color or light but of sound. When he visits the Buchanan mansion and first meets Jordan Baker, Nick recognizes the promise in Daisy's voice:

> It was the kind of voice that the ear follows up and down, as if each speech is an arrangement of notes that will never be played again. . . . [T]here was an excitement in her voice that men who had cared for her found difficult to forget: a singing compulsion, a whispered "Listen," a promise that she had done gay, exciting things just a while since and that there were gay, exciting things hovering in the next hour. (9)

Nick can never fully characterize the attraction of that tone of voice; but as he attempts to define it, Gatsby supplies the precise metaphor:

> "Her voice is full of money," he said suddenly.
>
> That was it. I'd never understood before. It was full of money—that was the inexhaustible charm that rose and fell in it, the jingle of it, the cymbals' song of it. . . . High in a white palace the king's daughter, the golden girl. . . .   (120; ellipses in orig.)

The sound of money that characterizes Daisy's voice suggests further limitations that restrict her from participating completely in the fulfillment of Gatsby's dream. Daisy functions as the motivating factor not only for Gatsby to recover an idea of himself but also for him to abandon all else to achieve the trappings of wealth necessary to attract Daisy. As such, Daisy becomes part of the "foul dust float[ing] in the wake of his dreams" (2) that eventually preys on Gatsby and serves as objective correlative to what William James called "the bitch-goddess SUCCESS. That—with the squalid cash interpretation put on the word success—is our national disease" (260).

Daisy has little trouble committing adultery, for the deterioration of her marriage fits who she is, one of those "careless people" who "smashed up things and creatures and then retreated back into their money or their vast carelessness, or whatever it was that kept them together, and let other people clean up the mess they had made" (179). She cannot become what Gatsby wants her to become, for she cannot transcend the limitation of materialism to believe in such a life-altering commitment as the denial of the passage of time. Sarah Beebe Fryer defends Daisy's actions as being derived from a "sense of security she so desperately craved" and concludes, "[S]he deserves more pity than blame" for eventually "abandon[ing] her dream of a romantic love to cling desperately to the unsatisfactory stability her husband represents" ("Beneath the Mask" 161, 163, 165). As Richard Lehan writes regarding Fitzgerald's style in the novel, "Poetic prose does not always hold up firmly under realistic scrutiny. To my mind, the weakest criticism of *Gatsby* involves readings that over-particularize the novel, robbing it of its romantic aura" (Great Gatsby: *The Limits* 132). Realistic scrutiny might do more than rob the relationship between Gatsby and Daisy of its romantic aura; it might also deny Daisy a truly sympathetic understanding. As Daisy tells Gatsby when he instructs her to deny that she ever loved Tom, "Oh, you want too much!" (132).

As I point out to my students, Gatsby wants the idealized conception more than the reality of Daisy's loving him. Indeed, something seems to go out of Gatsby as soon as he has staked a physical claim to Daisy: "He had been full of the idea so long, dreamed it right through to the end, waited with his teeth set, so to speak, at an inconceivable pitch of intensity. Now, in the reaction, he was running down like an overwound clock" (92). As Gatsby and Nick stroll the grounds of his mansion and Gatsby points out where they would see the green light at the end of

Daisy's dock if not for the fog, Nick conjectures, "Possibly it had occurred to him that the colossal significance of that light had now vanished forever" (93). Nick's concluding observation in that paragraph is most telling because the light has always been associated with Daisy and with Gatsby's idealized sense of self tied to loving her: "His count of enchanted objects had diminished by one" (93).

I try to show that Daisy's inability to join Gatsby in his vision renders him and Myrtle and George Wilson the most immediate victims of the Buchanans' carelessness. The Wilsons struggle to remain believers in the process of becoming, even as they find themselves mired in the vast wasteland of the ash heaps. Myrtle accepts the role of the other woman and with it Tom's facade of the rich philanderer, who lies that his wife is Catholic to deflect Myrtle's expectations of true love and marriage. Myrtle settles for the pretense of marriage to Tom, playing society maven at the parties that supplement their trysts. In all this she simply fools herself, taking on the airs of being without actually becoming anything. Despite her grand delusions, she services Tom's sexual needs as her husband services the automobiles of the rich who travel through the wasteland between East and West Egg and New York City. Tom will use her according to his needs and will abandon her once the "perceptible vitality about her as if the nerves of her body were continually smouldering" has been exhausted (25), leaving only the ashes behind. That she is willing to settle for such a facade suggests the degree to which she is attempting to deny that which she already has become. In her final attempt to escape her habitual confinement, she races from her home, where George has locked her up after discovering that she has taken a lover, toward the car that she thinks carries Tom and her means of liberation, only to be destroyed by it.

Meanwhile, George serves as another foil to Gatsby and the sense of becoming, one who has exhausted the possibilities of belief. Observing Tom and George Wilson together, Nick notes, "[I]t occurred to me that there was no difference between men, in intelligence or race, so profound as the difference between the sick and the well" (124). Devoid of religious faith or idealism, George is sickened by life, depleted even of the vitality that still lingers in his wife. It is important for students to understand that, in some ways, George actually has succeeded where Gatsby has failed; George Wilson has won the girl of his dreams. When asked why she married George, Myrtle replies, "I married him because I thought he was a gentleman. . . . I thought he knew something about breeding, but he wasn't fit to lick my shoe" (34). Myrtle is especially outraged to discover after their wedding day that George had borrowed the suit in which he was married, that he had created an illusion to win his lady. Described as a "ghost" (26) and as "spiritless" (25), "anæmic" (25), "sick" (124), and "hollow-eyed" (122), George is a lower-class version of Fitzgerald's characters who attain the girl of their dreams only to discover that nothing is left to sustain either themselves or their desires (e.g., Anthony Patch in *The Beautiful and Damned*). Wilson is a terminal case, as Tom's dismissive response to Nick first suggests: "Wilson? . . . He's so dumb he doesn't know he's alive" (26).

Nevertheless, George Wilson struggles to revive some hope in the possibility of becoming, even as Tom metaphorically buries him. With his last grasp at participation in the material wealth of America, George clings to the illusion that he can resurrect not simply his and Myrtle's lives but also the love between them, if only he can get some money together and move out West—a reflection of the boundless faith of the immigrant dream that echoes in the novel's closing passage. But for George and Myrtle Wilson, the fruit of faith in the West is no more real than a god who lingers above the ash heaps in the vacuous stare of Doctor T. J. Eckleburg.

I conclude my examination of the duality of becoming and being in *Gatsby* by having my students look at Nick. While his relationship with Jordan shadows Gatsby's relationship with Daisy, Nick remains too founded in either midwestern moralism or the pragmatic realism gained from age and experience to stretch himself beyond the scope of ordinary belief to embrace the idealism of possibility. But that foundation in ordinary belief allows Nick to render both the magnificence and the absurdity of Gatsby's obsession. Fitzgerald once wrote, "Reporting the extreme things as if they were the average things will start you on the art of fiction" (*Notebooks* 161). Nick provides the average perspective from which to view the extremism of Gatsby's "extraordinary gift for hope" (2).

Nick is an effective narrator in part because he operates as a judge of what others are or of what they are in the process of becoming. Introducing himself, Nick claims, " 'Whenever you feel like criticizing any one,' [my father] told me, 'just remember that all the people in this world haven't had all the advantages you've had.' . . . In consequence, I'm inclined to reserve all judgments" (1). Despite his protestation, Nick does judge the other characters, looking past the veneer of riches and respectability that both Tom and Gatsby project.

I point out to students that Nick's first mention of Gatsby foreshadows his vacillating feelings: "Only Gatsby . . . was exempt from my reaction—Gatsby, who represented everything for which I have an unaffected scorn. . . . Gatsby turned out all right at the end" (2). Nick is simultaneously fascinated and repelled by the same element in Gatsby's character: his "extraordinary gift for hope, a romantic readiness such as I have never found in any other person and which it is not likely I shall ever find again" (2). But Gatsby's "heightened sensitivity to the promises of life" (2) is countered by his naive attempt to "repeat the past" (110). I have students look closely at Nick's final encounter with Gatsby, in which Nick struggles to validate Gatsby; but his narration of that event belies his ability to judge decisively:

> "They're a rotten crowd," I shouted across the lawn. "You're worth the whole damn bunch put together."
> I've always been glad I said that. It was the only compliment I ever gave him, because I disapproved of him from beginning to end. First he nodded politely, and then his face broke into that radiant and understanding smile, as if we'd been in ecstatic cahoots on that fact all the time.   (154)

The novel's resolution reinforces Nick's failure to sustain that judgment. When he bumps into Tom following Gatsby's murder, Nick refuses to shake hands, saying, "You know what I think of you" (178). Yet, Nick subsequently shakes Tom's hand, rationalizing that it would be "silly not to" (179).

I try to have my students see that Nick's judgment of the other characters operates as a fundamental step not only in his narration of the story but also in his own process of becoming. Indeed, he has transposed his father's advice to put off becoming and thereby to retain the potential of life. "Reserving judgments"—like youth, in *The Great Gatsby* and throughout Fitzgerald's fiction—"is a matter of infinite hope" (2). But the process of narration itself denies the possibility of reserving judgment. At the Plaza Hotel, immediately after Tom's scathing attack on Gatsby's dream, Nick realizes that it is his thirtieth birthday. (Students will recognize the continuing significance in the American lexicon of thirty as a threshold year at both ends of a spectrum that stretches from the suspicions that accompanied the 1960s revival of Romantic idealism ["Don't trust anyone over thirty"] to the ambitions that drove the Reagan-era exaltation of materialism ["I'll make my first million by the time I'm thirty"].) Seeing "the portentous, menacing road of a new decade" (135) stretching before him, Nick is compelled to choose between the idealism of Gatsby and the materialistic realism of Tom Buchanan. Unable to find full satisfaction in either choice, Nick can become neither one nor the other; and so he retreats from the East, where the tenets fashioned by the innocent moralism and "provincial squeamishness" of the Midwest have been challenged and have proved wanting (179). In doing so, Nick unwittingly undertakes his own endeavor to repeat the past.

While his inability to sustain faith in Gatsby's limitless hope might be a product of his midwestern upbringing, Nick alludes to his age more than once late in the novel. While Nick is no Mencken, his pragmatic view of love mirrors that of the great social critic:

> Love, in the romantic sense, is based upon a view of women that is impossible to any man who has had extensive experience of them. . . . Find a man of forty who heaves and moans over a woman in the manner of a poet and you will behold . . . a man who ceased to develop intellectually at twenty-four.   (*Second Mencken Chrestomathy* 150)

What separates Jay Gatsby from Nick (as well as from Mencken) is Gatsby's indefatigable belief that his first love is powerful in the creation of self—and that the only path to realization of self lies not through the forward progress of experience but in repeating the past.

For most of our students, the intensity of first love is fresh in their minds, and some might even project a belief in the possibilities of love that rivals Gatsby's. Even those of us who have passed not only Nick's but also Mencken's threshold year will remember with a sense of regret how we first believed that love could do all those things that we now accept it cannot. Our students still believe in something akin to Gatsby's conception of love because they are still in the process of becoming; we no longer do because we already have become what we are. It is the interface of becoming and being that lies at the heart of Fitzgerald's fiction. And it is that interface that makes *The Great Gatsby* not only a truly great novel but a truly great novel to teach.

NOTE

[1] Because I teach primarily introductory and survey courses, I try to focus on the idea of becoming and being—which is closest to my students' experience and concerns—but this focus can be expanded easily into a larger consideration of the Platonic conception of self presented in *Gatsby*.

Teaching Mode, Style, and Politics in *The Great Gatsby*

Janet Giltrow and David Stouck

The initial response of most students to reading *The Great Gatsby* is to speculate on Fitzgerald's version of a timeless love story and to observe how beautifully the book is written. Astute readers in a class also recognize that the novel has much to say about American political life, but when a discussion of Nick Carraway's motives as narrator takes place a complicated question is likely to arise: Is Nick thoroughly progressive in his critique of Gatsby's romantic ambitions and the culture that formed them, or does Nick's suave talk conceal an inclination that is in fact conservative rather than progressive? Major statements about the novel in the last twenty years have identified important elements of cultural criticism in the text. Ross Posnock's Lukácsean reading, grounded in Marx's account of commodity fetishism, is a prime example of reading Fitzgerald (and Nick) as primarily a critic rather than an exponent of the American dream. Other critics such as Gregory S. Jay and Edward Wasiolek identify conservative attitudes in the novel's handling of sexuality and seem less certain about such positive claims. Investigating the text without reference to authorial intention, Meredith Goldsmith demonstrates that national identity and success in *The Great Gatsby* are figured linguistically in terms of racial and ethnic difference. In the same way, we suggest here a way of exploring the politics of this novel through mode and style (syntactic and discourse analysis), which builds on the student's initial response to both the love story and the novel's lavish writing. Our approach also invites students to refer to their own experience as language users—as readers and writers, listeners and speakers—and to consult that experience as a resource for literary analysis.

Naive Romance and Sentence Endings

The Great Gatsby can be viewed as embedded in a discourse known familiarly as the romance mode, which, in its barest outlines, is a reading of the individual life as an identity quest. Gatsby's story belongs to a particularly American version of naive or folk romance, the rags-to-riches story at the ideological heart of capitalism, wherein the hero's dream of success and romantic love is realized through the pursuit of material wealth. Presumably, it is the narrator's work to discredit this myth, and in scornful references to Gatsby's "appalling sentimentality" (111) and the "foul dust" that "floated in the wake of his dreams" (2) Nick does just that. But in some of the most beautifully wrought and memorable lines of the novel, Nick demonstrates not scorn for Gatsby but rather sympathy for his romantic aspirations. Nick tells us Gatsby's part of the story in what M. M. Bakhtin would describe as a lyrical style, without dialogue, words "suspended from any mutual interaction with alien discourse" (285). This lyricism is accomplished grammatically in the construction of sentences seemingly reluctant to end.

Looking at a characteristic Fitzgerald sentence, we show students that the first part does the work of the plot, moving the narrative forward in time and place and event; but the second part, often syntactically unnecessary, can go on to evoke feelings and indefinite excitements that exist only in the realm of possibility and the imagination: "For a while these reveries provided an outlet for his imagination; they were a satisfactory hint of the unreality of reality, *a promise that the rock of the world was founded securely on a fairy's wing*" (99; emphasis added). This sentence begins by establishing "reveries" as what is being talked about; then, after a semicolon and a second start, the sentence blossoms into an appositive, syntactically unnecessary surplus, seemingly engendered by sensitivity to words like "imagination" and "reverie." In the lush, improbable ending of the sentence occurs the "fairy's wing" that connects directly to the embodiment of Gatsby's dreaming, Daisy Buchanan, whose maiden name, Fay, is an archaic variant of *fairy*. Nick thus conveys an aura of magical destiny to Gatsby's quest, as does the ending of another trailing sentence where Daisy is described as "gleaming like silver, safe and proud above the hot struggles of the poor" (150). Frequently these elaborate sentence endings adumbrate the poetry of wealth and possessions, as when Gatsby, a young army officer, first views Daisy's house:

> There was a ripe mystery about it, *a hint of bedrooms upstairs more beautiful and cool than other bedrooms, of gay and radiant activities taking place through its corridors, and of romances that were not musty and laid away already in lavender, but fresh and breathing and redolent of this year's shining motor-cars and of dances whose flowers were scarcely withered.*   (148–49; emphasis added)

Everything contained in this massive appositive is suggestive, an elaboration of the mystery that surrounds Daisy. The sentence endings gather the emotional excitement that accumulates around ambition, money, romantic love, the passage of time, and the longings and commotions they generate. In drawing attention to the grammatical surplus of such sentences, we ask students to rewrite them without appositives—to prune the lush excess—and to consider the consequence for their reading of the narrator's attitude toward Gatsby's ambitions or aspirations.

Another type of sentence ending similar to the appositive is the "as if" (sometimes "as though") clause, which is the syntactic site for a range of romantic propositions. One of these (preceded by an appositive) appears when Nick first mentions Gatsby and attempts to suggest something of Gatsby's acute sensitivity and a heroic dimension spanning great distances in time and space:

> If personality is an unbroken series of successful gestures, then there was something gorgeous about him, *some heightened sensitivity to the promises of life,* as if he were related to one of those intricate machines that register earthquakes ten thousand miles away.   (2; emphasis added)

Yet another variant on the appositional structure is the sentence fragment where the momentum and surplus of one sentence carries beyond its boundary, producing evocative fragments: "It was full of money—that was the inexhaustible charm that rose and fell in it, *the jingle of it, the cymbals' song of it. . . . High in a white palace the king's daughter, the golden girl. . . .*" (120; ellipses in orig.; emphasis added). The appositions here are seemingly as inexhaustible as Daisy's charm; Fitzgerald's ellipses signify the sentence's resistance to closure, suggesting that the sentence like the dream has no conclusion. The fragments float free from the original sentence as a gesture to romance in its purest form, the fairy tale of the hero striving and attaining, his sights set on the transformative goal of the king's daughter.

Ironic Romance and Direct and Indirect Speech

Students aware of the complicated texture of this novel recognize that Nick also has an ironic version of Gatsby's story to tell. Where naive romance evokes the ambition of the individual, ironic romance details the frustration and stalling of those ambitions and draws on ways of speaking that make audible the dissonance of the social order. Nick's ironic stance is most prominent in his representation of others' speech, especially on those occasions when the domains of romantic possibility and suggestion have turned sour: when he has ventured too far into the actual world occupied by Gatsby and Daisy, when he portrays himself in the company of Myrtle Wilson or Meyer Wolfsheim, or when he lingers until the end of one of Gatsby's gaudy parties. Nick has an ear for the words and accents of daily usage and for the sociohistorical stratifications they embody. The way he speaks in turn allows us to hear both the sounds of his times—as Bakhtin phrases it, "language saturated with the conditions of the historical era" (263)—and his own response to those sounds. In moments when Nick comes into intimate contact with brute matters, he practices speech habits that distance him from other speakers, and an attitude of superiority and reserve becomes apparent between the formality of his own words and the words he reports or reproduces. In the following sentence, Nick finds a delicate, arm's-length way of saying that the people in Myrtle's apartment were rapidly getting drunk: "The bottle of whiskey—a second one—was now in constant demand by all present, excepting Catherine, who 'felt just as good on nothing at all' " (35).

We ask students, Who talks like this? Who at the party would be likely to say the bottle is "in constant demand"? Would Myrtle say this? What would Myrtle say? Our ear for speech registers tells us that some wordings come not from the party scene but from Nick's perspective on it: "a second one" indicates his measure of excess; "in constant demand by all present" converts the loud, indulgent talk of the partygoers to a formal register. Then, in the same sentence, words appear that are not Nick's at all and are isolated by quotation marks: Catherine "felt just as good on nothing at all." This construction tells us more than that Catherine does not drink. As artifacts, her words come with "conditions attached" (Bakhtin 75); they are words that have been attracted, as Bakhtin says, into the "orbits of certain social groups" (290), words that are the alien language, that produce art that is not "poetic" (or lyrical) but novelistic (Bakhtin 278, 287). Nick's way of handling Catherine's words, exposing them as artifacts of a lower social class, as not his way of speaking, represents his social distance from the figures he is closeted with and asserts an attitude of superiority.

Nick finds himself in such circumstances again at the end of one of Gatsby's parties. As the evening deteriorates into total confusion and disorder and Nick joins the crowd around the car wreck, he similarly distances himself with ironic wording: "The sharp jut of a wall accounted for the detachment of the wheel, which was now getting considerable attention from half a dozen curious chauffeurs" (53). Here the ironic wording achieves a conspicuous effect that perhaps has been immanent all along—an effect of high politeness. Buried in this formal statement is an account of drunk driving; somebody drove into a wall: "At least a dozen men, some of them a little better off than he was, explained to [the driver] that wheel and car were no longer joined by any physical bond" (55).

Especially at moments like this, when the world of romance has left him stranded in ugly confusion, Nick works most rigorously on capturing and transforming the speech of others. In so doing, he asserts his social distance and superiority not only from working-class people like the contemptuous butler (113) or the maid who spits (88) but also from the fashionable society of partygoers who collect around Gatsby. By their names they are identified as the nouveau riche, and Nick stands, with Gatsby, apart from them, at a distance. Very audible nonetheless are the sounds of the historical moment—the heteroglot voices of a turbulent, unceasingly transient, contradictory social order. Rumor and reputation resound; notoriety and slander amplify the publicity of the newsstands; medleys of popular lyrics play over and over. The clamor of the age, we tell our students, is what Nick flees from at the close, the El Greco nightmare of history (176), not the romantic dream of the king's daughter. Students can tune their ears to the sound of their own age, too: they can be asked what corresponds, in our times, to the newsstand exclamations and to the replaying of popular songs.

Pastoral and Maxims

Nick's instinct to flee the sordid is not limited to the novel's conclusion. Students may find curious an observation he makes in chapter 2 when Tom

Buchanan takes him into Manhattan for the party with his mistress Myrtle Wilson: "We drove over to Fifth Avenue, so warm and soft, almost pastoral, on the summer Sunday afternoon that I wouldn't have been surprised to see a great flock of white sheep turn the corner" (28). Directly after this reflection, Nick tries to leave the car, but Tom says, "No, you don't," and takes Nick against his will to the apartment he rents for his rendezvous with Myrtle and her friends.

Thus far, students have observed how the elaborate sentence endings are generated by the romance mode of the novel, and we have considered Nick's ironic version of romance and the conservative, restraining expressions that reveal his disapproving fastidiousness and elitist stance. But the glimpse of white sheep on Fifth Avenue suggests another mode of storytelling that informs *The Great Gatsby*—the pastoral, a discourse that privileges memory and order and complicates the narrative with feelings of escapism, nostalgia, and loss. Despite our reference to sheep, we use the term pastoral here to indicate not a rural subject but art based on memory and the human dream of a simplified, ordered existence from which social ills and natural process (change, decay, and death) are eliminated. (To activate this sense of a vanished but haunting perfection, we ask students if they themselves entertain images of another time, a time lost and long-ago but still close and touching in its appeal.) Beyond registering the voices of his social habitat, Nick attends to this other order of experience—an order that is original, stable, and seemingly timeless and that promotes his desire for "the world to be in uniform and at a sort of moral attention forever" (2).

At the beginning of his story, Nick tells us of his unusually close relationship to his father and conveys a certain pride in the Carraway clan, said to be "descended from the Dukes of Buccleuch" (3). He also turns over in his mind a piece of advice from his father: "Whenever you feel like criticizing any one . . . remember that all the people in this world haven't had the advantages that you've had" (1). Nick amplifies this counsel in a snobbish generalization, claiming that "a sense of the fundamental decencies is parcelled out unequally at birth" (2). Mr. Carraway's homily, his word of caution, has made a strong impression on his son. And it seems that it is the form as much as the content of the homily that impresses Nick, for, although his amplification somewhat distorts his father's intention, his speech habits often exactly preserve his father's voice. Despite his relative youth and his taste for partying, Nick makes a number of similar generalizations about life:

> There is no confusion like the confusion of a simple mind.   (125)

> [There is] no difference between men, in intelligence or race, so profound as the difference between the sick and the well.   (124)

Pointing out that, in linguistic terms, such statements are maxims, we ask students if they hear such proverbial claims in their own lives (and, if so, what the effects of hearing them are); we ask them to look for more maxims in *The Great Gatsby*. Occasionally maxims occur in the novel as independent clauses, as in the second example above; but more frequently they are embedded in longer sentences, sometimes compressed into referring expressions, as when Nick says that he is going to become "that most limited of all specialists, the 'well-rounded man.'" Insisting on the wisdom of this paradoxical observation, he continues to generalize, adding, "This isn't just an epigram—life is much more successfully looked at from a single window, after all" (4). Such statements and expressions are not only general in reference ("most," "a man," "life"), they have no specific time reference, their truth being neither particular nor contingent. They are somehow above, or beside, the narrative order of events and establish in the text the speaker's recourse to an order of permanent values beyond the contemporary world and even its ironic representation.

Maxims also convey a speaker's claim to knowledge, his or her access to established authority and steady truths; recognizing this, Aristotle said that while maxims were an effective tool for orators, young speakers should not use them (152). (Students might be asked what kind of speaker they imagine delivering a maxim.) Aristotle's advice acknowledges an incompatibility between lack of experience and wise sayings, yet Nick is prone to thinking in maxims, despite his youth and his resolve to reserve all judgments. Their incongruence draws our attention to that very divided nature of the novel's narrator who on the one hand is a heedless partygoer, imagining glamorous encounters with women in darkened doorways, and on the other hand is an apprentice in the banking and bond business and a judicious observer of human behavior. The voice of the maxim, grounded in paternal authority and wisdom from the past, is a regulating device for Nick—solemn, stable, even magisterial—negotiating the extravagance and moral confusion of West Egg and New York. Reflecting on the rumor that Jordan Baker has cheated in a major golf tournament, he observes, "Dishonesty in a woman is a thing you never blame deeply" (58). The posture of the maxims, distributed in the text beyond particular sentences and situations, signals for the reader further evidence of Nick Carraway's conservative, even regressive nature, qualifying those claims that *The Great Gatsby* is a radical critique of American values.

Pastoral and Cohesion

While Nick leans on maxims to guide him, he is at the same time acutely sensitive to the evocative power of more ephemeral aspects of language, to the overtones of words and especially to their power to evoke feelings of loss. As he listens to Gatsby tell his story one evening, he reflects:

> Through all he said . . . I was reminded of something—an elusive rhythm, a fragment of lost words, that I had heard somewhere a long time ago. For a moment a phrase tried to take shape in my mouth and my lips parted like a dumb man's, as though there was more struggling upon them than a

wisp of startled air. But they made no sound, and what I had almost remembered was uncommunicable forever.   (111)

In his essays and letters, as well as in his fiction, F. Scott Fitzgerald was obsessed
by impermanence. Style was its counterforce, he argued: "material, however,
closely observed," he wrote, "is as elusive as the moment in which it has its existence unless it is purified by an incorruptible style" (*Afternoon* 263). John Keats's
"fine excess" was his model: Keats's greatest poems, he wrote to his daughter, are
"a scale of workmanship for anybody who wants to know truly about words, their
most utter value for evocation, persuasion or charm" (*F. Scott Fitzgerald: A Life*
460–61). In a letter to Ernest Hemingway, he cites Joseph Conrad's preface to
The Nigger of the Narcissus as providing him with a theory of fiction: "the purpose of a work of fiction is to appeal to the lingering after-effects in the reader's
mind as differing from, say, the purpose of oratory or philosophy which respectively leave people in a fighting or thoughtful mood" (*F. Scott Fitzgerald: A Life*
263–64). And in a letter to Corey Ford about *Gatsby*, he writes that he "selected
the stuff to fit a given mood of 'hauntedness' or whatever you might call it" (*Letters* 551). "Evocation," "lingering after-effects," "hauntedness"—at the core of
these statements is a poetics of allusiveness and suggestiveness to describe high-
quality writing. So we take students on one last step in this investigation of style
and politics in *The Great Gatsby* to reveal the particular arrangement of words
that evokes this pastoral "hauntedness." We turn to another aspect of
language—the nonreferential capacity of words to call to mind other words,
thereby making a text both expansive and cohesive.

Pastoral art, figured, for example, in Renaissance paintings by a death's head
in a garden, is invariably distinguished by a style that is evocative of loss. In *The
Great Gatsby*, style cultivates this emotion through a feature of language
known as cohesion, the quality of sentences' depending on one another for
their interpretation, their quality as text, or their "texture" (Halliday and Hasan
2). Of the five types of lexical cohesion, lexical repetition is the one most open
to traditional measures of style. A particular word can recur in a text—in different localities, with different reference—and concordance techniques can cal-
culate these recurrences, which create a network of interdependencies beyond
plot or argument or image. So a concordance to *The Great Gatsby* lists 21 oc-
currences of the word "road," 16 of "dream[ed]," 14 of "flower[s]," (Crosland,
Concordance 272, 93, 121) and, according to Matthew Bruccoli's preface to the
1992 Scribner's paperback edition of the novel, some 450 words having to do
with time (xv). "Flower," reappearing after 15 pages, or 50 pages, evokes not
only its single instance but its earlier instance as well, however irrelevant at the
discursive level. As M. A. K. Halliday and Ruqaiya Hasan's model of cohesion
shows, words acquire a textual history, and the reader's memory is the archive
of this history.

The most subtle and poetic measure of a text's cohesiveness, however, can be
made by a study of collocations—the ties between words that have a tendency

to appear together, societies of words that have a history of accompaniment. Collocation registers the potential energies resting in words themselves, residual from their use. Textual collocations transform that potential to kinetic energy. If we take, as an example, a sentence two-thirds of the way through the book, one describing Daisy's and Gatsby's reactions to each other at the Plaza Hotel party in New York, we find that the words of this sentence seem to draw reverberations from the whole text:

> But with every word she was drawing further and further into herself, so he gave that up, and only the dead dream fought on as the afternoon slipped away, trying to touch what was no longer tangible, struggling unhappily, undespairingly, toward that lost voice across the room.   (134)

For the reader who already knows the text and has an ear for language, "fought on" anticipates the novel's last sentence, "beat on . . . against the current" (180), so that we hear "boat" in this sentence although the word is not there. But we have already been conditioned to hear "boat" because of a textual history of sea words. In the beginning of his story, Nick tells us that at the Buchanans' waterfront home the breeze "rippled over the wine-colored rug, making a shadow on it as wind does on *the sea*," and that Jordan and Daisy on the couch "were *buoyed up* as though upon an *anchored* balloon" (8; emphasis added). And carrying the association of the boat from these crucially situated sentences, "across the room" picks up an echo of across the bay, and Daisy's lost voice becomes one with the green light, one of Gatsby's "enchanted objects" (93). In this context, the "trying to touch" recalls Gatsby's hands stretched out across the bay at the end of the first chapter, which in turn recalls Gatsby trying to reconnect with the past "just out of reach of his hand" (110). This elusiveness, not only of object but of language as well, returns with the account of Gatsby's departure from Louisville: "He stretched out his hand desperately as if to snatch only a wisp of air, to save a fragment of the spot that she had made lovely for him" (153). Some of the words of this sentence ("wisp of air," "fragment") echo their own use, although with different reference, in the passage describing Nick's fleeting recollection, but most powerful is the word "stretch" which gathers up the aspiration of romance and the longing of pastoral and yields their full force in those lines of the resonant penultimate paragraph: "to-morrow we will run faster, stretch out our arms farther. . . ." (180).

Words' tracings, the imprint words make on a reader's memory, some connection audible but not quite understood—these "lost" but persistent fragments can be examined as they reach across spans of text. They create in the attuned reader the sensations we identify as Nick's unique way of speaking; they touch off fleeting and nearly uncommunicable recognition of the largest designs in the novel, its mythic dimension, referring us to light and dark, to strange and exotic gardens, to human migrations, to the sea, and to death. It is language used in this way that allows the reader of pastoral to hear "an elusive rhythm, a fragment of lost words" from an order of experience before speech and memory, that remains, in Nick's phrasing, "uncommunicable forever."

The effects of such language are among those that Dan Sperber and Dierdre Wilson term "poetic effects"—effects that writers provide for but whose meaning they do not guarantee—meanings for which readers take some responsibility as they construct the context in which sentences are understood, expanding these contexts as long as "contextual effects" reward each expansion (222, 125). Focusing on this level of style, gathering clusters of collocations, students can witness the process by which they as readers construct and expand the contexts for meaning.

To conclude, we point out to our students that an examination of mode and style in *The Great Gatsby* reveals a complex amalgam of social and political attitudes: on the one hand, Nick satirizes Tom Buchanan and his class by having him quote with admiration the racist writings of Lothrop Stoddard, while on the other hand, in the novel's famous last scene (and in one of those romantic appositives), he tells us of a Long Island that flowered once for Dutch sailors' eyes—"a fresh, green breast of the new world" (180)—a pastoral and Nordic vision of America's origins that directly echoes Stoddard's ideal. We ask our students then: Where has Fitzgerald located Nick? Where do Nick's interests lie? Even as Nick shows us the sordid actuality of the romance of wealth and status, that core myth of American culture still excites his stylistic homage, as we have seen in the elaborate sentence endings that outline Gatsby's romantic aspirations.

If this were the sum of the novel's stylistic resources—fascination balanced by exposé—we might read Nick as a disinterested observer, an objective witness of the scene around him. But we have shown students how his ironic representation of others' voices locates Nick in a socially elevated position, a trick of rank or hierarchy that derives from his acute sense of social differentials. The maxims, moreover, identify Nick's voice as issuing from a well-placed family, and they are supplemented by his ear for echoes and "lost words" that reveals his nostalgia for the past. Sharing political territory with the Gatsby myth of rags to riches and the self-made man, there is another equally conservative myth—that of a distinguished class aloof from the strivings of the marketplace, its rags phase long forgotten and its riches converted to moral authority. As Fitzgerald presents it, Nick's position in the social order is one from which visions of reform are not likely to develop. These circumstances are embodied in Nick's voice and reveal the complications of interest that are perhaps inherent in all forms of cultural criticism. In this light, finally, we point out that mode and style in *The Great Gatsby* are not motionless, unitary conditions of the text but source and substance, incessantly changing and engendering the novel's political complexity.

A Poetic "Capacity for Wonder": Fitzgerald and the Language of *The Great Gatsby*

Gail Sinclair

> This book will be a consciously artistic achievement and must depend on that. . . .
> —Fitzgerald, *The Letters of F. Scott Fitzgerald*

In February 1936, F. Scott Fitzgerald took stock of his personal life and his professional work and recorded those musings in "The Crack-Up." The stated thesis for this nostalgic piece, "that life has a varying offensive" (71), was the product not solely of reflective observation but also of a controlling practice that governed even his early writing. He believed "the test of a first-rate intelligence is the ability to hold two opposed ideas in the mind at the same time, and still retain the ability to function" (69). This theoretic stance posed by a seasoned writer also represents Fitzgerald's synthesis of style and meaning throughout his career, and it is nowhere more evident than in the narrative technique of *The Great Gatsby*.

Embedded in the novel, Fitzgerald's seemingly incongruous and innocuous linguistic units at first seem randomly thrown together, subtly adorning the prose and frequently confusing students. Soon, however, these unusual combinations become too numerous to explain as accidents or mere verbal play. They accumulate to reveal a carefully constructed pattern of mismatched pairings whose highly charged connotations go beyond surface interpretation. Fitzgerald corroborates such stylistic purposefulness, at one point guiding his daughter Scottie's writing by advising:

> If you have anything to say, anything you feel nobody has ever said before, you have got to feel it so desperately that you will find some way to say it that nobody has ever found before, so that the thing you have to say and the way of saying it blend as one matter—as indissolubly as if they were conceived together. (*F. Scott Fitzgerald: A Life* 313)

He elaborates on this thought in the next paragraph of the letter:

> I mean that what you have felt and thought will by itself invent a new style, so that when people talk about style they are always a little astonished at the newness of it, because they think that it is only *style* that they are talking about, when what they are talking about is the attempt to express a new idea with such force that it will have the originality of the thought. (313–14)

This is precisely what he demonstrates so artfully in his greatest work.

One of the joys I find in teaching *The Great Gatsby* is the sheer beauty of its prose, which comes as close to the demanding precision and explicit imagery of verse as any I have ever read. As a talented wordsmith, Fitzgerald infuses the text with a richness that still amazes me after nearly three decades of classroom exploration. From the first passages, students will likely be struck by the work's poetic quality and symbolic power, not to mention Fitzgerald's ability to do what he professes—to invoke fresh language. It is with his semantic units that I begin teaching *Gatsby*. By examining key phrases that exemplify those contradictory juxtapositions and unorthodox word combinations, I work to guide students toward a deeper sense of Fitzgerald's craftsmanship, his right to be considered one of the great modern literary masters, and this novel's standing as his *tour de force*.

Once I point out Fitzgerald's stylistic intent, students are prepared to dig more deeply for the text's hidden potential. I emphasize here his focus on life as a complicated attempt to

> hold in balance the sense of the futility of effort and the sense of the necessity to struggle; the conviction of the inevitability of failure and still the determinations to "succeed"—and, more than these, the contradiction between the dead hand of the past and the high intentions of the future.
> ("Crack-Up" 70)

Fitzgerald emphasizes polemic extremes, beginning with simple phrases, amassing them to imply life's fullness. The story, situated in the 1920s, becomes universal, still relevant to students many decades after the Jazz Age it depicts.

In his essay "Style as Meaning in *The Great Gatsby*," Jackson R. Bryer identifies what he calls "three simultaneous and deliberate objectives" for Fitzgerald's unusual linguistic choices and their importance in understanding *Gatsby*:

> they are marvelously descriptive and evocative;
> they are often so original and witty that they surprise and capture the
>   reader's attention; in Fitzgerald's own words, they astonish by their
>   "newness"; and
> they metaphorically encapsulate or suggest in microcosmic form the
>   meanings of the novel as a whole.   (124)

Bryer's third point holds most relevance for the classroom approach I discuss here. Looking closely at these "microcosmic" units, I ask students first to enjoy them and then to take notice of the information provided and to draw conclusions from it.

Fitzgerald uses creative and original descriptions to destabilize the concrete world of the novel. He underscores an aura of unreality in Gatsby's surrealistically fabricated world and emphasizes Nick's language as a force symbolically transforming surroundings. Objects become personified and caricatured. Wilson's car "crouched in a dim corner" (25), Gatsby's "lurched" "[w]ith fenders spread like wings" (63, 68), and Nick's taxi "groaned away" (81). Gatsby's "hulking" (92) cabinets hold his piles of shirts, and his house seems to have "winked into the darkness" (81). (Artistically talented students may have fun drawing their own cartoonlike versions of these descriptions.) Nick sees his midwestern towns as "bored, sprawling, swollen" (176). Nature also becomes transmogrified into "a fantastic farm where ashes grow like wheat" (23); "[t]he late afternoon sky bloomed in the window for a moment like the blue honey of the Mediterranean" (34); there are "twinkle-bells of sunshine" (89); redolent flowers have a "sparkling odor of jonquils and the frothy odor of hawthorn and plum blossoms and the pale gold odor of kiss-me-at-the-gate" (90); and Long Island is a "fresh, green breast," where the trees "pandered in whispers" (180). Gatsby's "capacity for wonder" and his world of wonder (180), contrasted with its often grotesque distortions, become merged into what Nick envisions as a "night scene by El Greco: a hundred houses, at once conventional and grotesque, crouching under a sullen, overhanging sky and a lustreless moon" (176). In this sense, Nick creates a dualistic world offering through both dream and nightmare a landscape even more vivid to readers because of its unusual descriptive qualities.

Fitzgerald also uses poetically evocative yet seemingly vacuous, nonsensical, or carelessly disjunctive language that serves more than a descriptive function. Very early in *Gatsby*, readers are forced to slow down, step back, and reexamine opinions the narrator has just given them. In the novel's third paragraph, Nick says, "I'm inclined to reserve all judgments" (1). But almost immediately he negates this statement, saying, "And, after boasting this way of my tolerance, I come to the admission that it has a limit" (2), and then proceeds indiscriminately to critique everyone he encounters. Nick calls himself a "well-rounded man" who nevertheless lives by a controlling philosophy that "life is much more successfully looked at from a single window" (4). In the next chapter, he reveals, "I was within and without, simultaneously enchanted and repelled by the inexhaustible variety of life" (35). Nick's odd or imprecise language and shifting assessments highlight his propensity for dramatically opposing views, as readers might begin to note.

This quality is clearly evinced in Nick's character descriptions, and finding examples can be an entertaining and instructive way to draw students into the text and help them experience Fitzgerald's wordplay in a more immediate way. He says Daisy has "an absurd, charming little laugh" and speaks with "tense gayety" (8, 15); Jordan possesses "a wan, charming, discontented" face (11); both women talk "at once, unobtrusively and with a bantering inconsequence that was never quite chatter" (12). Nick boasts of an "unaffected scorn" for Gatsby but sees "something gorgeous about him" (2); Tom has a "harsh, defiant wistfulness" (7); and Gatsby is an "elegant young roughneck" who wears a "gorgeous pink rag of a suit" (48, 154). George Wilson appears "anæmic, and faintly handsome" (25), and his wife carries her "surplus flesh sensuously" and exhibits "panting vitality" (25, 68). Even minor characters' descriptions are contradictory. Mrs. McKee is "shrill, languid, handsome, and horrible" (30); Meyer Wolfsheim eats "with ferocious delicacy" (71); Klipspringer is "wandering hungrily about the beach" (91); and Mr. Sloane "lounged back haughtily" (102). Nick's character descriptions present disparate elements of the persons and personalities he observes.

The mixed images these unusual pairings create, particularly as they deal with the more significant characters, work against clear, concise evaluation and hinder easy binary division into the good/bad, moral/immoral, heroic/villainous distinctions perpetuated by Nick. Many students ignore the destabilizing language, however, and see him as a reliable narrator. This view encourages a search for corresponding evidence backing up those assumptions. Asking students to identify contrasting points—to list them and, where they occur, to assess how they shape our feelings at that moment, and to express how they dovetail or diverge with other statements—leads them toward far more comprehensive and in-depth responses.

Even Nick is forced into such an exercise as he examines Gatsby's revelations for their veracity. The "man who gives his name to this book" (2), like much else in the novel, seems an amalgamation of the desirable and the undesirable. Students initially react positively to Jay Gatsby and to the word *great* in the novel's title. I ask them, however, What is great about Gatsby? This question often elicits lively conversation, and students passionately argue their personal stances. Being always the educator, I cheer such active engagement while continuing to require textual support justifying their opinions.

What careful students often find is that Jay Gatsby is a self-created man displaying spectacular flash and surface panache—a sorcerer who magically appears and disappears from his blue, unnatural gardens (39) and seems hardly present for most of the novel dedicated to revealing him. "The great Gatsby" is reminiscent of Barnum and Bailey's "Greatest Show on Earth" and "The Great Houdini," and students can be asked to search for other indications of Gatsby's elusiveness. The first time Gatsby appears, Nick describes "a figure [that] had emerged from the shadow of my neighbor's mansion" (20), but, glancing seaward momentarily, he turns back to discover, "[w]hen I looked once more for Gatsby he had vanished" (21). During his reintroduction to Daisy, Gatsby disappears from Nick's living room, reappears at the front door, and gets "himself into a shadow" while Nick and Daisy chat (87). At a luncheon in New York, after introducing Gatsby to Tom Buchanan, Nick turns back to Gatsby—"but he was no longer there" (74).

Gatsby weaves a web of illusion to transfigure his vision of reality and hide his shift from James Gatz, poor farmer's son, to Jay Gatsby, entrepreneur and socialite. In fact, Nick contends that Gatsby's whole world is based on "the unreality of reality" (99), where even Gatsby can happen "without any particular wonder" (69). Gatsby prefers his imaginative creation, believing "what a

grotesque thing a rose is and how raw the sunlight was upon the scarcely created grass" because they cannot match his capacity to transform them beyond
their temporal natures (161). He is a shadowy person who elicits innuendo
about himself because so little is known firsthand of this man who has sprung
from his "Platonic conception of himself" (98). He evokes an aura of disbelief
through his "strained counterfeit of perfect ease" (86), and the "dim background [that] started to take shape behind him" (49) gives Nick the sense that
forming a conception of his mysterious neighbor "was like skimming hastily
through a dozen magazines" (66). Students will likely begin drawing such a conclusion as well.

Focus on Gatsby's mysterious inconsistencies can demonstrate Fitzgerald's
balancing of oppositions. Nick finds "something gorgeous" about Gatsy's "heightened sensitivity to the promises of life" (2) but derides his "appalling sentimentality" (111). He professes an "unaffected scorn" for the person who "had
broken up like glass against Tom's hard malice" but declares Gatsby "worth
the whole damn bunch put together" (2, 148, 154). On the one hand, students
see that Gatsby represents the worst nouveau riche stereotype. He is garish,
materialist, shallow, and obsessively focused, and yet his quest exhibits the romantic propensity Nick finds honorable. Such faith in his envisioned world,
replicating the Dutch sailor's belief that the island holds "the last and greatest
of all human dreams" (180), makes Gatsby a figure to be faulted for his tendency toward romantic disillusionment but praised for the strength of his
convictions and creative vision. Both views are valid, and this recognition is
central to classroom discussion and deeper assessment of Gatsby's complex
character.

The power Jay Gatsby has to evade or reconfigure reality "he neither understood nor desired" can make him seem elusive and even remotely sinister when
he favors his conception of life over hard evidence to the contrary (180); con-
versely, such propensity bolsters a view of his greatness in the traditional sense
that students are now more fully prepared to address. Gatsby's inclination toward romantic speculation, inferred by the title's straightforward interpretation
of the word, saves him from "the foul dust float[ing] in the wake of his dreams"
and allows him to turn "out all right at the end." He is not mired down by the
"abortive sorrows and short-winded elations of men" that disgust Nick and
make him wish for "the world to be in uniform and at a sort of moral attention
forever" (2). Instead, the man who "had committed himself to the following of
a grail" is able to see in the blocks of the sidewalk a ladder he can climb skyward
to "suck on the pap of life, [and] gulp down the incomparable milk of wonder"
(149, 110). Like the original sailor's transcendent dreams for the "fresh, green
breast of the new world," Gatsby believes "in the green light, the orgastic future" (180) the youthful James Gatz had dreamed through the "constant, turbulent riot" (99) that was his "creative passion" (95). Many students have a great
appreciation for and a sense of connection to this young romantic's optimistic
spirit.

To a large degree, Gatsby's vision rests on Daisy, and, for students who find her an unworthy grail, this dependence creates another troubling incongruence in the picture Nick Carraway paints. They have difficulty reconciling admiration for Gatsby's hold on his "incorruptible dream" with their antipathy for the woman he loves (154). What they miss through this limited analysis is the same tendency toward personal complexity in Daisy that Nick has shown in the other players from that "riotous" summer (2). A good side discussion here can be identifying pejorative female archetypes such as the femme fatale, the siren, and Circe that permeate classical literature. Students can see Daisy, like those paradigms, unfairly presented as the scapegoat for men's moral faltering or failed quests.

While few students contend that Daisy deserves the same level of respect they have for Gatsby's romantic idealism, they may grant her some redemptive qualities. Gatsby detects in her a kindred spirit, confiding to Nick, "She used to be able to understand. We'd sit for hours——" (109). Nick, on the other hand, has judged her harshly despite admitting that he "had no sight into Daisy's heart" (6). Further, he fails to acknowledge elements of his own close observations as he notes "bright things" lurking in her sad demeanor (9), hears an excited quality in her voice relaying a tendency to "carry well-forgotten dreams from age to age" (135), and describes the sunshine falling "with romantic affection" on Daisy's "glowing face" (14). He instantly negates all this, however, as if Daisy couldn't really possess such depth:

> The instant her voice broke off ceasing to compel my attention, my belief, I felt the basic insincerity of what she had said. It made me uneasy, as though the whole evening had been a trick of some sort to exact a contributory emotion from me. I waited, and sure enough, in a moment she looked at me with an absolute smirk on her lovely face, as if she had asserted her membership in a rather distinguished secret society to which she and Tom belonged.   (17)

Nick's failure to acknowledge Daisy's complex nature here should alert students to his other equally simplistic conclusions. Contradictory images early in the novel expose his bias as he calls into question her sincerity while acknowledging its possibility. Describing his cousin's conversation as "only extemporizing," Nick reluctantly admits that "a stirring warmth flowed from her, as if her heart was trying to come out to you concealed in one of those breathless, thrilling words" (14). He reports that "she laughed with thrilling scorn" (17), inferring a callous nature, but admits, "I saw that turbulent emotions possessed her" (16). Nick disregards what his experiences have shown—that life is a mixed composite of observations—and instead establishes a hostile evaluation easily accepted by his audience. Only after Gatsby's death and his own reflection on the summer's events does Nick give us his vision of the East and its wealthy inhabitants as "haunted for me . . . distorted beyond my eyes' power of correction" (176).

Once again, close examination of Fitzgerald's language is important and points to the richer problematic vision ignored by his narrator and most critics when they speak of Daisy. I point out to students that he abandons incongruent pairings in one significant place in the novel—when he speaks of her capacity for love. Fitzgerald provides this information not from Nick's biased viewpoint but through Jordan Baker's less critical perspective. Jordan reveals Daisy's feelings for Gatsby and for her new husband, continuing for four pages without a single unusual word pairing (74–77). She describes the young ingenue as so "engrossed" in Gatsby that "she didn't see me until I was five feet away" (74) and so devastated by his loss on the night before her marriage to Tom Buchanan that she "cried and cried" and "wouldn't let go of the letter" (76)— presumably Gatsby's profession of love for her. Fitzgerald even expresses Daisy's perhaps sublimated, possibly genuine, love for Tom Buchanan in straightforward language as Jordan reports:

> I saw them in Santa Barbara when they came back, and I thought I'd never seen a girl so mad about her husband. If he left the room for a minute she'd look around uneasily, and say: "Where's Tom gone?" and wear the most abstracted expression until she saw him coming in the door. She used to sit on the sand with his head in her lap by the hour, rubbing her fingers over his eyes and looking at him with unfathomable delight. It was touching to see them together—it made you laugh in a hushed, fascinated way.   (76–77)

I point out to students that Fitzgerald presents this account uncritically without undercutting or enhancing his prose; in doing so, he portrays the strength of deeply felt young love between Daisy and the men on whom she bestows it. Students will no doubt fault her in not waiting for Gatsby and for corrupting her ideals by marrying Tom Buchanan, but though Daisy's early romantic dreams become tainted by reality, Fitzgerald avoids authorial interjections in his description of that time period. He does not devalue her ability for deep connection, however abandoned or misplaced it might become, and these few pages are the only noticeable place in the novel where he forgoes ambiguity to tell the story in straightforward, unadorned language not colored by Nick's subjective view or unconventional word pairings. He presents Daisy as a woman with great emotional capacity, and though she squanders or taints that power through faulty decisions, Fitzgerald, it seems, cannot pass sentence as unequivocally as most others do. Exploring this stance encourages students toward a more generous, less condemnatory view.

An almost essential aspect to explore, and a wonderful essay topic for students, then, is their response to Nick's, Gatsby's, or Daisy's character. If they have read the novel in its entirety before any class discussion occurs, getting initial reactions to these characters makes for an interesting starting point. Students will likely present a myopic opinion defending the worth or worthlessness of the figure they choose. The question then becomes, Can they support such a view after a thorough examination of the text? Without guidance, they will find identifying redeeming qualities in Daisy—some element of wonder straining toward Gatsby's capacity—particularly difficult. They will also resist investigating Gatsby as a pathetic Don Quixote wasting his dreams on a ridiculous quest or corrupting them through financial misdealing. This pre- and postwriting exercise is extremely useful because it helps students see the power of effective argument, especially if they have shifted opinions after discovering convincing textual support.

Finally, Fitzgerald's unique ordering of language works against limiting meaning in Nick's parting statements. The ancient Dutch sailor gazing on the old island with forward-looking vision mirrors Gatsby's anchoring in history while straining toward the future. Nick strengthens this dichotomy by describing Gatsby's dream as both "*behind* him, somewhere *back* in that vast obscurity" and "*beyond* the city" (180; emphasis added). In the next sentence, he sees "the future that year by year *recedes*" not just before Gatsby but before and away from an all-inclusive "us" as well (180; emphasis added). Nick, Gatsby, and we are concomitantly in the past, in the present, and in the future—today "we beat on," "to-morrow we will run faster," all the while knowing we are "borne back ceaselessly into the past" (180). Through the novel's last few paragraphs, Fitzgerald raises *The Great Gatsby* from a tale about a particular man's unfulfilled or tainted dream-quest to an allegory representing its author's complex view of the human condition.

For Nick, the "gorgeous" spirit in Jay Gatsby is his tenacious adherence to the pursuit and his ability to hold on to this beautiful vision even in the valley of ashes. Fitzgerald displays similar qualities through his capacity to recognize humanity's flaws without dismissing its redeeming qualities. Life's contradictions, perhaps responsible for creating Fitzgerald's own self-proclaimed divided nature, become a central theme in *The Great Gatsby*. By emphasizing Fitzgerald's unique use of language and by helping students examine his often connotatively complex word pairings and intricate characterizations, we can demonstrate how his style deliberately creates meaning and inspires his readers into an "æsthetic contemplation" of their own (180).

"Look Here, You See":
Focusing on Myopic Vision in
The Great Gatsby

Ted Billy

Teaching *The Great Gatsby* without referring to the eyes of Doctor T. J. Eckleburg looming over the Eliotic valley of ashes at the opening of chapter 2 would be unthinkable; but extending this image to the theme of the corruption of the American dream of success requires relating it to Fitzgerald's orchestration of the novel's pervasive eye motif, particularly to Gatsby's obsession with his extrinsic self. Warren Bennett has noted:

> The significance of Eckleburg is not in his presence as an isolated symbol, but in his presence as the full expression of a pattern of imagery that includes both the ocular imagery of Jay Gatsby and the spectacle imagery of Owl Eyes and Klipspringer. (221)

Gatsby's colossal mansion, his box-laden car (called by Malcolm Cowley "West Egg on wheels" [46]), and his opulent parties all testify to his compulsion to externalize his personal identity, for he believes that greatness must be manifested in the expansiveness of his vision and in the exhibition of his various possessions. Ronald Berman has observed that Fitzgerald's novel presents personality as a blank, to be filled in by "the addition of externalities" (Great Gatsby *and Modern Times* 113). Like a modern-day Trimalchio (a character in Petronius's *The Satyricon* famous for hosting lavish feasts), Gatsby surveys the materialistic excesses of his entertainments with "approving eyes" (50). By showing students how Fitzgerald foregrounds perception throughout the novel, I emphasize his ironic exposure of Gatsby's spiritual myopia.

Students often inquire how Gatsby is great. I usually respond that whatever claim to greatness Gatsby may have relates to the vast scope of his personal vision. Fitzgerald associates Nick's first glimpse of the title character, at the close of chapter 1, with the "stars" and "heavens" that he attempts visually to encompass (20). Moreover, Gatsby attempts to legitimize the loftiness of his grandiose aspirations by gaining the approval of admiring eyes, as in the following conversation with Nick:

> He saw me looking with admiration at his car.
> "It's pretty, isn't it, old sport!" He jumped off to give me a better view. "Haven't you ever seen it before?"
> I'd seen it. Everybody had seen it. (64)

Like Myrtle Wilson, another exhibitionist whom Fitzgerald links to regal glances and misperceptions ("Myrtle raised her eyebrows in despair at the shiftlessness

of the lower orders" [32]; "She looked around to see who was listening" [35]),
Gatsby requires an audience for his personality to glow, frequently using the
phrases "look here" and "you see" and variations thereof (65, 67, 71).

It is important, of course, to point out to students the analogy of Gatsby's aspiring selfhood and his mansion, which objectifies the colossal dream of its
meretricious owner. Gatsby's mansion is Fitzgerald's most conspicuous example
of its owner's aspiration to make his possessions the visible expression of his
lofty status. At the opening of chapter 5, the mansion is "lit from tower to cel-
lar," yet the wind "made the lights go off and on again as if the house had
winked into the darkness" (81). Here it is important to remind students of how
American authors, in particular, have often employed houses as metaphors for
the minds of the occupants (e.g., Poe's "The Fall of the House of Usher,"
James's "The Jolly Corner," and Gilman's "The Yellow Wall-Paper").

Fitzgerald again calls attention to the homology of Gatsby and his mansion
later in the chapter: " 'My house looks well, doesn't it?' he demanded. 'See how
the whole front of it catches the light.' . . . His eyes went over it, every arched
door and square tower" (89–90). After Gatsby's death, Mr. Gatz reinforces the
analogy between his son and the mansion:

> "Jimmy sent me this picture." He took out his wallet with trembling fin-
> gers. "*Look there.*"
>
> It was a photograph of the house, cracked in the corners and dirty with
> many hands. He pointed out every detail to me eagerly. "*Look there!*" and
> then *sought* admiration from my eyes. He had shown it so often that I
> think it was more real to him now than the house itself.
>
> (172; emphasis added)

For Mr. Gatz, the picture verifies his son's strange success story more so than
the mansion it represents. Fitzgerald emphasizes the old man's visual orienta-
tion repeatedly in the final chapter: "*Look here*, this is a book he had when he
was a boy. It just *shows* you. . . . It just *shows* you, don't it?" (173; emphasis
added).

When dealing with the final chapter, I encourage students to view Mr. Gatz
as a kind of surrogate for his son, who is no longer present in the novel that
bears his name. Mr. Gatz's eyes "blink anxiously" as he relates to his son's death
the only way he can—by evasion (174). Gatsby's myopic illusions about the future find a parallel in his father's necessary illusions about the past. Like Gatsby,
Mr. Gatz reveres lavish displays as measures of character: "[W]hen he *looked*
around him now for the first time and *saw* the height and splendor of the hall
and the great rooms opening out from it into other rooms, his grief began to be
mixed with an *awed pride*" (168; emphasis added).

Mr. Gatz displa͙   ͙ moral myopia typical of other characters in the book,
such as the ͙   ͙ ͙llenged and misperceiving Wilsons, Jordan Baker,
Gatsby, and ͙   himself: "[Mr. Gatz's] eyes leaked continuously with

excitement. . . . His eyes, seeing nothing, moved ceaselessly about the room. . . . [H]is face flushed slightly, his eyes leaking isolated and unpunctual tears" (167–68). "Unpunctual" may prompt students to recall Gatsby's efforts to recapture time. Both father and son retreat into the past to evade the present; Mr. Gatz's escapism seems mundane, but Gatsby's attempt to retrieve a previous phase of life has transcendent overtones.

Even when Gatsby temporarily attains his goal, Fitzgerald undermines the accomplishment with ironic ocular imagery. While Gatsby awaits Daisy's coming to tea at Nick's house, he resembles Doctor Eckleburg's Ozymandian situation: *"Gatsby looked with vacant eyes* through a copy of Clay's *Economics*, . . . *peering toward the bleared windows* from time to time as if a series of invisible but alarming happenings were taking place outside" (84; emphasis added). On Daisy's arrival, his eyes consistently reflect trepidation:

> Gatsby, pale as death, . . . was standing in a puddle of water glaring tragically into my eyes. . . . [H]is distraught eyes stared down at Daisy. . . . His eyes glanced momentarily at me, and his lips parted with an abortive attempt at a laugh.   (86)

Ironically, as Gatsby comes closest to achieving his transcendent goal, luring Daisy into his arms through external signs of his success, Fitzgerald undermines Gatsby's accomplishment. With Daisy finally in sight of his house, Gatsby should be ecstatic, but when Nick and Daisy start to make conversation, Gatsby "looked conscientiously from one to the other of us with tense, unhappy eyes" (87).

Asking students why Gatsby's eyes would look "unhappy" during the reunion scene with his beloved Daisy prompts them to begin to articulate the implications of a fraudulent American dream of success based on materialism. I point out that Fitzgerald foreshadows the tragic consequences of Gatsby's quest, counterpointing the romantic elements of this seriocomic scene. Gatsby and Daisy, during their reunion, seem like characters in a medieval melodrama of courtly love, as Nancy Y. Hoffman, William Bysshe Stein, and Deborah Davis Schlacks have suggested. Fitzgerald depicts their relationship as an eye romance, a love affair depending mainly on eye contact rather than tactile expressions for communication. Lovers in the courtly love tradition were often prohibited from touching by custom, convention, or circumstance. Consequently, their relations were carried out chiefly through visual contact. The eye-romance motif is prominent not only in Chaucer's *Troilus and Criseyde* but also in Sidney's *Astrophel and Stella* and the lyrics of Edmund Spenser; Thomas Wyatt; Henry Howard, Earl of Surrey; Michael Drayton; and John Davies. John Kuehl has documented Fitzgerald's familiarity with these poets ("Fitzgerald's Reading" 60–61).

In this way, Fitzgerald emphasizes the ocular aspect of the Daisy-Gatsby reunion: "They were sitting at either end of the couch, looking at each other as if some question had been asked, or was in the air, and every vestige of embarrassment was gone" (89). Their eye romance flourishes while Gatsby gives Daisy the grand tour of his mansion:

> He hadn't once ceased looking at Daisy, and I think he revalued everything in his house according to the measure of response it drew from her well-loved eyes. Sometimes, too, he stared around at his possessions in a dazed way, as though in her actual and astounding presence none of it was any longer real. Once he nearly toppled down a flight of stairs.   (91)

Gatsby's close call here brings to mind his earlier near accident, when he leans his head back against the "defunct mantelpiece clock," "star[ing] down at Daisy" with "distraught eyes," only to have it tumble into his trembling hands (86), suggesting the spiritual myopia of his vision that has left him time-blind.

Tom Buchanan's recognition of and reaction to the Daisy-Gatsby eye romance initiates the sequence of events leading to Gatsby's death. At the end of chapter 7, after the fatal accident, Gatsby assumes "the sacredness of the vigil," contemplating the exterior of Daisy's house, "standing there in the moonlight—watching over nothing" (145). Like the "vigil" kept by Doctor Eckleburg's "giant eyes" over the ash heaps on the edge of the wasteland (124), Gatsby unknowingly witnesses the transformation of his blessed isles into a solemn dumping ground. Victimized by his own cultivated delusion, he has foolishly attempted to use materialistic excess to reshape reality according to his visionary dreams. Ultimately, his final vigil outside Daisy's house links him inextricably with the "eternal blindness" of the absent oculist represented by the gigantic eyes of Doctor Eckleburg's billboard (24), a sign advertising what it cannot deliver. Indeed, Richard Lehan affirms that the Eckleburg-like spirit of blindness pervades the entire novel, suggesting the moral breakdown of the pioneering vision of America and Gatsby's vision of Daisy (Great Gatsby: *The Limits* 122–23). By juxtaposing the closing image of the Dutch sailors' first sighting the New World with the abandoned billboard advertisement of Doctor Eckleburg, I direct students' attention to the materialistic perversion of the American dream. The yellow spectacles reflect the corruption of Gatsby's endeavor to use the spectacle of affluence to objectify the "gorgeous" extrinsic identity that masks an intrinsic void (2). The "colossal vitality" of Gatsby's ambition stems from a moral blindness that is synonymous with futility (95).

I ask students to view the "eternal blindness" of the absent oculist in the oft quoted paragraph introducing Doctor Eckleburg's eyes in conjunction with the Eliotic passage immediately preceding it: "[T]he ash-gray men swarm up with leaden spades and stir up an *impenetrable cloud, which screens their obscure operations from your sight*" (23; emphasis added). Fitzgerald uses blindness and clouded vision, together with Eckleburg's spectacles, to deride the egoism of the avaricious oculist who once projected his image larger than life, just as Gatsby attempts to manifest his extrinsic self to attain his transcendent ends.

Moreover, much like the "wild wag of an oculist" (24), Gatsby absurdly clings to his misperception of reality, as evidenced in a frequently quoted conversation with Nick:

> "Can't repeat the past?" he cried incredulously. "Why of course you can!"
> He looked around him wildly, as if the past were lurking here in the shadow of his house, just out of reach of his hand.   (110)

Gatsby's myopic vision, in Fitzgerald's kingdom of the morally blind, is thus akin to the "grotesque gardens" in the "valley of ashes," a wasteland "where ashes take the forms of houses and chimneys and *rising smoke* and, finally, with *a transcendent effort*, of men who move dimly and already crumbling through the *powdery air*" (23; emphasis added). I focus on the word "grotesque" to show students how Fitzgerald connects the sterile scene with the "enormous" spectacles of the oculist, the "enormous" Gatsby mansion, and the "colossal vitality" of Gatsby's dream (the recovery of the illusory rose, Daisy). In the externalization of his personal identity, Gatsby loses his authentic self.

The Eckleburg–Owl Eyes linkage can also generate good discussion among students searching for the novel's deeper meanings. Whereas the Eckleburg billboard objectifies the magnitude of Gatsby's transcendent and materialistic aspirations, Owl Eyes (who also wears "enormous" spectacles [45]) provides insight into the shadowy Jimmy Gatz who existed before the accumulation of his vast fortune. (Milton Hindus, "Mysterious Eyes"; Robert F. McDonnell; David Savage; and Riley V. Hampton have all discussed the connection between Eckleburg and Owl Eyes.) Thus it is appropriate that Owl Eyes is the only other mourner besides Nick and Mr. Gatz at the funeral, for it is James Gatz who is being buried, not Jay Gatsby. When Fitzgerald first introduces the owl-eyed man in Gatsby's library, he is "staring with unsteady concentration" (45) at the bookshelves and has penetrated the fabulous facade: " 'See!' he cried triumphantly. 'It's a bona-fide piece of printed matter. It fooled me. . . . What realism! Knew when to stop, too—didn't cut the pages' " (45–46).

Owl Eyes is also associated with Gatsby through his involvement in the auto wreck after the party, an event that parallels the accident that kills Myrtle. Both men are passengers in cars driven by visually impaired drivers (Owl Eyes's driver is blind drunk, and Daisy has her vision clouded by the disturbing memory of the confrontation between Tom and Gatsby). The final reappearance of Owl Eyes in the novel occurs after Nick has said his last word about Mr. Gatz, a strategically important point because Gatsby's father has been extolling his son's virtues in idealistic terms. At the funeral, Fitzgerald again calls attention to Owl Eyes's weak eyesight: "The rain poured down his thick glasses, and he took them off and wiped them to see the protective canvas unrolled from Gatsby's grave. . . . He took off his glasses and wiped them again, outside and in" (174–75). Through the emphasis on the external and the internal ("outside and in") and the facade that conceals the reality (the "protective canvas" analogous to the pretense of Gatsby's library), Fitzgerald exposes the spiritual bankruptcy beneath the specious veneer of affluence as Owl Eyes utters his brief but fitting eulogy: "The poor son-of-a-bitch" (175).

This brief overview of how I guide my students to a richer understanding of Fitzgerald's orchestration of ocular imagery (in relation to the theme of Gatsby's preoccupation with his extrinsic identity) can extend to commentary on Tom, Daisy, Jordan, and Myrtle and George Wilson. Tom's restless, arrogant eyes and Daisy's ferocious winks and defiant glances mask their mutual moral blindness, a trait shared by Jordan, whose eyes reflect a cultivated strategic oblivion. George Wilson, a victim of his own desire for blind revenge, resembles Eckleburg in his symbolic sightlessness, his blue eyes framed by a yellow background.

But Nick Carraway's role is too often reduced by students to the status of a neutral observer, and it is important to call their attention to his problematic comments on perception early and late in the novel. In the opening pages, he seems to endorse the value of limited perception and professes his desire to have no more "privileged glimpses into the human heart" (2). Later, he laments having to look at things with "new eyes" (104), and, after Gatsby's death, instead of condemning the millionaire's pretense, he rationalizes that Gatsby was a westerner out of his depths in the East (176). Ultimately, Fitzgerald associates Nick with a vision "distorted beyond [his] eyes' power of correction" (176) and links that myopia to the eyes of Dutch sailors gazing for the first time on the "green breast of the new world" (180). Like those early Americans, Gatsby and even Nick cannot resist the temptation to incorporate everything they see into a colossal ego projection. After an in-depth critical analysis of Fitzgerald's eye narrative, my students come to see Gatsby's transcendent and meretricious quest as an amoral grand illusion.

Echoes of the Middle Ages:
Teaching the Medieval in *The Great Gatsby*

Deborah Davis Schlacks

In 1931, F. Scott Fitzgerald wrote an essay entitled "Echoes of the Jazz Age," in which he looked back on the previous decade. The title of that essay could fit much of Fitzgerald's canon, which eloquently describes the 1920s. While he never wrote an essay entitled "Echoes of the Middle Ages," oddly enough this title would also fit many of Fitzgerald's works. They often have a medieval flavor born of his fascination with the Middle Ages and of his recognition of medievalism as a significant social force during the 1920s. *The Great Gatsby*—with its emphasis on feudalism, the grail search, and courtly love—is a prime example. I teach *The Great Gatsby* in an upper-level undergraduate college course called Writers of the Jazz Age, in which students learn about 1920s American literature in historical context. I have found that discussing with the students the medieval motifs of the novel reveals to them a great deal about the preoccupations of Jazz Age society, particularly that era's complex attitudes toward social class distinctions.

I want students to understand that an emphasis on the medieval was part of the culture into which Fitzgerald was born. Medievalism has been described by Morton W. Bloomfield as "the idealization of medieval life and culture." It stresses "a rich, mysterious and imaginary world of nobility, honor, class-consciousness, defenders of women, battles and so forth that, it was believed, flourished in the Middle Ages" (14). Medievalism provided a model of what seemed a better way of life. Medievalists saw the Middle Ages as an era of faith and order, an era the chaotic nineteenth-century and twentieth-century world would do well to emulate (Moreland, *Medievalist Impulse* 119–20). This notion was extremely attractive to people in both England and the United States, particularly in the late nineteenth and early twentieth centuries, when forces ranging from Darwinism to a world war were producing anxiety and disillusion. American medievalism began in the mid-nineteenth century with the arrival in the United States of large numbers of Irish immigrants and continued into the early twentieth century with the arrival of various eastern European groups. Anti-immigration attitudes flourished, resulting in a desire for a medieval pedigree (real or imagined) to set one apart from the despised newcomers (Higham 9–10).

I also emphasize for students that Fitzgerald himself had a particular interest in the medieval. We know that, as a young man, he read such nineteenth-century medievalist works as Sir Walter Scott's *Ivanhoe* and Sir Arthur Conan Doyle's *The White Company*, works that emphasize knights and courtly love (Morsberger 122; Mandel 543). In *The White Company*, as Robert E. Morsberger puts it, a "penniless squire of the lesser nobility must perform feats of valor in order to be worthy of marriage to a lady above him" (122). Fitzgerald's apprentice writings, which often concern knights, show the influence of such works. He even wrote a poem imitating *Ivanhoe* called "Elavoe," and, later on, he briefed his daughter on Scott's novel (Mandel 543). He was also attracted to familiar national icons that derive from the medieval knight—namely, Hopalong Cassidy and the football player.

Besides popular medievalism, Fitzgerald was exposed to a more scholarly approach to the Middle Ages. His mentor Cyril Sigourney Webster Fay introduced a teenaged Fitzgerald to Henry Adams. Adams, Harvard University's first medieval historian, wrote such works as *The Education of Henry Adams* (which has been called a model for Fitzgerald's first novel [Wasserstrom 295]) and *Mont-Saint-Michel and Chartres*. Both works contrast the medieval and the modern. Adams uses the virgin and the cathedral to represent medieval faith and order and the dynamo and the world's fair to represent modern chaos. Through Fay, Fitzgerald was also acquainted with Ralph Adams Cram, who, like Fay, was part of Henry Adams's circle. Once at Princeton University, Fitzgerald came to know Cram's buildings, since Cram was then Princeton's chief architect, responsible for the Gothic buildings that Fitzgerald mentions in laudatory terms in his first novel, *This Side of Paradise*.

Fitzgerald's education in the Middle Ages continued in other ways at Princeton. The author assessed his Princeton education in a 14 September 1940 letter to his wife, Zelda: "I got nothing out of my first two years—in the last I got my passionate love for poetry and historical perspective and ideas in general (however superficially), it carried me full swing into my career" (*F. Scott Fitzgerald: A Life* 464). Notably, Fitzgerald stresses history and poetry. Of all historical periods, it was medieval history that held special interest for Fitzgerald, as evidenced by his comment to an interviewer not long after his Princeton days that he was enthusiastic about "all books about that period which lies between the V and XV centuries" (Bruccoli and Bryer 270). Much later he planned to write a historical novel set in ninth-century France, to be called "Philippe, Count of Darkness." He completed four short stories about Philippe, a young knight who organizes the peasants and establishes the beginnings of a feudal society (see J. Lewis).

During his last year at Princeton, Fitzgerald studied medieval poetry in the course Chaucer and His Contemporaries (N. Hoffman 149, 157n). In the unused preface to *This Side of Paradise*, he was to dedicate the novel "to all those argumentative and discoursive souls who once frequented a certain inn whose doors are now dark, whose fabled walls ring no more to the melody of Chaucer's lesser known poems" ("Preface" 2).

Turning to *The Great Gatsby*, I mention Fitzgerald's mindset as he composed the novel. In a May 1924 letter to Thomas Boyd, he said he was "going to read nothing but Homer & Homeric literature—and history 540–1200 A.D. until I finish my novel" (*F. Scott Fitzgerald: A Life* 68). The era was apparently much on Fitzgerald's mind at the time, with far-reaching results in the novel.

Presenting to students the medieval material in *Gatsby*, I first discuss feudalism, which is pictured in the novel as part of 1920s American society. In his self-
introduction, Nick Carraway says that his family has "a tradition" that they
descend from the (medieval) dukes of Buccleuch. Instead, the real founder is a
great-uncle who came to the United States in 1851, "sent a substitute to the
Civil War, and started the wholesale hardware business that my father carries
on to-day" (3). The bourgeois Carraways' choice of medieval nobility as ances-
tors points to the importance of medievalism in American society during the
early twentieth century. One wished to be linked to the medieval, to have roots
in that intensely hierarchical society; but Nick wryly speaks of this practice,
seemingly aware of the hypocrisy of pretending to such ancestry.

Nick also speaks of the brewer who was the original owner of Gatsby's mansion. This man "agreed to pay five years' taxes on all the neighboring cottages if
the owners would have their roofs thatched with straw." But the neighbors refused, and the man "went into an immediate decline" and died. "Americans,"
Nick concludes, "while occasionally willing to be serfs, have always been obsti-
nate about being peasantry" (88). André Le Vot has called this man's plans
"absurd efforts to connect with a bogus, pseudo-bucolic tradition, to identify
with a vanished historical order" (*F. Scott Fitzgerald* 149). The original owner's attempt to re-create what to him is an ideal past represents medievalism
gone amuck. Other people, including Nick, react negatively to the owner's attempts; the man takes his medievalism too far and too seriously, lacking Nick's
awareness.

Gatsby has added his own medieval touch to the mansion. He has a "high
Gothic library, panelled with carved English oak, and probably transported
complete from some ruin overseas" (45). Elsewhere, Nick calls the library
Gatsby's "Merton College Library" (91)—referring to the Oxford college
founded in 1264 by Walter de Merton. Like Nick's family and like the original
owner of the mansion, Gatsby creates a background for himself—a link, specifically, to the medieval past.

Fitzgerald once called the old-money American aristocracy "a silly, pretentious, vicious mockery of a defunct feudal regime" with "violently selfish and
unchivalric standards" (Bruccoli and Bryer 190). Yet in the novel it is not the
old-money Buchanans who speak of medieval ancestry or have homes with medieval touches; it is people such as Nick, Gatsby, and the original owner of
Gatsby's mansion who highlight their supposed medieval connections in these
ways. Gatsby and the original owner do so to an absurd degree. As modern-day,
"feudal" nobility, perhaps the old-money families need not bother making such
overt displays to realize their connections with the medieval.

Next I draw students' attention to the medieval plot, starring Jay Gatsby as a
knight in search of a grail and in pursuit of his lady fair. Indeed, the quests for
grail and lady become fused for him. After Gatsby and Daisy's affair initially began, back in 1917, Gatsby, Nick says, "found that he had committed himself to
the following of a grail. . . . He felt married to her, that was all" (149).

In courtly-love fashion, Daisy plays aloof lady fair to Gatsby's knight errant. William George Dodd summarizes the medieval author Andreas Capellanus's famed "rules" of the courtly love system: Courtly love is sensuous, illicit, secret, not too easily obtained (hence the lady's aloofness). The courtly lover suffers illness, insomnia, loss of speech on seeing the lady, trembling and paleness when near her, and a dread of being found out. The lady is a superior being, and the courtly lover willingly becomes her vassal, ready to serve her and sacrifice all for her (4–13). Aloof and high-born, ready for an illicit affair with Gatsby, ready to allow Gatsby to become her vassal, Daisy indeed is much like the courtly-love ladies of medieval (and medievalist) literature. This similarity is explicitly emphasized when Nick mentions Gatsby's comment that Daisy's voice is "full of money," and Nick realizes that the quality "was the inexhaustible charm that rose and fell in it, the jingle of it, the cymbals' song of it. . . . High in a white palace, the king's daughter, the golden girl. . . ." (120; ellipses in orig.).

Daisy's names further identify her with the courtly-love lady. During the Middle Ages in France, "marguerite poems," written in praise of the daisy (in French, *marguerite*), were a tradition (see Lowes). Chaucer brought the marguerite tradition into English poetry in his Prologue to *The Legend of Good Women*, which first describes a pretty, fresh, uncultivated, inspiring daisy and then describes a daisylike dream figure called Queen Alceste. But Alceste proves manipulative, convincing the poet-persona that he has written evil works about women and must repent by composing legends of good women (Higgs 87–94). The daisy seems like Gatsby's image of a pure and inspiring Daisy Buchanan, while Alceste is like the "real" Daisy, seemingly pure but actually corrupt (Schlacks, "Revisiting" 131–39).

The shasta daisy (Chrysanthemum maximus), the kind most familiar to people in the United States, is white on the outside and yellow in the center (Seymour et al. 422–23). The daisy spoken of in the marguerite poems, however, is the English daisy, which comes in pink or white and may be tipped in crimson (Stevens 79; Rowland). The intriguing possibility of a crimson-tipped daisy adds a new dimension to the usual symbolism; besides being outwardly pure but having a corrupt center, Daisy is tipped in crimson—that is, in bloody violence—after she kills Myrtle Wilson and is complicit in Gatsby's death.

Daisy's maiden name, Fay, also has medieval implications. Robert J. Ewald describes the fay, a common figure in medieval lore, as "a woman of great beauty with supernatural powers who comes from an 'other world' where ordinary laws of space and time do not apply" (4). She can heal, prophesy, shift shapes, and prompt a knight to perform chivalric deeds. She is also inconsistent; according to Ewald, "in one role, she is the helpful and maternal Dame du Lac, yet in another, the sinister and scheming Morgain la Fee [or Fay]" (2). In the Middle Ages, the fay was often blended with the courtly lady (Ewald 2). This description resembles not only Chaucer's Alceste but also the inconstant Daisy Fay Buchanan (see also Lupak 339; Stein).

In courtly-love fashion, the garden is important in *Gatsby* as the locus for the romance of Gatsby and Daisy. Gardens are, in Jerome Mandel's words, "central to medieval romance" (550), images of beauty and perfection. In his "blue gardens" (39), Gatsby holds parties to which he wishes to lure Daisy. In the "garden" of cut flowers that Gatsby creates in Nick's sitting room (84), Gatsby reunites with Daisy. And, back in his own garden, he woos her that same day with visions of his wealth.

Details of Daisy's incarnation scene are also significantly linked to medieval concepts of perfection. The incarnation takes place where "the blocks of the sidewalks really formed a ladder and mounted to a secret place above the trees" (110). Also, just before Gatsby kisses Daisy, he hears "the tuning fork that had been struck upon a star" (110–11). According to Kim Moreland, the sidewalk ladder is "reminiscent of that appropriated from Plato by the medieval Neoplatonists of Chartres"; Dante uses a similar image in *The Divine Comedy*. Furthermore, the tuning fork alludes to the music of the spheres, a popular medieval image of the perfect harmony of the universe (*Medievalist Impulse* 140).

Of course—and here is an especially important point for students to note—the perfection is a sham. The courtly-love portrait in *Gatsby* is full of bitter irony. Daisy is no ideal lady—except in Gatsby's deluded mind. She is not part of the perfect realm above the stars, nor should she be confused with the grail. In the end, Gatsby realizes (Nick thinks) "what a grotesque thing a rose is" (161)—a rose, that medieval symbol of love and beauty (Mandel 556).

In fact, the novel presents, long before Gatsby's sad end, an emblematic setting that is the very antithesis of the lovely medieval garden, of the beautiful medieval rose: the valley of ashes. This place is described in the novel as a "fantastic farm where ashes grow like wheat into ridges and hills and grotesque gardens" (23). A dumping ground for industrial wastes, the valley of ashes is antinature, antigarden. In the novel, it is a symbol of the corrupt modern world, corrupt both materially and spiritually, thus very unlike the idealized image of the medieval world. Fitzgerald's source for this setting was, at least in part, T. S. Eliot's *The Waste Land*, which offers a similar depiction of the modern world as a wasteland. In that poem, "April is the cruellest month" (*Complete Poems* 37), in which the spring rain merely hints at a renewal that does not really come. Meanwhile, the modern world offers "A heap of broken images, where the sun beats, / And the dead tree gives no shelter, the cricket no relief, / And the dry stone no sound of water" (*Complete Poems* 38). Eliot was influenced by Chaucer's General Prologue (Fitzgerald also undoubtedly knew *The Canterbury Tales* through his Chaucer course in college), whose first lines celebrate the perfect harmony of nature: "Whan that Aprill with his shoures soote / The droghte of March hath perced to the roote" (17). Here, April rains saturate the land; the drought utterly disappears. The beauty and harmony of nature are in abundance, and pilgrims set forth to visit a holy shrine. It is a scene of natural and spiritual harmony. Eliot's wasteland and Fitzgerald's valley of ashes could not provide any sharper contrast to Chaucer's vision of spring.

Furthermore, in Eliot's poem, the dry, barren land in need of renewal could be helped if a search for a grail were successful, but in the modern world, such a search proves fruitless. Eliot drew on Jessie L. Weston's *From Ritual to Romance*, which connects the medieval grail legend with ancient vegetation myths, in developing this motif. Gatsby searches fruitlessly for Daisy as a grail, thinking she will bring him a transcendent fulfillment. Having confused a highborn, wealthy lady with a grail, he is very much mistaken; Daisy is pictured as utterly unable to bring him the kind of fulfillment he longs for, just as all such fulfillment was elusive in Fitzgerald's 1920s America.

In short, the twentieth century as presented by Fitzgerald in *Gatsby* is not like the ideal medieval world. But then again, I point out to students, the medieval world was not really ideal. The courtly-love system of medieval literature was less a way of life among courtiers than a game—a serious game, a class marker. The courtiers and the best of the medieval poets who wrote about the system knew that ladies were not ideal and knights were not ordinarily self-sacrificing. The game became increasingly serious in the late Middle Ages, a time of social mobility (as in the 1920s, in Fitzgerald's United States). In England, men of the merchant class could now be knighted, and noblemen married daughters of merchants (Brewer 19; Schlacks, *American Dream Visions* 13). Such changes were disturbing to the old courtly class. Hence, the courtly-love system increasingly became a way to maintain differences between the aristocratic class and the wealthy bourgeoisie, who, when they tried to imitate courtly ways, did so without seeing courtly-love practices as a game (Ferrante and Economou 4–5).

I try to show my students that Fitzgerald uses this complex view of courtly love. Gatsby, the "wealthy bourgeois" with the non-Anglo-Saxon, immigrant roots, takes the system to heart. As Gatsby tells Nick the story of himself and Daisy, he is creating a courtly-love text in which Daisy is truly the lady fair—and the grail—and he, the self-sacrificing knight. Meanwhile, the aristocratic Daisy and Tom—old money threatened by new—create a very different courtly-love text, in which Gatsby's willingness to be self-sacrificing knight is manipulated, first by Daisy to make Tom jealous and then by both Buchanans to make Gatsby the fall guy in their cover story, developed and deployed in the aftermath of Myrtle's death. Nick's text—the novel itself—includes Gatsby's text and the Buchanans' text; Nick tries to make sense of both.

I teach *The Great Gatsby*, long hailed as the quintessential Jazz Age novel, as a novel that is also filled with the medieval. I contend that the medieval in the novel is not cosmetic, nor was Fitzgerald's interest in the Middle Ages a momentary whim. Instead, he brought to his writing a real knowledge of popular medievalism and of medieval history and literature. In so doing, he was able to reveal a great deal about Jazz Age attitudes toward social class.

I have presented rather detailed and comprehensive information and perspectives on the medievalist content of *The Great Gatsby*, an approach to the novel that might work best with advanced students in a class in which *Gatsby* and the 1920s are to be discussed in depth. Teachers of *Gatsby* at various levels, however, might select from the information and perspectives offered here in accordance with the proclivities of their students and the goals of their particular courses. To whatever extent it is done, presenting *Gatsby* to students through its medieval motif is a productive and interesting way of helping them learn about Fitzgerald, the novel, and 1920s American society.

Enough Guilt to Go Around:
Teaching Fitzgerald's Lesson in Morality

Peter L. Hays

I teach *The Great Gatsby* in both modern American novel classes and in modern American literature survey courses. In each, I teach the novel twice: the first time, slowly, almost page by page; the second time, more quickly. The first time through is essentially a standard interpretation; the subsequent reading looks at the implications of identifying with Nick, an unreliable narrator. I begin by pointing out how the novel details the corruption of the American dream as exhibited by life in the Roaring Twenties. I remind students that the novel takes place during Prohibition and yet everyone drinks, liberally, throughout— a waiter even asks openly if Nick and Gatsby want drinks (70). I also tell my students briefly how Prohibition encouraged the development of organized crime on a national scale for the first time in America. Other incidents of corruption in the novel are Gatsby's cozy relationship with the police commissioner (68), Gatsby's involvement with bootleg liquor and stolen bonds, and the characters' general disregard for marital vows.

Although Fitzgerald himself, in answer to Owen Davis, who dramatized *Gatsby*, was not sure whether Gatsby and Daisy were having sex during her afternoon visits to him (Mizener, *Far Side* 208), today's students cannot imagine them just playing Monopoly. Moreover, none of the guests whom Tom and Myrtle invite to their apartment on 158th Street offer moral objections to the adulterous relationship, even though its character is known: Nick is too complacent (he describes himself as nonjudgmental), Catherine supports her sister's right to have a "sweetie" (35), and the McKees see Tom as their entrée into

Long Island society and wish to do nothing to jeopardize that financial opportunity. Finally, the circumstances of Myrtle's death point out the immorality: Daisy is responsible for the hit-and-run, but she never tells Tom how Myrtle was killed (letting Gatsby take the blame), and Catherine commits perjury at the inquest into her sister's death.

After giving my students a brief account of "muscular Christianity"[1] and the ideal of the athlete, I introduce them to Dink Stover and Frank Merriwell, heroes of early-twentieth-century popular novels with athletic protagonists at Yale University (Nick and Tom Buchanan's alma mater). The Merriwell books, written by Burt L. Standish, a pseudonym for W. Gilbert Patten, are available as reprints; the originals sold over one hundred million copies. Jacket copy from one insists that these books stimulate "a boy's ambition to become a good athlete in order that he may develop into a strong, vigorous, right-thinking man" (Standish), and thus they provide a wonderful contrast to the portrait of athletes in *Gatsby*: adulterous Tom, lying Jordan, and those members of the Chicago White Sox who accepted Wolfsheim's bribe to throw the 1919 World Series (73). While the Merriwell books believe that only boys can be athletes, Fitzgerald is an equal opportunity employer, allowing Jordan to be as corrupt as her male peers. (I also show my students the 19 July 1924 *Saturday Evening Post* ad for the Jordan sports car, depicting a female golfer.) If Tom the philanderer and exemplar of domestic violence is "a national figure" (6) in football, essentially All-American, and if the great American pastime, baseball, has been fixed by a gambler, then corruption is pandemic, infecting all that is American.

I continue by exposing Gatsby's false belief in the equality postulated by the American dream. Gatsby's new money, even if it had not been criminally obtained, cannot buy him entrée into the social elite. He lives in déclassé West Egg, has shady "gonnegtion[s]" (70), dresses in flamboyant and inappropriate garb, and gives ostentatious parties attended by "all kinds of crazy fish" (103), as indicated by the guest list (61–63) and Daisy's aversion to them (107). His gaudy automobile, a perfect symbol for the social mobility promised by America's myth of equal opportunity for all, kills Myrtle and results in his death as well. Another example of a futile attempt to achieve equality and respect through money is the brief description of "three modish negroes, two bucks and a girl" (69), driven into New York by a white chauffeur. Besides the racism of the language in the entire passage (echoing Tom's racist concerns [12–13]), Nick's reaction displays the fixity of class status: "I laughed aloud as the yolks of their eyeballs rolled toward us in haughty rivalry" (69). The incident with the Sloanes (assuming that the woman, never named, is Mrs. Sloane) accentuates Gatsby's position as a socially unacceptable outsider: "My God, I believe the man's coming. . . . Doesn't he know she doesn't want him? . . . She has a big dinner party and he won't know a soul there" (103).

Gatsby cannot turn back the clock. Poor Richard and Horatio Alger myths of work hard, do your best, and you can achieve anything do not cancel time or its progress. Nor do they cancel the class consciousness of 1920s American society.

The dream of equality, opportunity, and security has been corrupted by greed and commercialism. Besides Wolfsheim's gambling activities, there is the bond and stock market, which Nick is not alone in entering during the flush 1920s. Others, too, were "agonizingly aware of the easy money in the vicinity and convinced that it was theirs for a few words in the right key" (42). Gatsby's heated conversation with Tom Buchanan about Gatsby's source of income paints a wider social picture:

> "I picked him for a bootlegger the first time I saw him, and I wasn't far wrong."
> "What about it?" said Gatsby politely. "I guess your friend Walter Chase wasn't too proud to come in on it."
> "And you left him in the lurch, didn't you? . . ."
> "He came to us dead broke. He was very glad to pick up some money, old sport."　　　　　　　　　　　　　　　　　　　　　　　　　(133–34)

The search for wealth in *Gatsby* crosses lines of class and legality. The border between honest business, shady business, and criminality is sometimes indistinguishable. Wolfsheim and Gatsby are clever businessmen—they "saw the opportunity" (73), much like the robber barons referred to in the text, John D. Rockefeller (27) and James J. Hill (168). Fitzgerald condemns the rampant, heedless commercialism of his era, as well as the rigid classism based on wealth, of which he felt he had been a victim, especially in losing his first love, the Chicago socialite Ginevra King. He records in his ledger what he overheard someone say of him: "Poor boys shouldn't think of marrying rich girls" (*F. Scott Fitzgerald's Ledger* 170). As he says in "The Crack-Up":

> It was one of those tragic loves doomed for lack of money. . . . [I] would always cherish an abiding mistrust, an animosity, toward the leisure class—not the conviction of a revolutionist but the smoldering hatred of a peasant. In the years since then I have never been able . . . to stop thinking that at one time a sort of *droit de seigneur* might have been exercised to give one of them my girl.　　　　　　　　　　　　　　　　　　(77)

At the novel's conclusion, Fitzgerald reminds the reader of when America was "a fresh, green breast of the new world" (180), when this country was founded by religious Pilgrims who sought to make it "a city on a hill," a moral exemplar to the corrupt Old World. Instead, the country is corrupt, the West no different from the East, from Dan Cody to Wolfsheim to Jordan and Tom. And instead of Puritan proscriptions or Poor Richard incitements to hard work, the evident motto "[o]n the white steps [is] an obscene word" (179–80), a manifestation of our moral entropy.

That emphasis on corruption concludes my first run-through of the novel, usually the first class session devoted to the novel; often this reading is not too different from students' readings in other classes, in high school or college. At the next class period, I go through a second reading of the novel. I ask how many of those few reading the novel for the first time hoped for a happy ending to Gatsby and Daisy's illicit romance. There are always a few. I then ask how many like Nick, struggling as he is to start a career and to find love. There are always several who identify with him. Then I begin to deconstruct Nick's reliability as a narrator by pointing to his statement on page 67 that Gatsby's mini-autobiography "was *all* true" (emphasis added). Since our campus is seventy-five miles from San Francisco, stated on page 65 to be in the Middle West, my students know it can't be all true. What else is not true? I ask them. I direct them to look at Nick's comments throughout the first chapter, particularly his description of Tom, and then compare those highly charged opinions with Nick's statement that he reserves judgments (2). Next, I ask them to compare his quotation from his father, "Whenever you feel like criticizing any one, . . . just remember that all the people in this world haven't had the advantages that you've had" (1), a statement with material implications, with his repetition of it a page later: "a sense of the fundamental decencies is parcelled out unequally at birth" (2). My students begin to see that Nick cannot be trusted; he has deceived them—and perhaps himself as well.

Next I ask them to turn to his self-praise—"I am one of the few honest people that I have ever known" (59)—self-congratulation stimulated by his letter to the rumored fiancée back in the Midwest. Nick's relationship with Jordan could develop into marriage, and thus he feels the need to be free—so the letter is understandable. But why, I ask my students, didn't Nick feel the same need three pages before while he "had a short affair with a girl who lived in Jersey City and worked in the accounting department" of his bank (56)? They quickly identify the social difference between the two women, a golf champion who moves from "Asheville and Hot Springs and Palm Beach" (18) and an office worker from Jersey City. Nick's snobbery, which he himself confessed on page 2, is evident here and in his sexist remark that "[d]ishonesty in a woman is a thing you never blame deeply" (58) (and his bank is ironically named Probity Trust [56]). The conjunction of these references, all within three pages of each other (56–59), cannot be coincidental: Fitzgerald is directing our attention to Nick's morality, and Nick, like Tom, assumes that morality only obtains between men of one's own social standing. When he declines Gatsby's offer of a job—"because the offer was obviously and tactlessly for a service to be rendered, I had no choice except to cut him off there" (83)—it is not because Nick objects to making money. He comes to the East to "learn the bond business" (3), and on his shelf at home are books "in red and gold like new money from the mint, promising to unfold the shining secrets that only Midas and Morgan and Mæcenas knew" (4). Rather, he has been asked to be a go-between, to arrange a private meeting between Daisy and her former lover, Gatsby, and he feels, perhaps subconsciously, that he will be less of a pander if he does not get paid for it.

Nick acts less than morally scrupulous when he praises Catherine's perjury (163–64) and when he conceals his knowledge of the driver who killed Myrtle from the police, making him an after-the-fact accessory to the hit-and-run killing. Concealing knowledge of a crime is a crime. Thus he prevents Daisy from being accused, allowing Wilson to seek his own vengeance, killing Gatsby and then himself. Nick correctly concludes, "I was responsible" (164).

I then ask those students who liked Nick, who identified with him, what it meant that they went along with him while he observed but did nothing to prevent immorality, not only condoning it (voyeuristically accompanying Tom and Myrtle to their apartment), but also participating in it (ignoring Prohibition, pandering for Gatsby, concealing evidence) and even praising it. I ask my students who romantically identified with Gatsby and Daisy what the moral difference was between their adultery and Tom and Myrtle's and what their support for Gatsby and Daisy's adultery said about them. I tell them that their complacency in accepting Gatsby and Daisy's adultery, in agreeing with Nick to cover up Daisy's crime, in not objecting to Nick's praise of Catherine's perjury, in not objecting to any of the immoral acts in the novel—beyond the obvious ones, Tom's breaking Myrtle's nose and Daisy's running over Myrtle—makes them morally complicit with Nick. He has been, as he calls himself, their "guide" (4) through the novel and into immorality, and they have not objected. Like Nick in the novel, they have witnessed criminality and not demurred. And in not objecting to immorality, they permit it to continue. As a final example, I point to our university's honor code. I ask how many know of cheating that has occurred. There are always many hands. Then when I ask how many have reported the cheaters to faculty members or administrators, there are almost never any hands. Like Nick, they see evil and may condemn it silently. Nick says that he wants the world "to be in uniform and at a sort of moral attention forever" (2) and that he is honest, but he does nothing to contest evil. My students, in observing cheating and not objecting or obstructing, are, like Nick, partly responsible for the continuation of that immorality.

In an interview, William Faulkner spoke of reactions to evil:

> There seem to be three stages: The first says, This is rotten, I'll have no part of it, I will take death first. The second says, This is rotten, I don't like it, I can't do anything about it, but at least I will not participate in it myself, I will go off into a cave or climb a pillar to sit on. The third says, This stinks and I'm going to do something about it.
>
> (qtd. in Gwynn and Blotner 245–46)

Nick, going back to the Midwest at the novel's end, is at the second stage—going off to a cave or climbing a hermit's pillar, not realizing that he has participated, and thus furthered, the wickedness he denounces. Those who tacitly agree with Nick's judgments in the novel, his complicity in immorality, do the same.

By using this double reading, I try to make *The Great Gatsby* not just a marvelously written novel of the 1920s but one with still current relevance to each of my students. On one level, it is the engaging story of a Horatio Alger character, who, with idealistic intentions but criminal means, fails to achieve his dreams. His failure points up the extent to which the American dream is a myth, a dangerous lie, a gasbag, like the air mattress supporting Gatsby in his pool at his death (162). On another level, it is a savage indictment of the corruption of the American dream, degenerated from its unlimited and moral potential to an obscene commercialism, figured in America's business practices, criminality, and pandemic immorality. But it is also an indictment of our own moral culpability, much like Nick's, our willingness to observe immorality and accept it more or less complacently.

NOTE

[1] Chris Armstrong defines muscular Christianity as "the belief that physical activity and sports, especially team sports, developed character, fostered patriotism, and instilled virtues that would serve their participants—and their participants' God—well in later life. In other words, team games taught their own high ethic, and that ethic could and should be a Christian one. 1857 serves as a convenient date to mark the origin of muscular Christianity—and of the notion that college sports should be the training ground for youths' spirits and consciences as well as their bodies. This was the year British author Thomas Hughes published his blockbuster school story, *Tom Brown's Schoolboys.*"

Doubting Nick:
Reading Nick Reading Gatsby Reading Daisy

Cecilia Konchar Farr

Recently, my colleagues and I got together to edit the catalog copy for the English major at our midwestern women's college. The work became an effort to justify our existence. Why, we were forced to ask, should students of the new century invest in an English major? An old answer turned up in new clothes: with careful reading skills, students can stroll confidently through the digital universe. Good reading skills invite students to be skeptical of information, to question texts of all forms: What is the source of this information? Whose interest does it serve? How much should we believe? These questions have long been in the arsenal of rhetorical critics, but now they are more often found in librarians' handouts on using the Internet.

In the midst of this discussion, I was preparing to teach *The Great Gatsby* again. Though I have often taught the concept of the unreliable narrator, I decided I would emphasize it more this time—after all, what better texts to train students in skepticism than modernist ones? At the beginning of the twentieth century, many writers lost their belief in what we have come to call master narratives, single, all-encompassing explanations of why the world works the way it does. Along with the painters of their day, these writers began to experiment with perspective and with time. What is true in this moment, they asked themselves, and how might another moment or another perspective change this truth? Texts such as *Gatsby*, Virginia Woolf's *The Waves*, Ernest Hemingway's *The Sun Also Rises*, and Willa Cather's *My Ántonia* engaged these questions through their narrators.

Nick Carraway is an especially effective narrator to use in teaching this concept because many students come to college having read *The Great Gatsby* in high school, but generally they have read it without questioning Nick's point of view. The change in their reading once they become skeptical is striking. Reading Nick reading Gatsby reading Daisy is a much more complex and interesting experience than simply believing Nick. In fact, for many of my students, reading *The Great Gatsby* as informed skeptics is what leads them to view themselves as English majors, even literary critics, rather than just as enthusiastic readers.

Reading Nick Reading Gatsby

When I assign my students to read *Gatsby*, I begin by briefly introducing the question of Nick's reliability. I want to plant a seed of distrust, so that they read (or reread) the novel doubting Nick. Many critics have addressed this issue, most significantly Scott Donaldson in "The Trouble with Nick" and Gary J. Scrimgeour in "Against *The Great Gatsby*." They point out that Nick's confession on the first page of the novel that he is "inclined to reserve all judgments" (1) is followed by more than one hundred fifty pages of judgments—of Daisy, Jordan, Tom, Gatsby, and the world. Nick admits that he often avoids the "intimate revelations of young men" (2), then doggedly pursues young Gatsby's.

Despite his tone of detached observation, Nick is a participant in all the summer revelry he describes. He purposely chooses a house that features the "consoling proximity of [the] millionaires" he says he disdains (5). He admits, at one point, that Gatsby's offer of a business deal he knows is shady, had it come "under different circumstances," might have been "one of the crises" of his life (83). In the end, Jordan pegs him not as the "honest, straightforward person" he claims to be but as a man like her—a "bad driver" in a novel where a car is a murder weapon (177).

Donaldson argues that Nick is "the right narrator for *The Great Gatsby*" because, despite Nick's early reservations about Gatsby, he commits to Gatsby and to his dream at the conclusion of the novel:

> In the end, and for the only time in his life, Nick makes a commitment himself. And it is because this decision is so difficult for him, a judgmental snob who invariably keeps his emotional distance, that it seems inevitable for the rest of us.   ("Trouble" 137)

The reader, as Donaldson points out, is drawn into reaffirming Nick's values. His narrator persona operates persuasively by working from an apparently firm midwestern morality and by taking this morality for granted as universally understood and approved by his readers. Certainly it works for my midwestern students. They discern quickly that Gatsby's "romantic readiness" and "extraordinary gift for hope" will dominate Nick's account of a summer in the Jazz Age (2). They understand why only Gatsby is exempt from Nick's cynical disillusionment with the world, why only Gatsby is worthy of admiration. They agree with Nick's observation that

> Gatsby turned out all right at the end; it is what preyed on Gatsby, what foul dust floated in the wake of his dreams that temporarily closed out my interest in the abortive sorrows and short-winded elations of men.   (2)

Thus reading Nick reading Gatsby sets the reader up to appreciate Gatsby as a romantic hero, a man who "had committed himself to the following of a grail" (149). Critics have followed this line, comparing Gatsby with King Arthur and Christ, Browning's Childe Roland and Keats's Porphyro. Bruce Michelson traces Fitzgerald's hero images back to classical myths of "the skyborne mortal ascending towards the heavens on feathered wings, flying madly far and high, shaking the world with his earthward plunge" (566). He demonstrates how the image patterns in the novel—white and golden light, fire, fantastic cars, sunshine, and heat—all contribute to the re-creation of the myth of Phaëthon, a god among mortals who dared assume the greatest powers of the gods. But readers are also confronted with Gatsby's craving for wealth, his shady beginnings, his "gonnegtion[s]" (70) with the underworld and his violent death. Nick's mostly admiring descriptions of his friend's goals are marred with adjectives like "gaudy" (40), "vulgar," and "meretricious" (98). Sometimes, my students begin to suspect, Nick is forcing us to look the other way.

Dancing with the Narrator

Once doubt about Nick begins to invade how my students read *The Great Gatsby*, they sometimes resist the change in perception that follows. In the online discussion for the course I taught that spring, a student observed, "It's rather frustrating if you can't trust a narrator of a story, because how do you know what's real and what's not? How can you trust anyone?" I assured her that the reader can take the lead in the story "because in modernism there is no Voice of Authority, no Absolute Truth of the text, and since you don't know what is 'real,' you invent, you fill in, you interpret." Modernist narrators tell *their* story, not *the* story, and they allow for new patterns of reader interaction and interpretation. I tried to persuade her that "reading is much more fun when you have to 'consider the source.'"

Where is the fun, another student replied, in "this endless circle of questions that in the end have no answer?" If you can't trust the narrator, "the tapestry of the story just starts unraveling and you are left with a big pile of threads." There has to be, she insisted, "some level of trust." In reading twentieth-century literature, I responded, you dance always "between fiction and truth, trust and skepticism, disbelief and the willing suspension of disbelief." When reality is called into question, you stand on shaky ground. "What we thought was solid and dependable is actually a mass of dancing particles," I pointed out. The only answer, then, is to "dance with that narrator. Believe him when you feel it's appropriate, doubt when you think you should. It depends on how the narrative voice confronts your values and prejudices. My approach is to dance with a range of perceptions—and keep moving among them."

Another student insisted that the dance could only begin on a second reading of a text: "The first time through, I tend to trust the narrator while I am reading in order to understand the book better." The first student concluded with her that the rereading is key. "Upon a second reading, I became very skeptical of what I could and couldn't believe. I had to weed through Nick's egotism to find the 'real' characters. But in a way, that made reading more challenging and worthwhile."

Later in the semester, another student affirmed that doubting Nick made reading more "challenging and realistic" because "novels, then, are not maps to meaning." She added, "I think it gives the text more vitality because challenging motives—especially the narrator's—causes you to think of the characters on a more human level." There was widespread agreement on this point, especially when one student noted that a breakthrough for her was in watching Nick's changing perceptions of Daisy. "He really sides with Gatsby and blames Daisy in the end," she wrote.

Reading Gatsby Reading Daisy

This last realization, I found, was central in drawing my women students to the idea of skeptical reading. When they realize that they dislike the women in the novel because they buy into Nick's and Gatsby's perceptions of them, they are more eager to try alternative readings. I, too, hated Daisy when I read *The Great Gatsby* as an undergraduate. I had good reason: she obviously rejects Gatsby's invitation to join him in his romantic vision and, both literally and figuratively, is responsible for his death. And because I, with Nick, identified with Gatsby, I had to hate the woman who destroys him.

Hating Daisy Buchanan seems to be a common response to *The Great Gatsby*. Critics have famously dubbed her "criminally amoral," the "Dark Destroyer," and "vulgar and inhuman" (Person 250). She is the "classical Siren" (Settle 115), the seductress who detours Gatsby's romantic quest through the wasteland and into destruction. She epitomizes the materialism that alienates him from society. She is the tarnished golden girl. Even feminist critics have few positive things to say about Daisy. Judith Fetterley takes a second look at the character, then decides with the consensus of critics before her that Daisy is "the foul dust that floats in Gatsby's wake" (86). She sees Daisy in a slightly different perspective, however, as the victim of "Gatsby/Carraway/Fitzgerald," not as his victimizer—"the object of the novel's hostility and its scapegoat" (72).

Calling on the reader's inevitable identification with Gatsby, the critical establishment has set up a polarity between Gatsby and Daisy. David F. Trask notes:

> Fitzgerald develops the tragedy of Jay Gatsby as the consequence of his quixotic quest for Daisy Buchanan. . . . The trouble with Gatsby's quest was that Daisy was completely incapable of playing the role assigned to her. She was as shallow as the other hollow people who inhabited Fitzgerald's Long Island. (214)

And Arthur Mizener states, "In contrast to the corruption which underlies Daisy's world, Gatsby's essential incorruptibility is heroic" (*Far Side* 193).

An understanding of Daisy's fallibility, it seems, is necessary to the acceptance of Gatsby's heroic infallibility. Marius Bewley writes, "Fitzgerald's illustration of the emptiness of Daisy's character—an emptiness that we see curdling into the viciousness of a monstrous moral indifference as the story unfolds—is drawn with a fineness and depth of critical understanding" (45). But could it be read as just the opposite—that it is Nick's (and the critics') lack of critical understanding that condemns Daisy for "monstrous moral indifference" while forgiving Gatsby's similar flaws?

Taking a different critical perspective on the novel, viewing Nick skeptically, invites and encourages students to adopt a broader view of Daisy. We can show that it may be instead that she, like Gatsby, heroically fails to make what she wanted of her life. Through Jordan's narration, Fitzgerald constructs a dream for Daisy as tangible and as admirable as Gatsby's. Both fall victim to their own illusions; both fail to create themselves as they had envisioned. In Daisy, Fitzgerald gives us a lightsome sun goddess, a golden girl to complement his heroic Gatsby. She is not only the object of Gatsby's grand illusion but also "his female double," as Leland S. Person, Jr., describes her (251). Theirs is "the story of the failure of a mutual dream," he argues (251). Their joint, futile romantic quest could be seen as the focus of the novel.

I point out that, in her way, Daisy can be read as having as much of the "extraordinary gift for hope" as Gatsby and much of his "romantic readiness" (2). She responds to young Gatsby, her prince, as strongly as even he could want. When Gatsby leaves, she "didn't play around with the soldiers any more," and she incited "[w]ild rumors" by attempting to go to New York to see Gatsby off to war (75). Jordan describes an unforgettable drunken Daisy on the day before her wedding—a woman struggling to hold onto her dream in the face of impossible opposition, clinging to it desperately in the form of the soggy letter from Gatsby. But it fell "to pieces like snow" (76), and she bore the loss silently.

As my student noted above, Nick's changing assessment of Daisy is telling. This shift is most readily apparent in his description of her voice early in the novel:

> It was the kind of voice that the ear follows up and down, as if each speech is an arrangement of notes that will never be played again. Her face was sad and lovely with bright things in it, bright eyes and a bright passionate mouth, but there was an excitement in her voice that men who had cared for her found difficult to forget: a singing compulsion, a whispered "Listen," a promise that she had done gay, exciting things just a while since and that there were gay, exciting things hovering in the next hour. (9)

When Nick relates how Gatsby fell in love with Daisy, he says, "she turned toward him and he kissed her curious and lovely mouth. She had caught a cold, and it made her voice huskier and more charming than ever" (150). Later, when Gatsby stages a reunion at Nick's house, Nick describes how Daisy sounds: "Her throat, full of aching, grieving beauty, told only of her unexpected joy" (89).

As the novel progresses, however, Daisy's voice changes for Nick, following Gatsby's lead:

> "She's got an indiscreet voice," I remarked. "It's full of—" I hesitated.
> "Her voice is full of money," [Gatsby] said suddenly.

> That was it. I'd never understood before. It was full of money—that was the inexhaustible charm that rose and fell in it, the jingle of it, the cymbals' song of it. (120)

The most severe indictment of Daisy, however, is that, in a novel where many characters' metaphoric relationships with cars identify them as potential reckless killers, only Daisy fulfills that potential. Gatsby collects gorgeous cars; Tom, George, and Nick are fascinated with them; and Jordan is a frighteningly bad driver. But Daisy, driving for the first time in the novel on the night Myrtle is killed, is the one who realizes the car's deadly potential. Daisy's careless disregard for Myrtle's death cannot be dismissed; however, it can no more be held against her than can Gatsby's similar unconcern for Myrtle ("He spoke as if Daisy's reaction [to the accident] was the only thing that mattered," Nick observes [143]). Nor is it less evocative than Gatsby's questionable connections with the machinations of the underworld (surely Wolfsheim's human molars don't come from a dentist's office). In the final act of their romance, Daisy and Gatsby are implicated together. Both of their hands are on the steering wheel. It is the end of both of them.

Reading Nick reading Gatsby, then, can give students a different Gatsby, one more open to criticism, more careless, corrupt, and capitalist—more like the traditional reading of Daisy. Reading Nick reading Daisy through Gatsby can give students a different Daisy, a Daisy who is a failed dreamer—as we have learned to see Gatsby.

In opening up the reading of *The Great Gatsby* in this way, by inviting my students to be skeptical of Nick, I have found that they engage the text more directly, with less awe. Locating Nick as a biased narrator directing their reading of the novel makes them more comfortable locating themselves and then critically and self-consciously constructing their own readings. They begin to possess the text more fully, to question and engage it, even, joyfully, to dance with it. In short, they become not just informed readers, not just practiced skeptics, but skilled critics of literature. And if we're lucky, even in the age of the Internet, they become English majors.

NOTE

I wish to thank my students, who are always teaching me and who have enriched my understanding of this novel, especially Kristina Anderson, Heather Carlson, Jenny Kordosky, Cat McBride, and Robin Walser, who agreed to be quoted in this paper.

Teaching *The Great Gatsby* through Examining Gender Roles

Marilyn Elkins

Written in the 1970s, my master's thesis, "F. Scott Fitzgerald's Use of the Bitch-Goddess Success," looked at how Fitzgerald's female characters serve as trophies for aspiring young men and function as recognizable signs of American masculine success. It also analyzed the gender roles in *The Great Gatsby* that seem to entrap members of both sexes. What I wrote was not, however, cast in such contemporary language, since I was studying at Vanderbilt University in the declining days of New Criticism, which lingered much longer in southern climes. But, unknowingly, I had already begun my investigation of how Fitzgerald's writing, more than that of most men of his period, reflects that women were always already the object, and not the subject, of American success narratives. While women were the other in Fitzgerald's depiction of the American dream, men were often as thwarted by their assigned roles in the pursuit of love and success as the women they pursued. Years later, examining the representation of gender roles in *The Great Gatsby*—especially its chronicling of the reality of women's lives in the 1920s—and questioning its underlying assumptions about gender still seem an appropriate means for teaching this important text. Such a methodology actually helps reclaim a portion of Fitzgerald's somewhat skeptical readership among today's college students, for it can demonstrate that he captured the gender problems of his era through his careful rendering of the period. This approach allows many students to join me in faulting that reality while praising the artistry of its chronicler.

For the past twenty years in my American literature survey classes, I have been fine-tuning an approach to teaching *The Great Gatsby* that emphasizes gender roles. I have designed this course to further students' introduction to literary discourse; to help them understand the importance of American literary traditions and historical perspectives; to acquaint them with major writers, themes, and critical and theoretical approaches; to enhance their critical thinking and close reading skills; and to offer some instruction in writing about literature. As a feminist, I also see the course as an opportunity to help students become more aware of how gender roles are constructed and how such constructions have varied throughout American history. I teach the novel to English majors—many of whom are first-generation Americans and often the first member of their families to attend college—by asking them to examine the power relationships in the text and to view the novel as a possible, perhaps unconscious, critique of 1920s patriarchy. Our investigation serves as a catalyst for students to develop their interpretation of the novel and to create a topic for their major writing assignment for the course.

At this point in their education, my students have usually mastered basic literary terms and definitions, and I have explained my own ideas about how critical theory has reshaped our response to and use of such terms and our response to and use of the canonical texts we are studying. I have provided them with a brief summary of the new historicism, reader response, Marxism, and feminism as approaches that have significantly altered our interpretations of literary texts. I have also distributed a questionnaire I created, "Reading in the Context of a Personal Economy," which was inspired by Barbara Herrnstein Smith's *Contingencies of Value* and which asks students to consider the effect of their race, class, ethnicity, and gender on their responses to a short poem; I frequently use Claude McKay's "If We Must Die." For this activity, I divide students into groups of four, since smaller groups allow them to talk freely about their personal economies. When we reconvene to discuss our findings, students are usually surprised to discover that their responses to various texts are, at least partially, socially constructed. I then ask students to keep the sheet and use it as the basis for a page of written responses to various texts throughout the course.

When we begin our discussion of *The Great Gatsby*, we discuss these written responses to the novel, and students usually see a pattern that emerges as class and gender lines quickly become apparent (there is typically some difference in how various ethnic groups respond to the novel as well). Some students sympathize or identify with Gatsby; they know from personal experience what it is to be denied participation in a social setting or relationship because of poverty and what it means to be the child of immigrants who have a limited understanding of their children's reality. These students frequently find fault with Daisy for not honoring what they view as a romantic pledge. They see nothing wrong with Gatsby's methods, because they accept him as a man who is willing to do anything for love. That his hard work isn't always legal does not seem to interfere with their ability to admire him. Others see Gatsby as a con man who deserves exactly what he gets. Only a few spend much time worrying about Myrtle's death or Daisy's acquiescence to Tom's demands, and these few are usually women.

This first discussion serves as a great introduction for helping students recognize what aspects of the text are most engaging or troubling for them and how this response is tied to their positions as readers. From this recognition, I can easily discuss the critical response to the novel and its variation since its publication, drawing on Frances Kerr's succinct summary of that history. I then use students' reactions to shape their homework for our next meeting, giving them individual assignments that require reading either a feminist essay, an essay about the role of women in the 1920s, an essay that looks at the class struggle of the period, or an essay that deals with feminists' attempts to regender the novel's literary assessment. My list for these assignments keeps evolving as work in the field continues to develop, and usually some zealous student provides me with welcome additions. I often assign chapters of books, such as

Rachel Blau DuPlessis's *Reading beyond the Ending*, Ann Douglas's *Terrible Honesty*, and Nancy Milford's and Linda Wagner-Martin's biographies of Zelda Fitzgerald.

In the next class, students meet briefly in groups that are loosely based on the outside reading they have been assigned (sometimes there are two groups looking at the same aspect). They present their findings to the class as a whole, explaining how the new information they gained in their reading has altered or deepened their response to the novel. I insist that they use passages from the novel to demonstrate exactly what they mean by this difference in interpretation. I usually ask one group who has read essays focused on considerations of class to begin the discussion by pointing out the distinct challenge that money poses for American novelists; earlier readings have invariably convinced students that as a nation we have clung to the dream of success and made wealth its chief symbol, even as we have declared ourselves a classless society that welcomes the poor. I sometimes remind them that William James called "the exclusive worship of the bitch-goddess Success" our national disease and that this "disease" followed logically from the Protestant ethic that "instructed men to lay up wealth for the greater glory of God" (qtd. in Lynn 248). The good Puritan cultivated monetary success in this life as a sign that he would be welcome in the next. Students are quick to acknowledge that this fusion of materialism and religion is at the core of American values and praise Fitzgerald's perceptive portrayal of this amalgam.

My students who are first-generation Americans or immigrants have much to offer in this discussion and can easily connect many of these ideals and assumptions with the closing images of the novel. Like the "Dutch sailors," their parents see America as "a fresh, green breast of [a] new world" and have held their breaths "in the presence of this continent" (180). Their parents sometimes fail to recognize the difficulties that their children encounter in this "new world"— the American educational system and its requirement to speak English—and yet still have great reverence for the country that they feel will offer their children a chance at success, often without analyzing what sacrifices are required to attain material measures of success.

After this discussion, students begin to understand and appreciate Fitzgerald's symbolism. They connect the "green breast of [a] new world" with the green cards that Daisy distributes to be used as tokens for kisses (104) and with the green of money and the quasi-religious treatment of materialism in American society. They see that West Egg and East Egg have parallels in east Los Angeles and west Los Angeles, even though east and west have different connotations in the Los Angeles economy; and they understand the role that class plays in a woman's ability to function as a symbol of success through Fitzgerald's use of Daisy's voice "full of money" (120). They see that in the world of the novel, a woman's desirability depends on her ability to be "[h]igh in a white palace the king's daughter, the golden girl. . . ." (120; ellipsis in orig.). Occasionally, a student will have read a Horatio Alger novel and will report on the similarities between its values and those that shape Gatsby's goals and life. I usually mention that romantic love is also a high priority for Americans and suggest that we can see the fusion of the values of love and money in the novels of Henry James (*The American, The Portrait of a Lady*, and *The Golden Bowl*) and Theodore Dreiser (*Sister Carrie* and *An American Tragedy*). Some students recognize that the role of women—as a result of this fusion of love, money, and success—has become a subject for American writers as we have moved through the twentieth century, pointing to Kate Chopin's *The Awakening*, Willa Cather's *The Song of the Lark*, and Edith Wharton's *The Custom of the Country* and *Summer*.

Looking at how Daisy becomes the embodiment of the bitch-goddess success is our next step, and students who have read recent feminist essays on the female body as sign have no trouble making connections to Fitzgerald's portrayal of women. Using theoretical work such as that found in Judith Butler's *Bodies That Matter* and *Gender Trouble* as a starting point, students point out how Daisy is objectified throughout the novel, and their interpretation of Myrtle's torn breast (137) becomes much more perceptive. They seem more aware of the artificiality of the virgin/whore dichotomy that is reflected in the characters of Daisy and Myrtle, and they are able to recognize that Daisy's social class is the main difference between her position and Myrtle's. They are also able to identify how class works in the construction of female identity and how society ostracizes women who break societal norms. They recognize that Daisy's money saves her life and her reputation and that Myrtle's lack of such resources is connected to her death.

Next we discuss what is—and is not—acceptable female behavior in the world of Fitzgerald's novel. Students frequently feel that Daisy is a woman without a conscience, but looking at the few opportunities that exist for women of the period makes it clear that she has little choice but to stay with Tom and to lie about her role in Myrtle's death. They see that Fitzgerald's women are trapped because their very desirability depends on their inaccessibility: if they capitulate, they inevitably lose their charm. Yet if they do not accept a suitor who carefully follows all the prescribed social rules, they appear cruel and fickle. Both human and abstract, Daisy is the bitch-goddess in the flesh. Fitzgerald makes her loss of innocence symbolize the loss of moral innocence in the American experience.

Students notice that Fitzgerald gives Daisy all the popular trappings of the American dream. She always wears white, and behind her is the American flag or a red-and-white Georgian colonial mansion. She also wraps bandages for the Red Cross. These observations usually lead students back to a consideration of the text, especially the lines that link Daisy's appeal to her wealth, her "indiscreet voice" that is "full of money" (120). Now they can see that this affluence gives her power over Gatsby, that this power is constructed by America's value system, and that it prevents him from doing what he had intended: "to take what he could and go" and continue pursuing his goals and dreams (149). They recognize that Daisy's wealth still renders her inaccessible and, therefore, desirable, whereas similar actions by a woman of a lower economic class would damage her value. Many students persist in blaming Daisy for her final indifference to Gatsby, until someone talks about the ways in which she has been shaped by patriarchal values.

Some students point out that Fitzgerald seems to incorporate the female perspective faithfully and speculate that he is drawing on Zelda's experiences; students who have read Milford's or Wagner-Martin's biography of Zelda point out that he did, in fact, occasionally publish some of her stories under his name and incorporate her writing into his work. They see this method as preferable to male-imagined experience because it validates women's experience and voice—even though the transcriber of that experience and voice is male. Fitzgerald's sensitivity to women's experience, they argue, is largely responsible for the novel's accurate depiction of female gender roles in the 1920s and for the novel's appeal to female readers.

Students often point out that the men in the novel are just as restricted by gender expectations as the women are. They suggest that Gatsby, Tom, and Nick seem confined to roles that prevent them from finding individual meaning and goals in life and that men discover that devotion is not enough to ensure a successful love relationship. They can see that men seem required to have money, to dress well, and to cultivate a charming manner for purposes of ingratiation, unless, of course, they have the power that Tom's money provides. My students usually stress that money is the essential ingredient in the formula for male success, because it is money that grants men the opportunity to develop the finer qualities of their nature and affords them the proper stature to make their advances acceptable or make other societal rules inconsequential. Tom uses his power in an openly forceful, and often boorish, manner. My students see him as the embodiment of the patriarchy: wealthy, physically strong, and capable of exercising the "paternal contempt" in his voice (7). Portrayed as brutish and hulking, he is the most powerful and successful man in the novel—and the most cruel. The irony of his influence and power seems to be, students suggest, Fitzgerald's wry comment on the speciousness of patriarchal expectations for men.

Near the end of our discussions, some students move toward a Marxist reading of *Gatsby* and see romance in the novel as a mutually agreeable business exchange. They suggest that men and women look at people as they would any other item that they intend to buy, trying to get the best value for what they can afford. If men are conditioned to be attracted to that which is already out of their reach, then they are compelled to enhance their market value and increase their romantic purchasing power. With this understanding, students recognize that Gatsby's kissing Daisy and leading her to believe that his financial status is greater than it is constitutes a serious breach of a tacit social contract. Gatsby's actions falsely signify that he is "fully able to take care of her," and he therefore takes her "under false pretenses" (149). This discussion also helps students understand the importance of Gatsby's colossal house and over-the-top wardrobe. The guided tour of his grounds that he gives Daisy when they meet again seems less foolish and ostentatious to them; it becomes clear that Gatsby is demonstrating that he now understands his proper role in a patriarchy and is capable of fulfilling it.

At this point in the course, students are quick to recognize that Tom's set of commodities offers him great marketing power in this bazaar of love, despite his obvious flaws. If love is a commodity, it becomes a prize awarded to the winner of the bargaining contest. Under such guidelines, men's love becomes a form of self-love that is temporarily projected on a love object, and women must never allow their hearts to lead without investigating their suitors' bank accounts. Students sometimes suggest that when there is no longer the challenge of a barrier to overcome, each participant seeks love with a new person who is tantalizingly out of reach, a ghost of the seeker's imagination who, in Fitzgerald's words, breathes "dreams like air" (161). Some students suggest that Daisy's dalliance with Gatsby renews Tom's interest in her precisely because he recognizes that she may not be entirely his possession. Others argue that Tom simply cannot accept losing her to a man who does not measure up to patriarchal standards.

Before our final meeting, I ask students to choose an essay to read and share with the class, drawing from a broad range of critical and theoretical articles. This list currently includes feminist theoretical work by Butler, Elaine Showalter, Judith Fetterley, Lois Tyson (*Critical Theory Today*), and Sue Ellen Case; approaches to modernism by Suzanne Clark and Rita Felski; more recent critical interpretations of the novel by Greg Forter, Linda C. Pelzer, and Kerr; historical approaches by John Lukacs and Robert Seguin; and Sarah Beebe Fryer's book-length analysis of Fitzgerald's women characters (*Fitzgerald's New Women*). This assignment enables students to uncover the supposedly unbiased ideology of many critical interpretations that treat the novel's universality, while it still encourages them to acknowledge Fitzgerald's unusual ability to "see" and capture the gender reality of the 1920s. Students are often surprised at how such critics have failed to look at the novel's events through the eyes of Daisy, Myrtle, or Jordan.

Even though we do not focus on a particular school of feminist thought, my approach is rooted in American feminist theory. While students use traditional close reading to understand the position of women in the novel, the essays they read and share with the class provide them with the necessary historical and theoretical tools to integrate feminism with a variety of other approaches as well. Finally, I ask students to compare Fitzgerald's treatment of women with other portrayals of the period and other portrayals in the literature we have been reading throughout the course. These texts vary, but usually include Wharton's *The Age of Innocence*; Cather's *A Lost Lady*, which Fitzgerald had described as "one of the best books of the fall" (qtd. in Wagner-Martin 78); Dreiser's *An American Tragedy*; and Ernest Hemingway's *The Sun Also Rises* or *Men without Women*. Students usually conclude that Fitzgerald is much more sympathetic to women's issues than they had originally thought. While we do not spend time looking at the gender of Fitzgerald's prose, I suspect that endeavor would be a welcome addition to our discussion of the novel.

Because I believe that students learn more when they participate in scholarly inquiry, I continue to revise this series of research activities to allow students to use more active and cooperative learning techniques. I carry this approach over into their writing assignment as well. Using both the Internet and a traditional library, students locate materials that look at women's increased participation in society as a result of World War I and women's suffrage. They also investigate the icon of the flapper, birth control as it existed in America at that time, the increasing importance of women in American popular culture (such as sports, the burgeoning film industry, and music), and regional differences with regard to women's roles, which allows them to see that Daisy's being southern is essential to her character. Because I want students to develop expertise in finding and evaluating their sources, I do not provide a list of texts to consult for this part of the project. (Douglas's *Terrible Honesty* is, however, an excellent resource that covers many of these aspects.) Without this additional information, students are apt to misinterpret many of the distinctions Fitzgerald draws among Myrtle, Daisy, and Jordan. They can then incorporate this material into their final paper, which they can choose to write as an individual or collaborative effort and which is often interdisciplinary.

Positioned at an interdisciplinary site of traditional criticism, contemporary theory, gender, and class, this feminist approach is not particularly innovative. Yet it helps students recognize that *The Great Gatsby* calls into question the ideologies and assumptions about gender roles that were prevalent during Fitzgerald's time. In this way, I can encourage students to view the text not merely as a cautionary tale but as a complicated social document that is always engaged with its history—at times contentious, as when Nick relates "what foul dust floated in the wake of [Gatsby's] dreams" (2)—and at times acquiescent, as when Daisy says "that's the best thing a girl can be in this world, a beautiful little fool" (17).

Studying the novel as if it is engaged in a dialogue with the reality it presents allows students to accomplish two important goals: it leads them into the past, looking at differences between their assumptions about women's roles during the period and the historical reality, and it returns them to the text itself so that they can distinguish between what the text says and what they assume it should say about gender roles. They come away from the class able to appreciate Fitzgerald's ability to perceive and depict the fissures in the social fabric of his time. They no longer blame him for his treatment of women; rather, they praise him for his unblinking look at the disastrous effect of socially constructed gender roles that destroy the individualism of men and women—and their relationships.

Defining one's identity is a problem that most of my students face in a very particular way since they are often torn between two sets of values: that of contemporary Los Angeles and that of their homes, which is still rooted in the land from which their parents emigrated. The west and east sides of Los Angeles offer other differences: the former is a world of movie stars and wealth; the latter is the world inhabited by most of my students, a world of immigrants, poverty, and gang activity. Perhaps these current realities of my students' lives make the men more empathetic with Gatsby. But by the end of our inquiry, many are willing to join the women in the class in sympathizing with Daisy and Myrtle as well. I am still working on Jordan, but I suspect that that may be what Fitzgerald intended. His presentation of this new woman as the athlete who dons the role of cheater and adopts the worst of patriarchal drives to win at any cost is perhaps intentionally ambivalent. Yet my students' investigation shows that this attitude clearly reflects the general response to such women at the time. To have written Jordan more sympathetically would have been, as one student pointed out, to render the novel unbelievable. This depiction, they decide, makes it important to continue to read and study *The Great Gatsby* as we move through the next century of its influence on American letters.

Fiction and Film: Teaching Aspects of Narrative in *The Great Gatsby*

Danuta Fjellestad and Eleanor Wikborg

More and more students first meet the classics on the screen. Indeed some of their—and our—most vivid memories of a work may be cinematic. At the same time, film adaptations of novels—particularly of complex novels—are frequently accused of simplification. In our experience, it is these very simplifications (omissions, condensations, and alterations) that may help students understand *The Great Gatsby* better. A study of the formal solutions that the two media use to tell the same story—the degree of sameness being one of the central cruxes— has the effect of diverting students' attention from the story to the discourse, to the how of representation rather than the what.

Cinema and literature are two different art forms, each with its specificity, opportunities, and limitations, but both are narrative forms and thus lend them- selves to the type of analysis developed by Seymour Chatman, Shlomith Rimmon-Kenan, Gerard Genette, and others. Moreover, we believe that plac- ing the text in the context of a medium with which students are comfortable makes them aware of how narrative strategies mediate ethical and ideological issues.

When teaching *The Great Gatsby* in the freshman course Introduction to Literature, we ask the students to view the film adaptation of the novel before they read Fitzgerald's text. We use Jack Clayton's 1974 version of the novel (screenplay by Francis Ford Coppola, starring Sam Waterston as Nick Car- raway, Mia Farrow as Daisy Buchanan, and Robert Redford as Jay Gatsby). In this way, students not only satisfy their initial propensity to read for the plot but also see explicitly many of the themes and issues that in the novel emerge only gradually and obliquely. By the time they turn to the book, they have achieved a certain distance from the events of the story, which makes it easier for them to observe the narrative strategies of both text and film. Our emphasis, how- ever, is on the novel; the movie is used as a tool for delving into aspects of Fitzgerald's narrative. For this reason, the film is not subjected to the kind of analysis that would be found in a film studies course.

Given the limited time allotted to work with the novel, we focus on only a few issues—primarily the representation of gender and the question of the nar- rative point of view. After a general discussion of the differences in the narra- tive strategies used by the two media forms, we restrict our detailed analysis to the opening passages in the book and the film and to the incident in which Nick confronts Tom Buchanan over Gatsby's death.

First, then, the students view the film, and we start by asking them to make a list of the themes and issues that seemed central. We also ask them to respond to their subsequent reading of the novel by writing a list of some main differences that they note between Fitzgerald's text and the movie. We then discuss their observations, focusing on those that allow us to deal with gender issues in the representation of Daisy.

Many students feel that in the movie the visual impact of the love scenes between Daisy and Gatsby, especially those with no dialogue (dancing alone in Gatsby's house, heads together by the swimming pool), activates love clichés that tip the romance over into sentimentality. Although the novel shares this tendency, the experience of a visual overdose of sentimentality may have a distancing effect and change the aesthetic response of the viewer: for some viewers the film resituates Fitzgerald's canonical text into the category of low culture. This issue raises the question of how categories such as classical and popular culture activate different horizons of expectations and set in motion different value systems.

Many students bring up the movie's representation of Daisy. While Daisy's first appearance in the novel is colored above all by the magic Nick feels in her "low, thrilling voice," with its promise of "gay, exciting things" (9), the scene in the film gives the impression that Daisy is a superficial woman. However different, the attribution of magic or silliness to a woman inevitably raises important gender issues.

Students also note that the movie's plotting of Nick's final confrontation with Tom fosters a condemnation of Daisy: Nick's attempt to tell Tom that it was Daisy and not Gatsby who drove the car that killed Myrtle is interrupted by Daisy's entrance into the scene. The image of Daisy glittering in steel blue (rather than the "innocent" white she has always worn before) and chattering about her plans for her new house suggests her total lack of remorse over the deaths she has caused. In the novel, Daisy is absent from this confrontation, a plot decision that makes Tom the primary moral agent. Nick judges both Tom and Daisy as "careless people" (179), but his final interaction is with Tom alone; Nick says, "I couldn't forgive him or like him" (179). The movie version thus helps students see that Fitzgerald has opted to remove Daisy from the novel's scene of moral confrontation.

Daisy's absence from this crucial scene in Fitzgerald's text and the issue of her superficiality versus her magic in the two versions of the opening scene lead us to discuss the representation of gender. We ask, To what degree do the narrative strategies assume women to be incapable of agency? Is the romanticization of women a way of concealing hostility? We recall the scene from the end of the movie in which Gatsby's father points at Daisy's photograph and asks, "Who is this girl?" Nick is shown trying to formulate an answer, but no words emerge. Does his failure to articulate a response suggest that Daisy (and woman in general) is an enigma, a mystery that baffled even Sigmund Freud?

We also discuss a certain ambiguity in the representation of Daisy in both the novel and the film. How are we to interpret her comment, "that's the best thing a girl can be in this world, a beautiful little fool" (17), or her statement (in the movie only) that "rich girls do not marry poor boys" (a phrase the film took from *F. Scott Fitzgerald's Ledger* [170])? By drawing attention to sexist clichés, does Daisy indicate an awareness of herself as a victim of patriarchy? Is she perhaps consciously playing the role of a foolish woman? If so, are her words to be interpreted as an act of subversion?

We continue our discussion of gender, but now in the wider context of the way the film emphasizes the glamour of fabulous wealth. We take a close look at the narrative strategies of the opening sequence in the film, which runs parallel with the printed credits. We show the film sequence on a player that allows us to freeze and to reverse the flow of images. The series of camera shots moves from the abandoned interior of a mansion to the opulent details of a bedroom and finally lingers over the objects on a man's dressing table. The camera shows us several photographs of a beautiful woman framed in silver, and it goes on to display a gold toilet set with the monogram *JG* as well as a watch, two war medals, and, intriguingly, a half-eaten sandwich with a fly crawling on it (at the end of the film we learn that the sandwich has been left there by Gatsby's father).

The gold of the monograms and the silver of the picture frames signal wealth and elegance, while the fly on the unfinished sandwich qualifies the splendor with suggestions of decay and mortality, two leitmotifs both in the movie and the novel. We ask the students to comment on the implications of the film's presentation of Daisy as a face in a series of silver-framed photographs on a man's dressing table along with the other objects. What do the framing and the setting communicate? That the woman is one of several collectable items? Or that right from the start she is made into an icon of wealth and glamorous desirability? This theme is in the novel as well (Nick describes her as a "silver idol" [115], "the golden girl" [120], and a figure "gleaming like silver" [150]), but here, we point out, such an interpretation takes far longer for the reader to form.

We next discuss the effects of the visual impact of film. As Seymour Chatman points out in *Coming to Terms*, camera shots can render pictures of people and settings with a degree of completeness that is simply not practicable in verbal description; "the evocation of detail is incessantly rich" (40), he writes. Chatman's point can also be illustrated by asking students to compare the novel's description of Gatsby's parties with their rendition in the movie. The richness of details in clothing, hair styles, and jewelry in combination with the period music has an immediate effect on the senses that is very different from the effects of the novel. In the movie's opening scene, the camera emphasizes the glamorous objects of Gatsby's dressing table. In the novel's first paragraphs, Nick presents Gatsby to us as "gorgeous," but he immediately links this quality to Gatsby's "heightened sensitivity to the promises of life" (2). Since it is Gatsby's material possessions that dominate the opening scene of the film, their visual effect—at this point in the film—privileges a material over a spiritual interpretation of Gatsby's "greatness."

We now turn to the question of the narrative point of view and the challenge of Nick Carraway as narrator. The cinematic media cannot maintain a first-person point of view other than in brief segments, such as voice-overs. Despite the many shots of Nick that remind us of his role as observer, most of the subjectivity of his narrative voice in the novel disappears in the film. For the most part, the movie follows the conventions of narrative film in that the presence of the camera eye seems to be neutralized to reproduce the so-called natural conditions of human perception and thus creates the illusion of objective reporting.

The camera eye produces only an illusion of neutrality, as pointed out by feminist film theorists and critics (esp. Mulvey; de Lauretis). Far from being objective, they have argued, the camera eye genders the gaze as male. At this point, we introduce the notions of voyeurism and scopophilia (the pleasure of looking), which enables us to link our earlier observations about the representation of Daisy in the film as an object of desire to the issue of the erotic charge of the viewer's gaze. We ask students to consider how the film's gaze positions its viewers, who, after all, are already gendered as male or female. What voyeuristic charge does this positioning imply, especially for women viewers? We then discuss the possibilities of resisting textual manipulation as presented by Judith Fetterley in *The Resisting Reader*.

By now, students have been alerted to the presence of the narrative I/eye in the text, and they are ready to discuss how Nick's judgments steer the reader's response to every aspect of the novel. We search for signs of Nick's angle of vision. In addition to his use of the word "gorgeous" for Gatsby (2), Nick characterizes Tom as a man with a "cruel body" and "arrogant eyes" (7) and Daisy as a woman with a "bright passionate mouth" (9). Nick not only attempts to guide the reader's proper response to characters and events but also indicates by his judgments his own positioning and, ultimately, his own desires. We ask students to reflect on the relation between Nick and Gatsby and on Nick's reasons for presenting Gatsby as a romantic hero. What happens, we ask, when a heterosexual man's gaze alights on a male figure and finds it attractive? What emotional and ideological involvement with the objects of his description does Nick's language imply? Students begin now to notice that Nick is always listening to, eavesdropping on, and watching other characters. Nick appears to be an obsessive voyeur.

The question is, If Nick's gaze constructs the relationship between Myrtle and Tom as tawdry and that between Daisy and Gatsby as chivalric, what does this tell us about Nick? How are his views to be linked to his class, race, and gender? Alerted to Nick's judgments in the text, students soon see how these contradict his earlier claim that he is "inclined to reserve all judgments" (1). Asked to find other examples of inconsistencies in Nick's account of himself, students may identify the passage at the end of chapter 3 in which he boasts of being "one of the few honest people that [he has] ever known" (59), although a few passages earlier we learn that he is dating Jordan at the same time that he is writing love letters to another woman. In the light of such inconsistencies and contradictions, can Nick's judgments and interpretations be trusted? Is he a reliable or an unreliable narrator? In the course of this discussion, we draw on

Wayne Booth's categories of the reliable and unreliable narrator, as presented in his *Rhetoric of Fiction*, as well as the revisions of these categories as suggested in James Phelan's "Reexamining Reality" and Elizabeth Preston's "Implying Authors."

We now return to the beginning of the movie to check its initial representation of Nick. We first see him, dressed in a white suit, ineptly struggling to maneuver a small boat around some impressively large yachts at the same time as we hear his voice telling us of his father's advice to reserve all judgments. In the film, there is no reason to doubt the accuracy of the rendition of what we see. Indeed, there is no discernable discrepancy between what the voice-over says on the few occasions that we hear it and the larger implied meaning of the movie. The question of Nick's reliability simply does not emerge in Clayton's adaptation of *The Great Gatsby*.

There are many other themes and issues raised by Fitzgerald's novel that can be fruitfully approached through its film adaptation. A starting point for a discussion of the theme of violence may be a comparison of the scene in the film in which the camera lingers on the blood trickling down Myrtle's face after Tom has hit her with the novel's far more muted reference to "bloody towels upon the bathroom floor" (37). To introduce class issues, it is useful to show how the movie juxtaposes the scene where Daisy bursts into tears at the beauty of Gatsby's shirts with a shot of Myrtle delightedly rubbing her cheek on Tom's gift of a silk robe (an invention of the movie). These scenes suggest gender parallels between Daisy and Myrtle despite the two women's different social standing.

Noteworthy also are the scenes in the movie in which Nick's absence is pronounced. He does not witness the fight between George Wilson and Myrtle or the conversation between Wilson and Michaelis after Myrtle's death; neither is he present when Daisy dances with Gatsby in his uniform in his mansion. These absences raise the question of the source and limits of the narrator's knowledge of facts in the novel. The kind of discussion these and other observations lead to, as well as the depth of theory-informed explanation decided on, depends on the design of the course in which *The Great Gatsby* is taught, the teacher's interests, and the students' backgrounds.

Using Music to Teach *The Great Gatsby*

Anthony Berret

Classics attract many cultural objects and interpretations and draw energy and meaning from them. *The Great Gatsby* encompasses motifs that range from sections of the country to times of the year and classes of people, from automobiles and alcohol to sports and music. These motifs form image patterns in the novel, but they also reflect and interpret the culture surrounding it. Music figures prominently in *Gatsby* because it plays in the background of the many party scenes and because F. Scott Fitzgerald used it to define the spirit of the times. He called the 1920s the Jazz Age. The songs in *Gatsby* also bring other artworks into its sphere of influence—other music, another novel, a play, a show, and a film. Since *Gatsby* names or quotes specific songs, and since these songs are accessible from various sources, music offers a convenient way to approach the novel through an outside cultural influence. Moreover, as an art form that is different yet akin to literature, music permits analysis by some of the same methods used for analyzing literature.

Sheet music provides words and music to the songs cited in *Gatsby* and should be available in either separate pieces or collections at local stores or libraries. Some collections, called fake books, contain a thousand or more songs. *The Greatest Legal Fake Book of All Time* has three of the songs mentioned in *Gatsby*. Once secured, this sheet music can be played and sung live in class by a student or teacher. Such a performance can reconstruct both the novel and its times since, in the early 1920s, sheet music sales (and therefore home performances) still matched record sales in determining hit songs, and six of the seven songs in *Gatsby* are performed live, four of them by amateurs.

Phonograph recordings exist for all the songs in *Gatsby* and might be available through a 78 rpm record collector or at an antique shop or used-record store, where early recordings of the songs or later reprints on LPs or cassettes may be in stock. Each song has also been recorded or reprinted on more than one compact disc. Both "The Sheik of Araby" (78) and "Ain't We Got Fun" (95) appear on the CD *The Roaring Twenties* (Proarte), Bix Beiderbeck plays "The Love Nest" (94) on *Riverfront Shuffle* (Naxos), Paul Whiteman conducts "Three O'Clock in the Morning" (108) on *Linger Awhile* (Asv Living Era), Alberta Hunter sings "Beale Street Blues" (151) on *Beale Street Blues* (TKO Coll. Blues), and the Irish tenor John McCormack does "The Rosary" (170) or "My Rosary" on *Celtic Gospel*, volume 1 (Platinum Disc). All these are period recordings and reflect the musical style of the early 1920s. The "Wedding March" (127) is from Felix Mendelssohn's *A Midsummer Night's Dream*. Recordings of these songs by other artists can be found in catalogs or online searches in retail stores. Several versions of each song in *Gatsby* can be found in the iTunes store.

Five songs from the novel appear in the 1974 film of *The Great Gatsby* and on its rentable DVD. The VHS version has a different sound track that includes only one of the songs, "Ain't We Got Fun." Although some of the songs occur at different places in the story in the film than in the novel, the VHS version does play "Ain't We Got Fun" in the same spot it appears in the novel and repeats it in the closing credits. The original sound track of the 1974 film (Paramount Records) contains three of the songs, but it is out of print, has not been produced on CD, and is available only at used-record stores and on eBay.

Sheet music for the songs can also be downloaded for free from the Internet. Duke University's *Historic American Sheet Music* (http://scriptorium.lib.duke .edu/sheetmusic) has "Beale Street Blues" and "The Rosary," and Johns Hopkins University's *Lester S. Levy Collection of Sheet Music* (http://levysheetmusic.mse .jhu.edu) has "The Sheik Of Araby," "The Love Nest," and "Three O'Clock in the Morning." The best site for period recordings of the songs is Scott Alexander's *The Red Hot Jazz Archive* (http://www.redhotjazz.com), which also includes historical introductions along with recording dates and personnel. Among its many possible choices, I recommend "The Sheik of Araby" (Waller, Whiteman), "Ain't We Got Fun" (Benson, Mitchell), "Love Nest" (Hickman), "Three O'Clock in the Morning," and "Beale Street Blues" (Lewis).

Playing the songs in class brings variety to a literature course and includes an art form that students enjoy. In addition, the songs offer glimpses of a world outside the novel and open up a historical approach to literature. Teachers can begin by analyzing the imagery and style of the lyrics and relating them to the scenes in which they appear. Ruth Prigozy sketches Fitzgerald's use of song lyrics to support images, set moods, and comment dramatically on the action (" 'Poor Butterfly' "). Philip Furia studies the poetic qualities of song lyrics, likening them to the traits of modern poetry fragmentation, and the daring juxtapositions of sentiment with wit, colloquialism, and banality. Most helpful for *Gatsby* are Furia's introductory chapter and his chapter on the 1920s; the latter contains a brief analysis of "Ain't We Got Fun" (76–77). The combination of romantic sentiment with wit and colloquialism in these lyrics also characterizes the general style of *Gatsby*. Those who analyze the musical qualities of songs (melody, rhythm, and harmony) find a similar combination, which they express as romance and rag, classical and jazz, or formal and casual. Charles Hamm summarizes these musical features in his chapter " 'It's Only a Paper Moon'; or, The Golden Years of Tin Pan Alley"; Arnold Shaw also gives helpful notes on songs of the time, including some in *Gatsby*.

Since *The Great Gatsby* includes at least one song in each chapter once Gatsby appears on the scene, the novel reflects the structure of a Broadway musical, whose action and dialogue are interspersed with songs. This Broadway quality fits the general tone of the story because Gatsby tries to mix literary types with show people at his parties. An interesting creative project would be to write up one scene and its song as a musical play and present it on stage. Surprisingly, there has been an opera version of *Gatsby*, but no Broadway musical.

"There was music from my neighbor's house through the summer nights" (39): so begins chapter 3 of *Gatsby*, which introduces Gatsby at one of his parties and stages the novel's first musical piece, requested by Gatsby and therefore applicable to him. Nick Carraway keeps his eyes on Gatsby all during the piece. "Vladimir Tostoff's *Jazz History of the World*" (49), a fictional piece, heralds Gatsby's entry and provides an overture for the musical show that the whole book may resemble. Like an overture, it probably includes melodies from many songs and announces the themes of the show. A more elaborate description of this piece in an earlier draft of *Gatsby* names some of the songs (Great Gatsby: A Facsimile 54–56). The theme announced by this piece is a mixture of classical and popular music, blending Carnegie Hall and a fictitious Russian composer with jazz. "Tostoff" could refer to the composer or to jazz, which is "tossed off," or improvised, on the spot. The orchestra carries both classical and jazz instruments—"oboes and trombones and saxophones and viols and cornets and piccolos" (40). The same combination occurs earlier at the party, when a "celebrated tenor had sung in Italian, and a notorious contralto had sung in jazz" (46). Art mirrors the social classes too; the party absorbs both *Follies* girls and "the staid nobility of the countryside" (41, 44). These images can spark a discussion on the classical and the popular. What other images in the novel fit these categories? How do the categories relate to each other? Where does Gatsby stand in relation to them?

Although fictional, *The Jazz History* might have been influenced by actual performances of the time. Darrel Mansell finds in it characteristics of Richard Strauss's *Also Sprach Zarathustra*, which Strauss conducted in a concert tour of America in 1921. The famous fanfare that begins this piece and the figure of the modern superman in the book of Nietzsche from which Strauss drew his title evoke Gatsby. Critics cite Whiteman's *Experiment in Modern Music*, played at the Aeolian Hall in New York on 12 February 1924 and later at Carnegie Hall, as another possible source or model for *The Jazz History* (Breitwieser, "Great Gatsby" 62; Henson 43, 133 n3).[1] This performance took place after the action in *Gatsby*, which is set in 1922, but it came just before Fitzgerald began to write his novel in earnest. The concert also claimed to be a history of jazz and featured George Gershwin playing his *Rhapsody in Blue*, a famous combination of jazz and classical music. Available on the CD *The Birth of* Rhapsody in Blue (MusicMasters), the performance is especially representative in music of what Fitzgerald attempted in his novel.

After hearing from Jordan Baker the story of Gatsby's affair with Daisy five years before and his dream of renewing it, Nick listens to little girls in Central Park singing "The Sheik of Araby" (78). The lyrics of this song add another Eastern image to the East/West pattern that runs through the novel. Students might list examples of this pattern and interpret them and then decide what "The Sheik" adds to their meaning. It certainly brings a foreign, extravagant, backward, and phony aura to Gatsby's pursuits. Talking with Nick earlier, Gatsby calls himself "a young rajah" (65), and Nick sees him as a "turbaned 'character' leaking sawdust" (66). Later, Gatsby dismisses his "caravansary" of servants (114). These Near or Far Eastern images support the song and show the extremity of Gatsby's intents. New York and East Egg and West Egg become Arabia or India. The melody of the song sounds exotic too, with diminished thirds and fifths in the first eight bars of the verses and stress on the sixth tone in the chorus—the note on which the syllables *Sheik, Ar-, -by, love, -sleep,* and *creep* are sung.

"The Sheik of Araby" also leads the reader outside *Gatsby* to E. M. Hull's novel *The Sheik* and to the film based on it, starring Rudolph Valentino; both appeared in 1921 and are celebrated by the song. Teachers can show scenes from the film (available on video and DVD) in class and ask how a modern, aristocratic, and liberated English woman, after venturing into the Algerian desert and being abducted by a sheik, can gradually become enthralled by him. Does this reflect the social forces at work in Daisy's affair with Gatsby?

The two songs in chapter 5, played by the houseguest Klipspringer while Gatsby, Daisy, and Nick relax after a tour of Gatsby's mansion, contrast two moods and styles, the romantic dream of "The Love Nest" and the carefree cynicism of "Ain't We Got Fun" (94, 95). The songs bring out the conflicting themes of Gatsby and Daisy's relationship: love and money, dream and suspicion. After pointing out examples of these conflicting themes in the lyrics to the songs, teachers can ask students to give further instances of this conflict in other scenes and images of the novel. Furia studies this conflict in American popular songs, and it applies to *Gatsby* as well and helps make *Gatsby* a modern novel, not just a conventional romance.

"The Love Nest" has a cozy feel, with notes on the beat and on the chords or falling easily down the scale. "Ain't We Got Fun" also puts notes right on the beat, but with a forced and mechanical feel that supports the cynicism; and the stops before "Ain't" and after "dear" interrupt the flow and arouse suspicions about the couple's complacency. "The Love Nest" appeared in the Broadway show *Mary* (1920), which, like *Gatsby*, is set on Long Island and treats the conflict between love and money, especially concerning houses. The theater collection of the New York Public Library for the Performing Arts, at Lincoln Center, houses librettos for old Broadway shows. One can also find a plot summary of a show in Gerald Bordman's *American Musical Theatre: A Chronicle*.

In chapter 6, Gatsby and Daisy reach a kind of fulfillment—they dance together at his party (105), but he fears that "[s]he didn't like it" (109). The song "Three O'Clock in the Morning" plays inside the house as Daisy leaves, possibly the song that she sings along with "in a husky, rhythmic whisper" (108). This song supports a pattern of time images to which students can be asked to add further examples. The lyrics and the bridge—a melody of hour chimes—express weariness and finality, a time too late yet too early. Because of rising suspicions, Gatsby and Daisy must soon face a showdown, with Tom, at least.

"Three O'Clock in the Morning" was recorded by Whiteman, whose orchestra played at the Palais Royal, a club on Broadway, and at high-class parties. He exemplifies the kind of composed and arranged jazz, sophisticated jazz, that Fitzgerald probably heard most. His recordings provide fitting background music for Fitzgerald's works in general. Other period bandleaders in this category include Ted Lewis, Vincent Lopez, and Joseph C. Smith. "Three O'Clock in the Morning" also appeared in another type of Broadway show, the revue, specifically *The Greenwich Village Follies* of 1921. Black-and-white figures danced to the song before a blue setting to evoke a fin de siècle decadence (Bordman 411), a theme that also applies to the scene in *Gatsby*.

A showdown finally occurs in chapter 7, at the Plaza Hotel in New York. Gatsby, Tom, Daisy, Nick, and Jordan rent a suite and hear Mendelssohn's "Wedding March" playing at a marriage ceremony downstairs (127). The piece stirs up memories of Tom and Daisy's wedding and eventually causes a confrontation between Tom and Gatsby about Daisy's love. Perhaps the "jazz" that follows the ceremony downstairs echoes this conflict and discord (128). (Smith directed the house orchestra at the Plaza, and so his recordings show the kind of jazz played there.) Unlike most weddings, which play Wagner's march for the processional and end with Mendelssohn's march, this one seems to begin with Mendelssohn. Did Fitzgerald intend to shuffle time here, having a wedding end before it began, as he would later do with the title of a short story collection, *Taps at Reveille*? Or did he want the reader to recall that this march is part of Mendelssohn's *A Midsummer Night's Dream*, incidental music to accompany Shakespeare's play? The word *mid-summer* appears twice in *Gatsby*, once in the scene when Gatsby and Daisy meet again (92; see also 57), and Daisy watches for "the longest day in the year" (11). Shakespeare's play operates on a contrast between town (Athens) and forest (where strange things happen, mainly to correct a bad marriage arrangement). Do the New York / Long Island contrast and love themes in *Gatsby* echo this?

Chapter 8 describes the aftermath of the hit-and-run death of Myrtle Wilson. It also recounts the early scenes of Gatsby and Daisy's meetings and of his departure for the war. The delay in his return and the nervous excitement of the postwar years cause Daisy to seek some security by marrying Tom. "Beale Street Blues" (151) expresses the excitement of this time and represents a step back from the sophisticated jazz of Whiteman or Smith. But it does not go too far back, because it was composed, arranged, and published in sheet music, not "sung by the blind man on the corner" as the lyrics say. Nonetheless, W. C. Handy, its African American composer and lyricist, tried to capture the original style and sentiment of the blues sung on the street. A brief survey of his career can give students a more authentic picture of the racial origins of the blues and jazz. The song itself shows the complex mixture of emotions that the blues evokes— sadness, longing, protest, sarcasm, and despair. A similar unsettling mixture of freedom, wildness, and instability in postwar America, when jazz and blues became nationally recognized by recordings, causes Daisy to stop waiting for Gatsby and marry Tom. The blues remains strong today, having almost classical stature, and students can study it as contemporary music and a key influence on jazz and rock. They could also analyze how and why these musical forms from African American culture have been so popular and expressive for mainstream listeners.

The last song in *Gatsby*, "The Rosary," could serve as Gatsby's funeral song in chapter 9. Referring to love, devotion, and the cross, yet whistled by a Jewish gangster who elects not to attend the funeral, it brings out the ironies of Gatsby's life (170). It is semiclassical rather than popular or jazzy, but the chromatic notes of the melody lean toward sentimentality. It also fits other religious images in the novel—the eyes of Doctor Eckleburg (159–60) and Nick's imagining Gatsby a "son of God . . . [who] must be about His Father's business" (98). When Fitzgerald first planned the novel that would become *Gatsby,* he set it back in the late nineteenth century and gave its hero a Catholic background. All that remains of this plan is Fitzgerald's short story "Absolution" (available in *Short Stories* 259–72). Could the adolescent boy's experience in this story, especially with its religious conflicts, lead to the life of a man like Gatsby?

A musical approach to *The Great Gatsby* in the classroom opens the novel to the music of the 1920s, an innovative and influential art form that defined the decade. This approach leads to other period artifacts related to the music—a novel, a show, a play, and a film. The songs, with their images of place, time, and religion, support the image patterns of the book, and the mixture of sentiment and sauciness in their style characterizes not only this book but modernist literature in general. A musical approach also provides interdisciplinary study and affords an opportunity to invite a member of the music or popular culture department to visit a literature class and discuss the relations between the two art forms. Studying songs in connection with a major work of fiction can add to the songs' value and meaning. Gilbert Seldes, a good friend of Fitzgerald and an appreciative reviewer of *Gatsby*, supported the value of popular art forms in his book *The Seven Lively Arts*, published just a year before *Gatsby*. Chapters 3, 4, and 5 of Seldes's book treat popular songs, ragtime, and jazz and refer to some of the songs cited in *Gatsby*. Seldes may have inspired Fitzgerald to incorporate songs as signs of the novelty and exuberance of the times.

NOTE

1. Henson gives an excellent study of class and race in *The Jazz History* scene and in the music of *Gatsby*.

NOTES ON CONTRIBUTORS

Jonathan N. Barron is associate professor of English at the University of Southern Mississippi. He is coeditor of *Jewish American Poetry*, *Roads Not Taken: Rereading Robert Frost*, and *New Formalist Poets* and editor of the *Robert Frost Review*. He is working on a history of the media and poetry in America.

Anthony Berret, SJ, is associate professor of English at Saint Joseph's University in Philadelphia. He is author of *Mark Twain and Shakespeare: A Cultural Legacy* and has published articles on Toni Morrison and F. Scott Fitzgerald. His current project is a book on the function of music in Fitzgerald's works.

Robert Beuka is associate professor of English at Bronx Community College, City University of New York. He is author of *SuburbiaNation: Reading Suburban Landscape in Twentieth-Century American Fiction and Film* and is editor of the *F. Scott Fitzgerald Society Newsletter*. He is working on a book project for Camden House entitled "American Icon: Fitzgerald's *The Great Gatsby* in Critical and Cultural Context."

Ted Billy is professor and chair of English at Saint Mary's College in Notre Dame, Indiana. He is editor of *Critical Essays on Joseph Conrad*, author of *A Wilderness of Words: Closure and Disclosure in Conrad's Short Fiction*, and coeditor of *A Joseph Conrad Companion*. He is working on a book on nineteenth-century American gothic fiction.

Stephen Brauer is associate professor of English and associate dean for first-year programs at St. John Fisher College. His articles on American literature have appeared in *Working Papers on the Web*, *F. Scott Fitzgerald Review*, *CEA Critic*, and *American Quarterly*. His current book project is titled "Criminality and the Modern: American Culture in the 1920s and 1930s."

Jackson R. Bryer is professor emeritus of English at the University of Maryland. He is cofounder and president of the F. Scott Fitzgerald Society and coeditor of the *F. Scott Fitzgerald Review*. Among the books on Fitzgerald he has written, edited, or coedited are *F. Scott Fitzgerald in the Twenty-First Century*; *Dear Scott, Dearest Zelda: The Love Letters of F. Scott and Zelda Fitzgerald*; *New Essays on F. Scott Fitzgerald's Neglected Stories*; *The Short Stories of F. Scott Fitzgerald: New Approaches in Criticism*; *The Critical Reputation of F. Scott Fitzgerald: A Bibliographical Study, Supplement One through 1981*; and *The Critical Reputation of F. Scott Fitzgerald: A Bibliographical Study*.

Kirk Curnutt is professor of English at Troy University, Montgomery. He is author of *Wise Economics: Brevity and Storytelling in American Short Stories*, *Ernest Hemingway and the Expatriate Modernist Movement*, and *Alienated-Youth Fiction* and editor of *The Critical Response to Gertrude Stein* and *A Historical Guide to F. Scott Fitzgerald*. His essays on Fitzgerald and other American writers have appeared in *F. Scott Fitzgerald Review*, *Critique*, *Journal of Modern Literature*, and *College Literature* and in *F. Scott Fitzgerald in the Twenty-First Century*, and *French Connections: Hemingway and Fitzgerald Abroad*. His most recent works are *The Cambridge Introduction to F. Scott Fitzgerald*, *Coffee with Hemingway*, and *Breathing Out the Ghost: A Novel*.

Marilyn Elkins is professor of English at California State University, Los Angeles. She is author of *Metamorphosizing the Novel: Kay Boyle's Narrative Innovations* and editor of *Critical Essays on Kay Boyle* and *August Wilson: A Casebook*. She has published essays on Hemingway, Boyle, and Evelyn Scott and on pedagogy. Her current book project is "The Writer as a Cultural Icon of American Modernism."

Cecilia Konchar Farr is professor of English and women's studies at the College of Saint Catherine. She is the author of *Reading Oprah: How Oprah's Book Club Changed the Way America Reads* and editor of *The Reflective Woman Reader*. She has published essays on Hemingway and Martha Gelhorn, Thoreau, Melville, Henry Roth, and Cynthia Ozick. She is coediting a volume, "The Oprah Effect: Critical Essays on Oprah's Book Club."

Jonathan P. Fegley is associate professor of English at Middle Georgia College. He has given papers on Fitzgerald at international conferences in Hempstead, Vevey, Saint Paul, Asheville, Princeton, and Paris. He is working on the article "Hemingway's Dialogic Model."

Danuta Fjellestad is professor of American literature at Uppsala University in Sweden. She is author of *Eros, Logos, and (Fictional) Masculinity*, coauthor of *Reading Texts: An Introduction to Strategies of Interpretation*, and coeditor of *Criticism in the Twilight Zone: Postmodern Perspectives on Literature and Politics* and *Authority Matters: Rethinking the Theory and Practice of Authorship*. She is working on a book, "Masters and Monsters: Intellectual Self-Fashioning in American Autobiography."

Janet Giltrow is professor of English at the University of British Columbia. She is editor of *Academic Writing, Academic Reading*, and *Introduction to Academic Writing*. She has published essays on Fitzgerald, Anita Brookner, Kiran Nagarkar, and Antonine Mailler. Her current projects include a book on theories of linguistic type and instance, work on judicial reasons as a genre, and a coedited collection on linguistic, pragmatic, rhetorical, and literary theories of genre, applied to computer-mediated communication.

Peter L. Hays is professor emeritus of English at the University of California, Davis, and author of *Teaching Hemingway's* The Sun Also Rises. His essays on Fitzgerald have appeared in *Fitzgerald/Hemingway Annual*, *Southern Folklore Quarterly*, *Edith Wharton Newsletter*, *Studies in the Humanities*, *F. Scott Fitzgerald Review*, and *Études Anglaises* and in the books *Hemingway in Our Time* and *New Essays on F. Scott Fitzgerald's Neglected Stories*.

Pearl James is assistant professor of English at the University of Kentucky. Her edition, "Picture This! Reading World War I Posters," is forthcoming. She has published essays on Cather, Faulkner, and Fitzgerald. She is working on a book on World War I and American modernism.

Heidi M. Kunz is associate professor of English at Randolph College and serves as board administrator of the F. Scott Fitzgerald Society. Her essay on "The Last of the Belles" appeared in *New Essays on F. Scott Fitzgerald's Neglected Stories*. She currently has two research interests: maritime Fitzgerald and the cultural phenomenon of Maria Mitchell.

Veronica Makowsky is vice provost for undergraduate education at the University of Connecticut, Storrs. She is the author of *Susan Glaspell's Century of American Women* and *Caroline Gordon: A Biography* and the editor of R. P. Blackmur's *Studies in Henry James* and of Blackmur's *Henry Adams*. She has published essays on Fitzgerald and Faulkner, Glaspell, Kaye Gibbons, Edith Wharton, Stark Young, Walker Percy, and Eudora Welty. She is editor emerita of *MELUS*.

Kim Moreland is professor of English at George Washington University. She is author of *The Medievalist Impulse in American Literature: Twain, Adams, Fitzgerald, and Hemingway* and of essays on Fitzgerald, Hemingway, Adams, Twain, Sherwood Anderson, and Jack London. She serves on the editorial board of the *F. Scott Fitzgerald Review*. She is working on the fiction of Martha Gellhorn.

Michael Nowlin is professor of English at the University of Victoria. He is the author of *F. Scott Fitzgerald's Racial Angles and the Business of Literary Greatness* and the editor of Broadview editions of *The Great Gatsby* and Edith Wharton's *The Age of Innocence*. His essays on several twentieth-century American writers, including Fitzgerald, Wharton, Ralph Ellison, and Toni Morrison, have appeared in *American Literature*, *Arizona Quarterly*, the *Journal of American Studies*, *African American Review*, and *College Literature*.

James Phelan is Distinguished Professor of English at Ohio State University, Columbus. He is author of *Experiencing Fiction: Judgments, Progressions, and the Rhetorical Theory of Narrative*; *Living to Tell about It: A Rhetoric and Ethics of Character Narration*; *Narrative as Rhetoric: Technique, Audiences, Ethics, Ideology*; *Reading People, Reading Plots: Character, Progression, and the Interpretation of Narrative*; *Worlds from Words: A Theory of Language in Fiction*; and *Beyond the Tenure Track: Fifteen Months in the Life of an English Professor*. He is the editor of *Reading Narrative: Form, Ethics, Ideology* and coeditor of the Blackwell *Companion to Narrative Theory* and *Understanding Narrative*. He is the editor of *Narrative*, the journal of the Society for the Study of Narrative Literature. He is preparing books on the twentieth-century American novel and on contested concepts in narrative theory.

Deborah Davis Schlacks is professor of English at the University of Wisconsin, Superior. She is author of *American Dream Visions: Chaucer's Surprising Influence on F. Scott Fitzgerald* and of essays on Meridel Le Sueur and Fitzgerald. She is working on an article on Fitzgerald and ethnicity.

Mark Shipman is associate professor of English at Tarleton State University. He presented a paper on Fitzgerald's "Crazy Sunday" at the International Fitzgerald Centennial Conference in Princeton. His current research interests include Arthur Miller's *The Misfits* and its depiction of the American West and Fitzgerald's treatment of aesthetic matters in his short fiction.

Gail Sinclair is scholar in residence and executive director for the Winter Park Institute at Rollins College. Her essays and reviews have appeared or are scheduled to appear in the *F. Scott Fitzgerald Newsletter*, *F. Scott Fitzgerald Review*, and *Hemingway Review* and in *Hemingway's Women: Female Critics and the Female Voice in Hemingway*, *Hemingway and War*, and *Teaching* A Farewell to Arms. She is coediting "Key West Hemingway."

David Stouck is professor of English at Simon Fraser University. He is author of *Willa Cather's Imagination* and of biographies of Ethel Wilson and Sinclair Ross; editor of a scholarly edition of Cather's *O Pioneers!*; author of an essay on Fitzgerald in *Genre*; and coauthor of essays on Fitzgerald in *Studies in the Novel* and in *F. Scott Fitzgerald in the Twenty-First Century* and of essays on mode and language in the work of Hawthorne, Cather, and Michael Ondaatje.

Nancy P. VanArsdale is professor of English at East Stroudsburg University of Pennsylvania. Her essay on Fitzgerald's *This Side of Paradise* appeared in *F. Scott Fitzgerald: New Perspectives*. Her research interests include Edith Wharton, George Bernard Shaw, and professional communication. She served on the Curriculum Advisory Board of the *Time Magazine* Education Program, which helped develop print and Web-based resources for teachers of college composition.

James L. W. West III is Edwin Erle Sparks Professor of English at Penn State University, University Park. He is author of *The Making of* This Side of Paradise, *William Styron: A Life*, and *The Perfect Hour: The Romance of F. Scott Fitzgerald and Ginevra King, His First Love*. The general editor of The Cambridge Edition of the Works of F. Scott Fitzgerald, he has edited for the series *This Side of Paradise, Flappers and Philosophers, Trimalchio: An Early Version of* The Great Gatsby, *Tales of the Jazz Age, My Lost City: Personal Essays, 1920–1940, All the Sad Young Men*, and *The Beautiful and the Damned*.

Eleanor Wikborg is professor emerita of English at Stockholm University. She is coauthor of *Reading Texts: An Introduction to Strategies of Interpretation* and *Reading Texts: Teaching Suggestions* and has published work on coherence breaks in student writing. Her latest publications are *The Lover as Father Figure in Eighteenth-Century Women's Fiction* and a coauthored essay on Jane Austen's reception in Sweden.

SURVEY PARTICIPANTS

Jonathan N. Barron, *University of Southern Mississippi*
Anthony Berret, *Saint Joseph's University*
Robert Beuka, *Bronx Community College, City University of New York*
Winifred Farrant Bevilacqua, *University of Turin*
Ted Billy, *Saint Mary's College*
Stephen Brauer, *St. John Fisher College*
Dan Coleman, *Stuyvesant High School, New York, NY*
Robert D. Cowser, *Saint Lawrence University*
Michael Coyle, *Colgate University*
Kirk Curnutt, *Troy University, Montgomery*
Wheeler Winston Dixon, *University of Nebraska, Lincoln*
Marilyn Elkins, *California State University, Los Angeles*
Tabb Farinholt, *Saint Catherine's School*
Cecilia Konchar Farr, *College of Saint Catherine*
Jonathan P. Fegley, *Middle Georgia College*
Danuta Fjellestad, *Uppsala University*
Janet Giltrow, *University of British Columbia*
Darren Harris-Fain, *Shawnee State University*
Peter L. Hays, *University of California, Davis*
Jamey Hecht, *Castleton State College*
David Garrett Izzo, *Fayetteville State University*
Pearl James, *University of Kentucky*
Yoshitada Kobayashi, *Ehime University*
Joe Kraus, *University of Scranton*
Horst H. Kruse, *University of Münster*
Heidi M. Kunz, *Randolph College*
Veronica Makowsky, *University of Connecticut, Storrs*
Robert A. Martin, *Michigan State University*
Michael J. Meyer, *DePaul University*
Kim Moreland, *George Washington University*
Rama Nair
Michael Nowlin, *University of Victoria*
Dave Page, *Inver Hills Community College*
James Phelan, *Ohio State University, Columbus*
Richard Pioreck, *Hofstra University*
James Plath, *Illinois Wesleyan University*
Edward J. Rielly, *Saint Joseph's College*
Dennis Ryan, *Buena Vista University*
Deborah Davis Schlacks, *University of Wisconsin, Superior*
Mark Shipman, *Tarleton State University*
Gail Sinclair, *Rollins College*
David Stouck, *Simon Fraser University*
Khachig Toloyan, *Wesleyan University*

Kiyohiko Tsuboi, *Kobe Women's University*
Michael Viel, *University of Paris, Sorbonne*
Jane Vogel, *Ithaca College*
Joseph Waldmeir, *Michigan State University*
James L. W. West III, *Pennsylvania State University, University Park*
Eleanor Wikborg, *Stockholm University*

WORKS CITED

Adams, Henry. *The Education of Henry Adams*. 1905. New York: New Amer. Lib., 1961.

——. *Mont-Saint-Michel and Chartres*. 1905. Boston: Houghton, 1933.

Aldridge, John W. *After the Lost Generation*. New York: McGraw, 1951.

——. "Afterthoughts on the Twenties." *Classics and Contemporaries*. Columbia: U of Missouri P, 1992. 69–78.

Alexander, Scott. *The Red Hot Jazz Archive*. Apr. 2006 <http://www.redhotjazz.com>.

Alger, Horatio. *Ragged Dick*. 1868. New York: Signet, 1990.

Allen, Frederick Lewis. *Lords of Creation*. New York: Harper, 1935.

Allen, Joan M. *Candles and Carnival Lights: The Catholic Sensibility of F. Scott Fitzgerald*. New York: New York UP, 1978.

Anderson, Hilton. "From the Wasteland to East Egg: Houses in *The Great Gatsby*." *University of Mississippi Studies in English* 9 (1991): 114–18.

Aristotle. *The Rhetoric*. Trans. Lane Cooper. Englewood Cliffs: Prentice, 1960.

Armstrong, Chris. "College Sports: Prodigal Son of 'Muscular Christianity.' " *Christianity Today* 15 Aug. 2003. 3 Sept. 2007 <http://www.christianitytoday .com/history/newsletter/2003/aug15.html>.

Astro, Richard, and Jackson J. Benson, eds. *Hemingway in Our Time*. Corvallis: Oregon State UP, 1974.

Audhuy, Letha. "*The Waste Land*: Myth and Symbolism in *The Great Gatsby*." *Études Anglaises* 33 (1980): 41–54.

Babb, Howard S. " 'The Great Gatsby' and the Grotesque." *Criticism* 5 (1963): 336–48.

Baker, Charles R. "F. Scott Fitzgerald's *The Great Gatsby*." *American Writers: Classics*. Ed. Jay Parini. Vol. 2. New York: Scribner's, 2004. 109–24.

Bakhtin, M. M. *The Dialogic Imagination: Four Essays*. Trans. Caryl Emerson and Michael Holquist. Austin: U of Texas P, 1981.

Baldwin, James. *Collected Essays*. Ed. Toni Morrison. New York: Lib. of Amer., 1998.

Barbour, Brian M. "*The Great Gatsby* and the American Past." 1973. Claridge 2: 350–58.

Barrett, Laura. " 'Material without Being Real': Photography and the End of Reality in *The Great Gatsby*." *Studies in the Novel* 30 (1998): 540–57.

Barton, Bruce. *The Man Nobody Knows*. 1925. New York: Dee, 2000.

Battle of the Somme. Dir. Geoffrey H. Malins and J. B. McDowell. 1916. London: Imperial War Museum, Dept. of Film and Dept. of Information Retrieval, 1987.

Baumgarten, Murray. "Seeing Double: Jews in the Fiction of F. Scott Fitzgerald, Charles Dickens, Anthony Trollope, and George Eliot." *Between "Race" and Culture: Representations of "the Jew" in English and American Literature*. Ed. Bryan Cheyette. Stanford: Stanford UP, 1996. 44–61.

Bender, Bert. " 'His Mind Aglow': The Biological Undercurrent in Fitzgerald's *Gatsby* and Other Works." *Journal of American Studies* 32 (1998): 399–420.

Bennett, Warren. "Prefigurations of Gatsby, Eckleburg, Owl Eyes, and Klipspringer." *Fitzgerald/Hemingway Annual* 11 (1979): 207–23.

Berman, Ronald. *Fitzgerald, Hemingway, and the Twenties*. Tuscaloosa: U of Alabama P, 2001.

———. The Great Gatsby *and Fitzgerald's World of Ideas*. Tuscaloosa: U of Alabama P, 1997.

———. The Great Gatsby *and Modern Times*. Urbana: U of Illinois P, 1994.

Bewley, Marius. "Scott Fitzgerald's Criticism of America." 1954. Lockridge, *Twentieth Century Interpretations* 37–53.

Bicknell, John W. "The Waste Land of F. Scott Fitzgerald." 1954. Claridge 4: 156–67.

The Birth of a Nation. Dir. D. W. Griffiths. Epoch, 1915. Videocassette. Blackhawk, 1990.

Bloom, Harold, ed. F. Scott Fitzgerald's The Great Gatsby. New York: Chelsea, 1986.

———, ed. F. Scott Fitzgerald's The Great Gatsby. New York: Chelsea, 1999.

———, ed. *Major Literary Characters: Gatsby*. New York: Chelsea, 1991.

———, ed. *Modern Critical Views: F. Scott Fitzgerald*. New York: Chelsea, 1985.

Bloomfield, Morton W. "Reflections of a Medievalist: America, Medievalism, and the Middle Ages." *Medievalism in American Culture*. Ed. Bernard Rosenthal and Paul E. Szarmach. Binghamton: Center for Medieval and Renaissance Studies, State U of New York, Binghamton, 1989. 13–29.

Booth, Wayne C. *The Rhetoric of Fiction*. 1961. Rev. ed. Chicago: U of Chicago P, 1983.

Bordman, Gerald. *American Musical Theatre: A Chronicle*. 3rd ed. New York: Oxford UP, 2001.

Bourne, Randolph. "Trans-national America." *War and the Intellectuals: Essays by Randolph Bourne, 1915–1919*. Ed. Carl Resek. New York: Harper, 1964. 107–23.

Brauer, Stephen. "Jay Gatsby and the Prohibition Gangster as Businessman." *F. Scott Fitzgerald Review* 2 (2003): 51–71.

Breitwieser, Mitchell. "*The Great Gatsby*: Grief, Jazz, and the Eye-witness." *Arizona Quarterly* 47.3 (1991): 17–70.

———. "Jazz Fractures: F. Scott Fitzgerald and Epochal Representation." *American Literary History* 12 (2000): 359–81.

Brewer, Derek. *Chaucer and His World*. 2nd ed. Cambridge: Brewer-Boydell, 1992.

Brogan, Jacqueline Vaught. "Strange Fruits in *The Garden of Eden*: 'The Mysticism of Money,' *The Great Gatsby*—and *A Moveable Feast*." Kennedy and Bryer 235–56.

Brooke, Rupert. *The Collected Poems of Rupert Brooke: With a Memoir*. 2nd ed. London: Sedgwick, 1928.

Brooks, Cleanth. "The American 'Innocence' in James, Fitzgerald, and Faulkner." 1964. Claridge 4: 482–94.

Brooks, Cleanth, and Robert Penn Warren. *Understanding Fiction*. New York: Crofts, 1943.

Bruccoli, Matthew J. *F. Scott Fitzgerald: A Descriptive Bibliography*. Rev. ed. Pittsburgh: U of Pittsburgh P, 1987.

————, ed. *F. Scott Fitzgerald's* The Great Gatsby: *A Literary Reference*. New York: Carroll, 2000.

————. *Getting It Right: Resetting* The Great Gatsby. Columbia: n.p., 2005.

————. " 'How Are You and the Family Old Sport?' Gerlach and Gatsby." *Fitzgerald/Hemingway Annual* 7 (1975): 33–36.

————, ed. *New Essays on* The Great Gatsby. Cambridge: Cambridge UP, 1985.

————. *Some Sort of Epic Grandeur: The Life of F. Scott Fitzgerald*. 2nd rev. ed. Columbia: U of South Carolina P, 2002.

Bruccoli, Matthew J., ed., with Jennifer McCabe Atkinson. *As Ever, Scott Fitz—: Letters between F. Scott Fitzgerald and His Literary Agent Harold Ober, 1919–1940*. Philadelphia: Lippincott, 1972.

Bruccoli, Matthew J., and Judith S. Baughman, eds. *Conversations with F. Scott Fitzgerald*. Jackson: UP of Mississippi, 2004.

Bruccoli, Matthew J., and Jackson R. Bryer, eds. *F. Scott Fitzgerald in His Own Time*. Kent: Kent State UP, 1971.

Bruccoli, Matthew J., and Margaret M. Duggan, eds., with Susan Walker. *Correspondence of F. Scott Fitzgerald*. New York: Random, 1980.

Bruccoli, Matthew J., Scottie Fitzgerald Smith, and Joan P. Kerr, eds. *The Romantic Egoists: A Pictorial Autobiography from the Scrapbooks and Albums of Scott and Zelda Fitzgerald*. New York: Scribner, 1974.

Bryer, Jackson R. "The Critical Reputation of F. Scott Fitzgerald." Prigozy, *Cambridge Companion* 209–34.

————. *The Critical Reputation of F. Scott Fitzgerald: A Bibliographical Study*. Hamden: Archon, 1967.

————. *The Critical Reputation of F. Scott Fitzgerald: A Bibliographical Study, Supplement One through 1981*. Hamden: Archon, 1984.

————. "Four Decades of Fitzgerald Studies: The Best and the Brightest." *Twentieth Century Literature* 26 (1980): 247–67.

————, ed. *F. Scott Fitzgerald: The Critical Reception*. New York: Franklin, 1978.

————, ed. *Sixteen Modern American Authors: A Review of Research and Criticism*. Durham: Duke UP, 1974.

————, ed. *Sixteen Modern American Authors: Volume 2, a Survey of Research and Criticism since 1972*. Durham: Duke UP, 1990.

————. "Style as Meaning in *The Great Gatsby*: Notes toward a New Approach." Donaldson, *Critical Essays* 117–29.

Bryer, Jackson R., Alan Margolies, and Ruth Prigozy, eds. *F. Scott Fitzgerald: New Perspectives*. Athens: U of Georgia P, 2000.

Bryer, Jackson R., Ruth Prigozy, and Milton R. Stern, eds. *F. Scott Fitzgerald in the Twenty-First Century*. Tuscaloosa: U of Alabama P, 2003.

Bufkin, E. C. "A Pattern of Parallel and Double: The Function of Myrtle in *The Great Gatsby*." *Modern Fiction Studies* 15 (1969–70): 517–24.

Burnam, Tom. "The Eyes of Dr. Eckleburg: A Re-examination of 'The Great Gatsby.' " *College English* 14 (1952): 7–12.

Butler, Judith. *Bodies That Matter: On the Discursive Limits of "Sex."* London: Routledge, 1993.

———. *Gender Trouble: Feminism and the Subversion of Identity.* London: Routledge, 1990.

Cahan, Abraham. *The Rise of David Levinsky.* 1917. New York: Penguin, 1993.

Cain, William E. "F. Scott Fitzgerald (1896–1940)." *American Literature.* Ed. Cain. New York: Pearson, 2004. 600–01.

Callahan, John F. *The Illusions of a Nation: Myth and History in the Novels of F. Scott Fitzgerald.* Urbana: U of Illinois P, 1972.

Carlisle, E. Fred. "The Triple Vision of Nick Carraway." 1966. Claridge 2: 307–15.

Carnes, Mark C., ed. *Novel History: Historians and Novelists Confront America's Past and Each Other.* New York: Simon, 2001.

Cartwright, Kent. "Nick Carraway as an Unreliable Narrator." *Papers on Language and Literature* 20 (1984): 218–32.

Case, Sue Ellen, ed. *Performing Feminisms: Feminist Critical Theory and Theatre.* Baltimore: Johns Hopkins UP, 1990.

Cass, Colin S. " 'Pandered in Whispers': Narrative Reliability in *The Great Gatsby.*" *College Literature* 7 (1980): 113–24.

Castille, Philip. "Jay Gatsby: The Smuggler as Frontier Hero." *University of Mississippi Studies in Fiction* 10 (1992): 227–37.

Cather, Willa. *A Lost Lady.* 1923. London: Virago, 2001.

———. *The Song of the Lark.* 1915. Mineola: Dover, 2004.

Chambers, John B. *The Novels of F. Scott Fitzgerald.* New York: St. Martin's, 1989.

Chard, Leslie F., III. "Outward Forms and the Inner Life: Coleridge and Gatsby." *Fitzgerald/Hemingway Annual* 5 (1973): 189–94.

Chase, Richard. *The American Novel and Its Tradition.* 1957. Baltimore: Johns Hopkins UP, 1983.

Chatman, Seymour. *Coming to Terms: The Rhetoric of Narrative in Fiction and Film.* Ithaca: Cornell UP, 1990.

Chaucer, Geoffrey. General Prologue. Chaucer, *Works* 17–25.

———. "Prologue to *The Legend of Good Women.*" Chaucer, *Works* 482–96.

———. *The Works of Geoffrey Chaucer.* 2nd ed. Boston: Houghton, 1961.

Chopin, Kate. *The Awakening.* 1899. New York: Bantam, 1981.

Claridge, Henry, ed. *F. Scott Fitzgerald: Critical Assessments.* 4 vols. Robertsbridge, Eng.: Helm, 1991.

Clark, Suzanne. *Sentimental Modernism: Women Writers and the Revolution of the Word.* Bloomington: Indiana UP, 1991.

Clymer, Jeffory A. " 'Mr. Nobody from Nowhere': Rudolph Valentino, Jay Gatsby, and the End of the American Race." *Genre* 29 (1996): 161–92.

Cobley, Evelyn. *Representing War.* Toronto: U of Toronto P, 1993.

Cohen, Richard. "The Inessential Houses of *The Great Gatsby.*" *Husson Review* 2.1 (1968): 48–57.

Coleman, Dan. " 'A World Complete in Itself': *Gatsby*'s Elegaic Narration." *Journal of Narrative Technique* 27 (1997): 207–33.

Corso, Joseph. "One Not-Forgotten Summer Night: Sources for Fictional Symbols of American Character in *The Great Gatsby.*" *Fitzgerald/Hemingway Annual* 8 (1976): 9–34.

Cowley, Malcolm. "Fitzgerald: The Romance of Money." *A Second Flowering: Works and Days of the Lost Generation.* New York: Viking, 1973. 19–47.

Crim, Lottie R., and Neal B. Houston. "The Catalogue of Names in *The Great Gatsby.*" *Research Studies* 36 (1968): 113–30.

Crosland, Andrew T. *A Concordance to F. Scott Fitzgerald's* The Great Gatsby. Detroit: Bruccoli, 1975.

———. "*The Great Gatsby* and *The Secret Agent.*" *Fitzgerald/Hemingway Annual* 7 (1975): 75–81.

Cuddon, J. A. *The Penguin Dictionary of Literary Terms and Literary Theory.* 4th ed. London: Penguin, 1999.

Curnutt, Kirk. "Fitzgerald's Consumer World." Curnutt, *Historical Guide* 85–128.

———, ed. *A Historical Guide to F. Scott Fitzgerald.* New York: Oxford UP, 2004.

Curry, Steven, and Peter L. Hays. "Fitzgerald's *Vanity Fair.*" *Fitzgerald/Hemingway Annual* 9 (1977): 63–75.

Deats, Sara Munson, and Lagretta Tallent Lenker, eds. *The Aching Hearth: Family Violence in Life and Literature.* New York: Plenum, 1991.

DeKoven, Marianne. *Rich and Strange: Gender, History, Modernism.* Princeton: Princeton UP, 1991.

de Lauretis, Teresa. *Alice Doesn't: Feminism, Semiotics, Cinema.* Bloomington: Indiana UP, 1984.

Dessner, Lawrence Jay. "Photography and *The Great Gatsby.*" 1979. Donaldson, *Critical Essays* 175–86.

Diner, Hasia. *The Jews of the United States.* Berkeley: U of California P, 2004.

Dinnerstein, Leonard. *Anti-Semitism in America.* New York: Oxford UP, 1994.

Dixon, Wheeler Winston. "The Three Film Versions of *The Great Gatsby.*" *Literature/Film Quarterly* 31 (2003): 287–94.

Dodd, William George. *Courtly Love in Chaucer and Gower.* 1913. Gloucester: Smith, 1959.

Donaldson, Scott, ed. *Critical Essays on F. Scott Fitzgerald's* The Great Gatsby. Boston: Hall, 1984.

———. *Fool for Love: F. Scott Fitzgerald.* New York: Congdon, 1983.

———. "Possessions in *The Great Gatsby.*" *Southern Review* 37 (2001): 187–210.

———. "The Trouble with Nick." Donaldson, *Critical Essays* 131–39.

Dos Passos, John. *Manhattan Transfer.* 1925. Boston: Mariner, 2003.

Douglas, Ann. *Terrible Honesty: Mongrel Manhattan in the 1920s.* New York: Farrar, 1995.

Doyno, Victor A. "Patterns in *The Great Gatsby.*" 1966. Donaldson, *Critical Essays* 94–105.

Dreiser, Theodore. *An American Tragedy.* 1925. New York: Signet, 2000.

———. *Sister Carrie.* 1900. New York: Signet, 2000.

DuPlessis, Rachel Blau. *Writing beyond the Ending: Narrative Strategies of Twentieth-Century Women Writers.* Bloomington: Indiana UP, 1985.

Eble, Kenneth. "The Craft of Revision: *The Great Gatsby*." 1964. Donaldson, *Critical Essays* 85–94.

———. *F. Scott Fitzgerald*. Rev. ed. New York: Twayne, 1977.

———. "*The Great Gatsby*." *College Literature* 1 (1974): 34–47.

Eby, Clare. "Of Gold Molars and Golden Girls: Fitzgerald's Reading of Norris." *American Literary Realism* 35 (2003): 130–58.

Eksteins, Modris. *Rites of Spring: The Great War and the Birth of the Modern Age*. New York: Doubleday, 1989.

Eliot, T. S. *The Complete Poems and Plays, 1909–1950*. 1952. New York: Harcourt, 1980.

———. "Gerontion." 1920. Eliot, *Complete Poems* 21–22.

———. "Three Letters about 'The Great Gatsby.'" E. Wilson 308–10.

———. *The Waste Land*. 1922. Eliot, *Complete Poems* 37–55.

———. *The Waste Land*. Read by T. S. Eliot. *The Caedmon Treasury of Modern Poets*. 1957. 2 cassettes. New York: Caedmon, 1988.

———. The Waste Land: *A Facsimile and Transcript of the Original Drafts including the Annotations of Ezra Pound*. Ed. Valerie Eliot. New York: Harcourt, 1971.

Elkins, Marilyn. "F. Scott Fitzgerald's Use of the Bitch-Goddess Success." MA thesis. Vanderbilt U, 1970.

Ellison, Ralph. *Going to the Territory*. New York: Random, 1986.

Elmore, A[lbert] E. "Color and Cosmos in *The Great Gatsby*." *Sewanee Review* 78 (1970): 427–43.

———. "*The Great Gatsby* as Well-Wrought Urn." T. D. Young 57–92.

———. "Nick Carraway's Self-Introduction." *Fitzgerald/Hemingway Annual* 3 (1971): 130–47.

Emmitt, Robert J. "Love, Death and Resurrection in *The Great Gatsby*." *Aeolian Harps: Essays in Literature in Honor of Maurice Browning Cramer*. Ed. Donna G. Fricke and Douglas C. Fricke. Bowling Green: Bowling Green UP, 1976. 273–89.

Evans, Oliver H. "'A Sort of Moral Attention': The Narrator of *The Great Gatsby*." *Fitzgerald/Hemingway Annual* 3 (1971): 117–29.

Ewald, Robert J. "The Jungian Archetype of the Fairy Mistress in Medieval Romance." Diss. Bowling Green State U, 1977.

Ewen, Stuart. *All Consuming Images: The Politics of Style in Contemporary Culture*. New York: Basic, 1988.

Fass, Paula. *The Damned and the Beautiful: American Youth in the 1920s*. New York: Oxford UP, 1977.

Felman, Shoshana, and Dori Laub. *Testimony: Crises of Witnessing in Literature, Psychoanalysis, and History*. New York: Routledge, 1992.

Felski, Rita. *The Gender of Modernity*. Cambridge: Harvard UP, 1995.

Ferrante, Joan M., and George D. Economou. Introduction. *In Pursuit of Perfection: Courtly Love in Medieval Literature*. Ed. Ferrante and Economou. Port Washington: National U–Kennikat, 1975. 3–15.

Fetterley, Judith. "*The Great Gatsby*: Fitzgerald's *Droit de Seigneur*." *The Resisting Reader: A Feminist Approach to American Fiction*. Bloomington: Indiana UP, 1978. 72–100.

Fitzgerald, F. Scott. "Absolution." *American Mercury* 2 (1924): 141–49.

———. *Afternoon of an Author: A Selection of Uncollected Stories and Essays.* New York: Scribner's, 1958.

———. *All the Sad Young Men.* New York: Scribner's, 1926.

———. *The Apprentice Fiction of F. Scott Fitzgerald, 1909–1917.* Ed. John Kuehl. New Brunswick: Rutgers UP, 1965.

———. *The Beautiful and Damned.* New York: Scribner's, 1922.

———. *The Beautiful and Damned.* Fitzgerald, *Novels* 435–802.

———. *Before* Gatsby: *The First Twenty-Six Stories.* Ed. Matthew J. Bruccoli. Columbia: U of South Carolina P, 2001.

———. "The Crack-Up." E. Wilson 69–84.

———. "Echoes of the Jazz Age." E. Wilson 13–22.

———. *Flappers and Philosophers.* New York: Scribner's, 1920.

———. "The Four Fists." Fitzgerald, *Novels* 417–34.

———. *F. Scott Fitzgerald: A Life in Letters.* Ed. Matthew J. Bruccoli with Judith S. Baughman. New York: Scribner, 1994.

———. *F. Scott Fitzgerald: Manuscripts.* Ed. Matthew J. Bruccoli. Vol. 3. New York: Garland, 1990.

———. *F. Scott Fitzgerald on Authorship.* Ed. Matthew J. Bruccoli and Judith S. Baughman. Columbia: U of South Carolina P, 1996.

———. *F. Scott Fitzgerald's Ledger: A Facsimile.* Washington: Natl. Cash Register–Microcard, 1973.

———. *F. Scott Fitzgerald: The Princeton Years: Selected Writings, 1914–1920.* Ed. Chip Deffaa. Fort Bragg: Cypress, 1996.

———. *The Great Gatsby.* New York: Scribner's, 1925.

———. *The Great Gatsby.* 1925. Ed. Matthew J. Bruccoli. Cambridge: Cambridge UP, 1991.

———. *The Great Gatsby.* 1925. Ed. Matthew J. Bruccoli. New York: Scribner, 1992.

———. *The Great Gatsby.* 1925. New York: Scribner, 2004.

———. The Great Gatsby: *A Facsimile of the Manuscript.* Ed. Matthew J. Bruccoli. Washington: Microcard, 1973.

———. *The Last Tycoon: An Unfinished Novel.* New York: Scribner's, 1941.

———. *The Letters of F. Scott Fitzgerald.* Ed. Andrew Turnbull. New York: Scribner's, 1963.

———. "My Lost City." E. Wilson 23–33.

———. *The Notebooks of F. Scott Fitzgerald.* Ed. Matthew J. Bruccoli. New York: Harcourt, 1978.

———. *Novels and Stories: 1920–1922.* Ed. Jackson R. Bryer. New York: Lib. of Amer., 2000.

———. " 'O Russet Witch!' " Fitzgerald, *Novels* 988–1018.

———. "Preface to 'This Side of Paradise.' " *Fitzgerald/Hemingway Annual* 3 (1971): 1–2.

———. *The Price Was High: The Last Uncollected Stories of F. Scott Fitzgerald.* Ed. Matthew J. Bruccoli. New York: Harcourt, 1979.

———. "The Rich Boy." 1926. Fitzgerald, *Short Stories* 317–49.

————. *The Short Stories of F. Scott Fitzgerald: A New Collection.* 1989. Ed. Matthew J. Bruccoli. New York: Scribner, 2003.

————. *Tales of the Jazz Age.* New York: Scribner's, 1922.

————. *Taps at Reveille.* New York: Scribner's, 1935.

————. *Tender Is the Night.* New York: Scribner's, 1934.

————. *This Side of Paradise.* New York: Scribner's, 1920.

————. *This Side of Paradise.* Fitzgerald, *Novels* 1–252.

————. *Trimalchio: An Early Version of* The Great Gatsby. Ed. James L. W. West III. Cambridge: Cambridge UP, 2000.

————. *Trimalchio by F. Scott Fitzgerald: A Facsimile Edition of the Original Galley Proofs for* The Great Gatsby. Columbia: U of South Carolina P, 2000.

————. *The Vegetable.* New York: Scribner's, 1923.

Forrey, Robert. "Negroes in the Fiction of F. Scott Fitzgerald." *Phylon* 28 (1967): 293–98.

Forter, Greg. "Against Melancholia: Contemporary Mourning Theory, Fitzgerald's *The Great Gatsby*, and the Politics of Unfinished Grief." *Differences* 14.2 (2003): 134–70.

Foster, Richard. "The Way to Read *Gatsby*." *Sense and Sensibility in Twentieth-Century Writing.* Ed. Brom Weber. Carbondale: Southern Illinois UP, 1970. 94–108.

Franklin, Benjamin. *Autobiography.* 1791. New York: Vintage, 1988.

Fraser, Keath. "Another Reading of *The Great Gatsby*." 1979. Donaldson, *Critical Essays* 140–53.

Friedman, Norman. "Versions of Form in Fiction: 'Great Expectations' and 'The Great Gatsby.' " 1954. Claridge 2: 415–31.

Fryer, Sarah Beebe. "Beneath the Mask: The Plight of Daisy Buchanan." Donaldson, *Critical Essays* 153–66.

————. *Fitzgerald's New Women: Harbingers of Change.* Ann Arbor: UMI, 1988.

Furia, Philip. *The Poets of Tin Pan Alley: A History of America's Greatest Lyricists.* New York: Oxford UP, 1990.

Fussell, Paul. *The Great War and Modern Memory.* New York: Oxford UP, 1975.

Gabler, Neal. *An Empire of Their Own: How the Jews Invented Hollywood.* New York: Anchor, 1988.

Gallagher, Catherine, and Stephen Greenblatt. *Practicing New Historicism.* Chicago: U of Chicago P, 2000.

Gamson, Joshua. *Claims to Fame: Celebrity in Contemporary America.* Berkeley: U of California P, 1994.

Genette, Gerard. *Narrative Discourse: An Essay in Method.* 1972. Trans. Jane E. Lewin. Ithaca: Cornell UP, 1980.

Gervais, Ronald. "The Trains of Their Youth: The Aesthetics of Homecoming in 'The Great Gatsby,' 'The Sun Also Rises,' and 'The Sound and the Fury.' " *Americana* 5 (1980): 51–63.

Gidley, M. "Notes on F. Scott Fitzgerald and the Passing of the Great Race." *Journal of American Studies* 7 (1973): 171–81.

Gilbert, Sandra M., and Susan Gubar. *No Man's Land: The Place of the Woman Writer in the Twentieth Century*. 3 vols. New Haven: Yale UP, 1988.

Giles, Paul. "Aquinas vs. Weber: Ideological Esthetics in *The Great Gatsby*." *Mosaic* 22.4 (1989): 1–12.

Giltrow, Janet, and David Stouck. "Pastoral Mode and Language in *The Great Gatsby*." Bryer, Prigozy, and Stern 139–52.

———. "Style as Politics in *The Great Gatsby*." *Studies in the Novel* 29 (1997): 476–90.

Gleason, William. *The Leisure Ethic: Work and Play in American Literature, 1840–1940*. Stanford: Stanford UP, 1999.

The Godfather. Dir. Francis Ford Coppola. Paramount, 1972.

The Godfather: Part III. Dir. Francis Ford Coppola. Paramount, 1990.

The Godfather: Part II. Dir. Francis Ford Coppola. Paramount, 1974.

Goldsmith, Meredith. "White Skin, White Mask: Passing, Posing, and Performing in *The Great Gatsby*." *Modern Fiction Studies* 49 (2003): 443–68.

Gollin, Rita. "The Automobiles of *The Great Gatsby*." *Studies in the Twentieth Century* 6 (1970): 63–83.

GoodFellas. Dir. Martin Scorsese. Warner Brothers, 1990.

Grant, Madison. *The Passing of the Great Race*. New York: Scribner's, 1916.

Grant, Mary Kathryn, R. S. M. "The Search for Celebration in *The Sun Also Rises* and *The Great Gatsby*." *Arizona Quarterly* 33 (1977): 181–92.

The Greatest Legal Fake Book of All Time. Secaucus: Warner Brothers, 1985.

The Great Gatsby. Dir. Jack Clayton. Paramount, 1974.

Greenblatt, Stephen. *Shakespearean Negotiations: The Circulation of Social Energy in Renaissance England*. Berkeley: U of California P, 1988.

Gross, Barry Edward. "Jay Gatsby and Myrtle Wilson: A Kinship." *Tennessee Studies in Literature* 8 (1963): 57–60.

Gross, Dalton. "The Death of Rosy Rosenthal: A Note on Fitzgerald's Use of Background in *The Great Gatsby*." *Notes and Queries* 23.1 (1976): 22–23.

Gross, Dalton, and Maryjean Gross, eds. *Understanding* The Great Gatsby: *A Student Casebook to Issues, Sources, and Historical Documents*. Westport: Greenwood, 1998.

Guerin, Wilfrid Louis. "Christian Myth and Naturalistic Deity: *The Great Gatsby*." *Renascence* 14 (1962): 80–89.

Gwynn, Frederick L., and Joseph Blotner, eds. *William Faulkner at the University*. 1959. New York: Vintage, 1965.

Halliday, M. A. K., and Ruqaiya Hasan. *Cohesion in English*. London: Longman, 1976.

Hamm, Charles. " 'It's Only a Paper Moon'; or, The Golden Years of Tin Pan Alley." *Yesterdays: Popular Song in America*. New York: Norton, 1979. 326–90.

Hampton, Riley V. "Owl Eyes in *The Great Gatsby*." *American Literature* 48 (1976): 229.

Hanzo, Thomas A. "The Theme and Narrator of 'The Great Gatsby.' " 1957. Lockridge, *Twentieth Century Interpretations* 61–69.

Harvey, W. J. "Theme and Texture in *The Great Gatsby*." 1957. Donaldson, *Critical Essays* 75–84.

Hays, Peter L. "*Gatsby*, Myth, Fairy Tale, and Legend." *Southern Folklore Quarterly* 41 (1977): 213–23.

———. "Hemingway and Fitzgerald." Astro and Benson 87–97.

Hays, Peter L., and Pamela Demory. "*Nostromo* and *The Great Gatsby*." *Études Anglaises* 41 (1988): 405–17.

Hemingway, Ernest. *A Farewell to Arms*. 1929. New York: Scribner, 2003.

———. *Men without Women*. 1927. New York: Simon, 1997.

———. "The Snows of Kilimanjaro." 1936. *The Complete Short Stories of Ernest Hemingway*. New York: Scribner, 1998. 39–56.

———. *The Sun Also Rises*. 1926. New York: Scribner, 2003.

Henretta, James, et al., eds. *America's History*. Vol. 2. New York: Worth, 1993.

Henson, Kristin K. *Beyond the Sound Barrier: The Jazz Controversy in Twentieth Century American Fiction*. New York: Routledge, 2003.

Heracleitus of Ephesus. *Herakleitos and Diogenes*. Trans. Guy Davenport. Bolinas: Grey Fox, 1979.

Hermansson, Clyde. " 'An Elusive Rhythm': *The Great Gatsby* Reclaims *Troilus and Criseyde*." *Studies in American Fiction* 25 (1997): 57–80.

Higgs, Elton Dale. "The Dream as Literary Framework in the Works of Chaucer, Langland, and the Pearl Poet." Diss. U of Pittsburgh, 1965.

Higham, John. *Strangers in the Land: Patterns of American Nativism, 1860–1925*. New Brunswick: Rutgers UP, 1955.

Hilgart, John. "*The Great Gatsby*'s Aesthetics of Non-Identity." *Arizona Quarterly* 59.1 (2003): 87–116.

Hindus, Milton. "F. Scott Fitzgerald and Literary Anti-Semitism: A Footnote on the Mind of the 20's." *Commentary* June 1947: 508–16.

———. *F. Scott Fitzgerald: An Introduction and Interpretation*. New York: Holt, 1968.

———. "The Mysterious Eyes of Dr. T. J. Eckleburg." *Boston University Studies in English* 3.1 (1957): 22–31.

Historic American Sheet Music. Rare Book, Manuscript, and Special Collections Lib., Duke U. 18 Apr. 2006 <http://www.scriptorium.lib.duke.edu/sheetmusic>.

Hochman, Barbara. "Disembodied Voices and Narrating Bodies in *The Great Gatsby*." *Style* 28 (1994): 95–118.

Hoffman, Frederick J., ed. The Great Gatsby: A Study. New York: Scribner's, 1962.

———. *The Twenties*. New York: Viking, 1955.

Hoffman, Nancy Y. "*The Great Gatsby*: Troilus and Criseyde Revisited?" *Fitzgerald/Hemingway Annual* 3 (1971): 148–58.

Hook, Andrew. *F. Scott Fitzgerald*. London: Arnold, 1992.

Howard, Leon. "Raymond Chandler's Not-So-Great Gatsby." *Mystery and Detection Annual* 2 (1973): 1–15.

Hughes, G. I. "Sub Specie Doctor T. J. Eckleburg: Man and God in 'The Great Gatsby.' " *English Studies in Africa* 15 (1972): 81–92.

Hull, E. M. *The Sheik: A Novel*. Boston: Small, 1921.

Humma, John B. "Edward Russell Thomas: The Prototype for *Gatsby*'s Tom Buchanan?" *Markham Review* 4 (1974): 38–39.

Hyland, Drew A. *The Origins of Philosophy: Its Rise in Myth and the Pre-Socratics*. 1973. Atlantic Highlands: Humanities, 1984.

Irwin, John T. "Compensating Visions: *The Great Gatsby*." *Southwest Review* 77 (1992): 536–45.

Ishikawa, Akiko. "From 'Winter Dreams' to *The Great Gatsby*." *Persica* 5 (1978): 79–92.

Jacobson, Matthew Frye. *Whiteness of a Different Color: European Immigrants and the Alchemy of Race*. Cambridge: Harvard UP, 1998.

James, Henry. *The American*. 1877. New York: Signet, 2005.

———. *The Golden Bowl*. 1904. New York: Penguin, 2001.

———. *The Portrait of a Lady*. 1881. New York: Doubleday, 1983.

James, William. *The Letters of William James*. Ed. Henry James. Vol. 4. Boston: Atlantic Monthly, 1920.

Jay, Gregory S. *America the Scrivener: Deconstruction and the Subject of Literary History*. Ithaca: Cornell UP, 1990.

Johnson, Carroll B. Don Quixote: *The Quest for Modern Fiction*. Boston: Twayne, 1990.

Johnson, Christiane. "*The Great Gatsby*: The Final Vision." 1976. Donaldson, *Critical Essays* 112–17.

Johnson, James Weldon. *The Autobiography of an Ex-Colored Man*. 1912. New York: Penguin, 1990.

———. *Black Manhattan*. 1930. New York: DaCapo, 1991.

Johnson, Robert, Jr. "Say It Ain't So, Jay: Fitzgerald's Use of Baseball in *The Great Gatsby*." *F. Scott Fitzgerald Review* 1 (2002): 30–44.

Kallen, Horace. "Democracy versus the Melting-Pot." *Nation* 18 Feb. 1915: 190–94; 25 Feb. 1915: 217–20.

Keable, Robert. *Simon Called Peter*. New York: Dutton, 1921.

Kehl, D. G. "Writing the Long Desire: The Function of *Sehnsucht* in *The Great Gatsby* and *Look Homeward, Angel*." *Journal of Modern Literature* 24 (2000–01): 309–19.

Kehl, D. G., and Allene Cooper. "Sangria in the Sangreal: *The Great Gatsby* as Grail Quest." *Rocky Mountain Review of Language and Literature* 47 (1993): 203–17.

Kennedy, J. Gerald, and Jackson R. Bryer, eds. *French Connections: Hemingway and Fitzgerald Abroad*. New York: St. Martin's, 1998.

Kerr, Frances. "Feeling 'Half-Feminine': Modernism and the Politics of Emotion in *The Great Gatsby*." *American Literature* 68 (1996): 405–31.

Kirk, G. S., and J. E. Raven. *The Presocratic Philosophers: A Critical History with a Selection of Texts*. London: Cambridge UP, 1957.

Klug, M. A. "Horns of Manichaeus: The Conflict of Art and Experience in *The Great Gatsby* and *The Sun Also Rises*." *Essays in Literature* 12 (1985): 111–24.

Knodt, Kenneth S. "The Gathering Darkness: A Study of the Effects of Technology in *The Great Gatsby*." *Fitzgerald/Hemingway Annual* 8 (1976): 130–38.

Koestenbaum, Wayne. *Double Talk: The Erotics of Male Literary Collaboration*. New York: Routledge, 1989.

Kopf, Josephine Z. "Meyer Wolfsheim and Robert Cohn: A Study of a Jewish Type and Stereotype." *Tradition* 10.3 (1969): 93–104.

Korenman, Joan S. " 'Only Her Hairdresser . . .': Another Look at Daisy Buchanan." *American Literature* 46 (1975): 574–78.

———. "A View from the (Queensboro) Bridge." *Fitzgerald/Hemingway Annual* 7 (1975): 93–96.

Koster, Katie de, ed. *Readings on* The Great Gatsby. San Diego: Greenhaven, 1998.

Krumrey, Ami M. "Nick Carraway's Process of Individuation." *Journal of Evolutionary Psychology* 15 (1994): 249–58.

Kruse, Horst. "*The Great Gatsby*: A View from Kant's Window—Transatlantic Crosscurrents." *F. Scott Fitzgerald Review* 2 (2003): 72–84.

———. "The Real Jay Gatsby: Max von Gerlach, F. Scott Fitzgerald, and the Compositional History of *The Great Gatsby*." *F. Scott Fitzgerald Review* 1 (2002): 45–83.

Kuehl, John. "Scott Fitzgerald's Reading." *Princeton University Library Chronicle* 22 (1961): 58–89.

Kuehl, John, and Jackson R. Bryer, eds. *Dear Scott / Dear Max: The Fitzgerald-Perkins Correspondence*. New York: Scribner's, 1971.

Kuhnle, John L. "*The Great Gatsby* as Pastoral Elegy." *Fitzgerald/Hemingway Annual* 10 (1978): 141–54.

LaHurd, Ryan. " 'Absolution': *Gatsby's* Forgotten Front Door." *College Literature* 3 (1976): 113–23.

Langford, Richard E., ed. *Essays in Modern American Literature*. DeLand: Stetson UP, 1963.

Langman, F. H. "Style and Shape in *The Great Gatsby*." 1973. Donaldson, *Critical Essays* 31–53.

Larsen, Nella. *Passing*. 1929. New York: Penguin, 1997.

Lauricella, John A. "The Black Sox Signature Baseball in *The Great Gatsby*." *Aethlon* 10 (1992): 83–98.

Lauter, Paul. "Plato's Stepchildren, Gatsby and Cohn." 1964. Claridge 2: 282–89.

Lehan, Richard D. *F. Scott Fitzgerald and the Craft of Fiction*. Carbondale: Southern Illinois UP, 1966.

———. "*The Great Gatsby* and Its Sources." Donaldson, *Critical Essays* 66–74.

———. The Great Gatsby: *The Limits of Wonder*. Boston: Twayne, 1990.

———. "*The Great Gatsby*—The Text as Construct: Narrative Knots and Narrative Unfolding." Bryer, Margolies, and Prigozy 78–89.

Lena, Alberto. "Deceitful Traces of Power: An Analysis of the Decadence of Tom Buchanan in *The Great Gatsby*." *Canadian Review of American Studies* 28.1 (1998): 19–41.

Lessa, Richard. " 'Our Nervous, Sporadic Games': Sports in *The Great Gatsby*." *Arete* 1.2 (1984): 69–79.

The Lester S. Levy Collection of Sheet Music. Special Collections, Milton S. Eisenhower Lib., Johns Hopkins U. 18 Apr. 2006 <http://www.levysheetmusic.mse.jhu.edu>.

Le Vot, André. "Fitzgerald and Proust: Connoisseurs of Kisses." Bryer, Margolies, and Prigozy 90–101.

———. *F. Scott Fitzgerald: A Biography*. Trans. William Byron. Garden City: Doubleday, 1983.

Lewis, David Levering. *W. E. B. DuBois: Biography of a Race, 1868–1919*. New York: Holt, 1993.

Lewis, Janet. "Fitzgerald's 'Philippe, Count of Darkness.' " *Fitzgerald/Hemingway Annual* 7 (1975): 7–32.

Lhamon, W. T., Jr. "The Essential Houses of *The Great Gatsby*." Donaldson, *Critical Essays* 166–75.

Lisca, Peter. "Nick Carraway and the Imagery of Disorder." *Twentieth Century Literature* 13 (1967): 18–28.

Little Caesar. Dir. Mervyn LeRoy. Warner Brothers, 1930.

Locke, Alain, ed. *The New Negro*. 1925. New York: Simon, 1992.

Lockridge, Ernest. "F. Scott Fitzgerald's *Trompe l'Oeil* and *The Great Gatsby*'s Buried Plot." *Journal of Narrative Technique* 17 (1987): 163–83.

———, ed. *Twentieth Century Interpretations of* The Great Gatsby. Englewood Cliffs: Prentice, 1968.

Long, Robert Emmet. *The Achieving of* The Great Gatsby: *F. Scott Fitzgerald, 1920–1925*. Lewisburg: Bucknell UP, 1979.

———. "The Vogue of Gatsby's Guest List." *Fitzgerald/Hemingway Annual* 1 (1969): 23–25.

Loos, Anita. *Gentlemen Prefer Blondes*. 1925. New York: Liveright, 1998.

Lowes, John L. "The Prologue to the *Legend of Good Women* as Related to the French *Marguerite* Poems and *Filostrato*." *PMLA* 19 (1904): 593–683.

Lukacs, John. "*The Great Gatsby*? Yes, a Historical Novel." Carnes 235–44.

Lupak, Barbara Tepa. "F. Scott Fitzgerald's 'Following of a Grail.' " *Arthuriana* 4 (1994): 324–47.

Lynn, Kenneth S. *The Dream of Success: A Study of the Modern American Imagination*. 1955. Westport: Greenwood, 1972.

MacPhee, Laurence E. "*The Great Gatsby*'s 'Romance of Motoring': Nick Carraway and Jordan Baker." *Modern Fiction Studies* 18 (1972): 207–12.

Mallios, Peter. "Undiscovering the Country: Conrad, Fitzgerald, and Meta-national Form." *Modern Fiction Studies* 47 (2001): 356–90.

Malone, Michael. *James J. Hill: Empire Builder of the Northwest*. Norman: U of Oklahoma P, 1996.

Mandel, Jerome. "The Grotesque Rose: Medieval Romance and *The Great Gatsby*." *Modern Fiction Studies* 34 (1988): 541–58.

Mansell, Darrel. "*The Jazz History of the World* in *The Great Gatsby*." *English Language Notes* 25.2 (1987): 57–62.

Margolies, Alan. "Novel to Play to Film: Four Versions of *The Great Gatsby*." Donaldson, *Critical Essays* 187–200.

Marren, Susan Marie. "Passing for American: Establishing American Identity in the Work of James Weldon Johnson, F. Scott Fitzgerald, Nella Larsen and Gertrude Stein." Diss. U of Michigan, 1995.

Martin, Albro. *James J. Hill and the Opening of the Northwest.* New York: Oxford UP, 1976.

Martin, Robert A. "The Hot Madness of Four O'Clock in Fitzgerald's 'Absolution' and *Gatsby.*" *Studies in American Fiction* 2 (1974): 230–38.

Matterson, Stephen. The Great Gatsby. London: Macmillan, 1990.

May, Rollo. "Gatsby and the American Dream." *The Cry for Myth.* New York: Norton, 1991. 125–47.

McCall, Dan. " 'The Self-Same Song That Found a Path': Keats and *The Great Gatsby.*" 1971. Claridge 2: 406–14.

McDonald, Jarom Lyle. *Sports, Narrative, and Nation in the Fiction of F. Scott Fitzgerald.* New York: Routledge, 2007.

McDonnell, Robert F. "Eggs and Eyes in *The Great Gatsby.*" *Modern Fiction Studies* 7 (1961): 32–36.

McKay, Claude. "If We Must Die." *The Norton Anthology of American Literature.* 6th ed. Ed. Nina Baym et al. *Vol. D: American Literature Between the Wars, 1914–1945.* New York: Norton, 2003. 1461.

McMichael, George. "F. Scott Fitzgerald (1896–1940)." *Anthology of American Literature.* Ed. McMichael et al. 7th ed. 2 vols. Upper Saddle River: Prentice, 2000. 1317–18.

McNally, John J. "Boats and Automobiles in *The Great Gatsby*: Symbols of Drift and Death." *Husson Review* 5.1 (1971): 11–17.

Melnick, Jeffrey. *A Right to Sing the Blues: African Americans, Jews, and American Popular Song.* Cambridge: Harvard UP, 1999.

Mencken, H. L. "As H. L. M. Sees It." Claridge 2: 156–59.

———. *A Second Mencken Chrestomathy.* Ed. Terry Teachout. New York: Knopf, 1995.

Messenger, Christian K. *Sport and the Spirit of Play in American Fiction: Hawthorne to Faulkner.* New York: Columbia UP, 1981.

———. "Tom Buchanan and the Demise of the Ivy League Athletic Hero." *Journal of Popular Culture* 8 (1974): 402–10.

Messent, Peter. "Speech Representation, Focalization, and Narration in *The Great Gatsby.*" *New Readings of the American Novel.* New York: St. Martin's, 1990. 8–43.

Meyer, Michael J., ed. *Literature and Musical Adaptation.* Amsterdam: Rodopi, 2002.

Michaels, Walter Benn. *Our America: Nativism, Modernism, and Pluralism.* Durham: Duke UP, 1995.

———. "The Souls of White Folks." *Literature and the Body: Essays on Population and Persons.* Ed. Elaine Scarry. Baltimore: Johns Hopkins UP, 1988. 185–209.

Michelson, Bruce. "The Myth of Gatsby." *Modern Fiction Studies* 26 (1980–81): 563–77.

Milford, Nancy. *Zelda: A Biography.* New York: Harper, 1970.

Miller, James E., Jr. "Fitzgerald's *Gatsby*: The World as Ash Heap." 1975. Donaldson, *Critical Essays* 242–58.

———. *F. Scott Fitzgerald: His Art and His Technique.* New York: New York UP, 1964.

Miller, Michael Vincent. *Intimate Terrorism: The Deterioration of Erotic Life.* New York: Norton, 1995.

Millgate, Michael. "Scott Fitzgerald as Social Novelist: Statement and Technique in 'The Great Gatsby.'" *Modern Language Review* 57 (1962): 335–39.

Mitchell, Giles. "The Great Narcissist: A Study of Fitzgerald's Jay Gatsby." *American Journal of Psychoanalysis* 51 (1991): 387–96.

Mizener, Arthur. *The Far Side of Paradise: A Biography of F. Scott Fitzgerald.* 1951. Rev. ed. New York: Vintage, 1959.

———. "F. Scott Fitzgerald, *The Great Gatsby.*" Stegner 180–91.

Monteiro, George. "James Gatz and John Keats." *Fitzgerald/Hemingway Annual* 4 (1972): 291–94.

Moreland, Kim. *The Medievalist Impulse in American Literature: Twain, Adams, Fitzgerald, and Hemingway.* Charlottesville: UP of Virginia, 1996.

———. "Music in *The Great Gatsby* and *The Great Gatsby* as Music." Meyer 29–45.

Morris, Wright. "The Function of Nostalgia: F. Scott Fitzgerald." *The Territory Ahead.* New York: Harcourt, 1958. 157–70.

Morrison, Toni. *Playing in the Dark: Whiteness and the Literary Imagination.* Cambridge: Harvard UP, 1992.

Morsberger, Robert E. "The Romantic Ancestry of *The Great Gatsby.*" *Fitzgerald/Hemingway Annual* 5 (1973): 119–30.

Moses, Edwin. "Tragic Inevitability in *The Great Gatsby.*" *College Language Association Journal* 21 (1977): 51–57.

Most, Andrea. *Making Americans: Jews and the Broadway Musical.* Cambridge: Harvard UP, 2003.

Moyer, Kermit W. "*The Great Gatsby*: Fitzgerald's Meditation on American History." 1972. Donaldson, *Critical Essays* 215–28.

Mulvey, Laura. "Visual Pleasure and Narrative Cinema." *Contemporary Film Theory.* Ed. Antony Easthope. London: Longman, 1993. 111–24.

Nafisi, Azar. *Reading* Lolita *in Tehran: A Memoir in Books.* New York: Random, 2003.

Neuhaus, Ron. "*Gatsby* and the Failure of the Omniscient 'I.'" Claridge 2: 359–68.

Nowlin, Michael E. "F. Scott Fitzgerald's Elite Syncopations: The Racial Make-up of the Entertainer in the Early Stories." *English Studies in Canada* 26 (2000): 409–43.

———. *F. Scott Fitzgerald's Racial Angles and the Business of Literary Greatness.* New York: Palgrave, 2007.

———, ed. *The Great Gatsby.* Peterborough, ON: Broadview, 2007.

O'Meara, Lauraleigh. "Medium of Exchange: The Blue Coupé Dialogue in *The Great Gatsby.*" *Papers on Language and Literature* 30 (1994): 73–87.

Oriard, Michael. *Sporting with the Gods: The Rhetoric of Play and Game in American Culture.* New York: Cambridge UP, 1991.

Ornstein, Robert. "Scott Fitzgerald's Fable of East and West." 1956. Lockridge, *Twentieth Cer   Interpretations* 54–69.

Owen, Guy. "I_   _eaning in 'The Great Gatsby.'" Langford 46–54.

Parker, David   _sby*: Two Versions of the Hero." Bloom, *Modern Critical View*

Parr, Susan Resneck. "Individual Responsibility in *The Great Gatsby*." *Virginia Quarterly Review* 57 (1981): 662–80.

Pasley, Fred. *Al Capone: Biography of a Self-Made Man*. New York: Washburn, 1930.

Paulson, A. S. "*The Great Gatsby*: Oral Aggression and Splitting." *American Imago* 35 (1978): 311–30.

Pauly, Thomas H. "Gatsby as Gangster." *Studies in American Fiction* 21 (1993): 225–36.

Pearson, Norman Holmes. "Reading a Novel—*The Great Gatsby*." 1962. Donaldson, *Critical Essays* 21–31.

Peek, Charles A. " 'The Tug of a Far Away Invisible Force': American Idealization of 'Home' and Its Impact on Two Signature Novels." *Platte Valley Review* 24.1 (1996): 60–75.

Pelzer, Linda C. "Beautiful Fools and Hulking Brutes: F. Scott Fitzgerald's *The Great Gatsby*." *Women in Literature: Reading through the Lens of Gender*. Ed. Jerilyn Fisher and Ellen S. Silber. Westport: Greenwood, 2003. 127–29.

Pendleton, Thomas A. *I'm Sorry about the Clock: Chronology, Composition, and Narrative Technique in* The Great Gatsby. Selingsgrove: Susquehanna UP, 1993.

Perkins, George, and Barbara Perkins. "F. Scott Fitzgerald (1896–1940)." *The American Tradition in Literature*. Ed. G. Perkins and B. Perkins. 10th ed. New York: McGraw, 2002. 1137–39.

Perosa, Sergio. *The Art of F. Scott Fitzgerald*. Trans. Charles Matz and Sergio Perosa. Ann Arbor: U of Michigan P, 1965.

Perrett, Geoffrey. *America in the Twenties: A History*. New York: Simon, 1982.

Person, Leland S., Jr. " 'Herstory' and Daisy Buchanan." *American Literature* 57 (1985): 250–57.

Petry, Alice Hall. "James Gatz's Mentor: Traces of Warren G. Harding in *The Great Gatsby*." *Canadian Review of American Studies* 16 (1985): 189–96.

Phelan, James. *Experiencing Fiction: Judgments, Progressions, and the Rhetorical Experience of Narrative*. Columbus: Ohio State UP, 2007.

———. *Living to Tell about It: A Rhetoric and Ethics of Character Narration*. Ithaca: Cornell UP, 2004.

———. *Reading People, Reading Plots: Character, Progression, and the Interpretation of Narrative*. Chicago: U of Chicago P, 1989.

———. "Reexamining Reality: The Multiple Functions of Nick Carraway." *Narrative as Rhetoric: Technique, Ethos, Audience, Ideology*. Columbus: Ohio State UP, 1996. 105–18.

Pinsker, Sanford. "Seeing *The Great Gatsby* Eye to Eye." *College Literature* 3 (1975): 69–71.

Piper, Henry Dan, ed. *Fitzgerald's* The Great Gatsby: *The Novel, the Critics, the Background*. New York: Scribner's, 1970.

———. *F. Scott Fitzgerald: A Critical Portrait*. New York: Holt, 1965.

———. "The Fuller-McGee Case." Piper, *Fitzgerald's* The Great Gatsby 171–84.

Plath, James. "*The Sun Also Rises* as 'a Greater Gatsby': 'Isn't It Pretty to Think So?' " Kennedy and Bryer 257–75.

———. "'What's in a Name, Old Sport?': Kipling's *The Story of the Gadsbys* as a Possible Source for Fitzgerald's *The Great Gatsby*." *Journal of Modern Literature* 25 (2001–02): 131–40.

Podis, Leonard A. "'The Unreality of Reality': Metaphor in *The Great Gatsby*." *Style* 11 (1977): 56–72.

Polek, Fran James. "From Renegade to Solid Citizen: The Extraordinary Individual in the Community." *South Dakota Review* 15.1 (1977): 61–72.

Posnock, Ross. "'A New World, Material without Being Real': Fitzgerald's Critique of Capitalism in *The Great Gatsby*." Donaldson, *Critical Essays* 201–13.

Preston, Elizabeth. "Implying Authors in *The Great Gatsby*." *Narrative* 5 (1997): 143–64.

Prigozy, Ruth, ed. *The Cambridge Companion to F. Scott Fitzgerald*. Cambridge: Cambridge UP, 2002.

———. "Gatsby's Guest List and Fitzgerald's Technique of Naming." *Fitzgerald/ Hemingway Annual* 4 (1972): 99–112.

———. "'Poor Butterfly': F. Scott Fitzgerald and Popular Music." *Prospects* 2 (1976): 41–67.

Public Enemy. Dir. William Wellman. Warner Brothers, 1931.

Pulp Fiction. Dir. Quentin Tarantino. Miramax, 1994.

Pyle, Joseph G. *The Life of James G. Hill*. 2 vols. Garden City: Doubleday, 1917.

Quirk, Tom. "Fitzgerald and Cather: *The Great Gatsby*." *American Literature* 54 (1982): 576–91.

Rabinowitz, Peter J. *Before Reading: Narrative Conventions and the Politics of Interpretation*. 1987. Columbus: Ohio State UP, 1998.

Raleigh, John Henry. "Fitzgerald's *The Great Gatsby*." *University of Kansas City Review* 13 (1957): 283–91.

———. "F. Scott Fitzgerald's *The Great Gatsby*: Legendary Bases and Allegorical Significances." 1957. Claridge 2: 256–60.

Randall, Monica. *The Mansions of Long Island's Gold Coast*. New York: Hastings, 1979.

Rimmon-Kenan, Shlomith. *Narrative Fiction: Contemporary Poetics*. London: Methuen, 1983.

Roark, James L., et al., eds. *The American Promise: A History of the United States*. Boston: Bedford, 1998.

Roberts, Kenneth. *Why Europe Leaves Home*. Indianapolis: Bobbs, 1922.

Roberts, Ruth E. "Nonverbal Communication in *The Great Gatsby*." *Language and Literature* 7 (1982): 107–29.

Rodewald, F. A. "Faulkner's Possible Use of *The Great Gatsby*." *Fitzgerald/Hemingway Annual* 7 (1975): 97–101.

Rohrkemper, John. "The Allusive Past: Historical Perspective in *The Great Gatsby*." *College Literature* 12 (1985): 153–62.

Roulston, Robert. "Something Borrowed, Something New: A Discussion of Literary Influences on *The Great Gatsby*." Donaldson, *Critical Essays* 54–66.

———. "Tom Buchanan: Patrician in Motley." *Arizona Quarterly* 34 (1978): 101–11.

————. "Traces of *Tono-Bungay* in *The Great Gatsby*." 1980. Claridge 2: 439–46.

Roulston, Robert, and Helen H. Roulston. *The Winding Road to West Egg: The Artistic Development of F. Scott Fitzgerald*. Lewisburg: Bucknell UP, 1995.

Rowe, Joyce A. "Closing the Circle: *The Great Gatsby*." *Equivocal Endings in Classic American Novels*. Cambridge: Cambridge UP, 1988. 100–26.

Rowland, Beryl. "Chaucer's Daisy (Prol. *LGW*, F 120–3; G 109–11)." *Notes and Queries* 208 (1963): 210.

R. V. A. S. Rev. of *This Side of Paradise*, by F. Scott Fitzgerald. *F. Scott Fitzgerald: The Man and His Work*. Ed. Alfred Kazin. 1951. New York: Collier, 1962. 49–50.

Samuels, Charles Thomas. "The Greatness of 'Gatsby.'" *Massachusetts Review* 7 (1966): 783–94.

Sanders, Barbara Gerber. "Structural Imagery in *The Great Gatsby*: Metaphor and Matrix." *Linguistics in Literature* 1.1 (1975): 53–75.

Sanders, J'aimé L. "Discovering the Source of Gatsby's Greatness: Nick's Eulogy for a 'Great' Kierkegaardian Knight." *F. Scott Fitzgerald Review* 3 (2004): 108–27.

Saposnik, Irving S. "The Passion and the Life: Technology as Pattern in *The Great Gatsby*." *Fitzgerald/Hemingway Annual* 11 (1979): 181–88.

Sarotte, Georges-Michel. "Francis Scott Fitzgerald: Self-Virilization and Its Failure." *Like a Brother, Like a Lover*. New York: Doubleday, 1978. 212–28.

Savage, David. "Who Is 'Owl Eyes' in *The Great Gatsby*?" *American Notes and Queries* 13 (1975): 72–74.

Scarface. Dir. Howard Hawks. United Artists, 1932.

Schlacks, Deborah Davis. *American Dream Visions: Chaucer's Surprising Influence on F. Scott Fitzgerald*. New York: Lang, 1994.

————. "Revising a Tribute: *The Great Gatsby*." Schlacks, *American Dream Visions* 117–60.

Schneider, Daniel J. "Color-Symbolism in *The Great Gatsby*." *University Review* 31 (1964): 13–17.

Scribner, Charles, III. "Celestial Eyes: From Metamorphosis to Masterpiece." *Princeton University Library Chronicle* 53 (1992): 140–55.

Scrimgeour, Gary J. "Against *The Great Gatsby*." 1966. Lockridge, *Twentieth Century Interpretations* 70–81.

Seguin, Robert. "*Ressentiment* and the Social Poetics of *The Great Gatsby*: Fitzgerald Reads Cather." *Modern Fiction Studies* 46 (2000): 917–40.

Seiters, Dan. "*The Great Gatsby*." *Image Patterns in the Novels of F. Scott Fitzgerald*. Ann Arbor: UMI, 1986. 57–87.

Seldes, Gilbert. *The Seven Lively Arts*. 1924. Mineola: Dover, 2001.

Settle, Glenn. "Fitzgerald's Daisy: The Siren Voice." *American Literature* 57 (1985): 115–24.

Seymour, E. L. D., et al., eds. *Favorite Flowers in Color*. New York: Wise, 1949.

Shaw, Arnold. *The Jazz Age: Popular Music in the 1920s*. New York: Oxford UP, 1987.

The Sheik. Dir. George Melford. Paramount, 1921. VCR, Paramount Home Video, 1998.

Showalter, Elaine, ed. *The New Feminist Criticism: Essays on Women, Literature, and Theory.* New York: Pantheon, 1985.

Shulman, Robert. "Myth, Mr. Eliot, and the Comic Novel." *Modern Fiction Studies* 12 (1966–67): 395–403.

Sipiora, Philip. "Vampires of the Heart: Gender Trouble in *The Great Gatsby*." Deats and Lenker 199–220.

Skinner, John. "The Oral and the Written: Kurtz and Gatsby Revisited." *Journal of Narrative Technique* 17 (1987): 131–40.

Sklar, Robert. *F. Scott Fitzgerald: The Last Laocoön.* New York: Oxford UP, 1967.

Slater, Peter Gregg. "Ethnicity in *The Great Gatsby*." *Twentieth Century Literature* 19 (1973): 53–62.

Smith, Barbara Herrnstein. *Contingencies of Value: Alternative Perspectives for Critical Theory.* Cambridge: Harvard UP, 1988.

Smith, David Geoffrey. *Pedagon: Interdisciplinary Essays in the Human Sciences, Pedagogy, and Culture.* New York: Lang, 1999.

Smith, Felipe. "The Dark Side of Paradise: Race and Ethnicity in the Novels of F. Scott Fitzgerald." Diss. Louisiana State U, 1989.

Sperber, Dan, and Dierdre Wilson. *Relevance: Communication and Cognition.* 2nd ed. Oxford: Blackwell, 1995.

Stafford, William T. "Benjy Compson, Jake Barnes, and Nick Carraway—Replication in Three 'Innocent' American Narrators of the 1920s." *Books Speaking to Books: A Contextual Approach to American Fiction.* Chapel Hill: U of North Carolina P, 1981. 25–50.

Stallman, R. W. "Conrad and *The Great Gatsby*." 1955. Claridge 2: 447–55.

———. *The Houses That James Built and Other Literary Studies.* East Lansing: Michigan State UP, 1961.

Standish, Burt L. [W. Gilbert Patten]. *Frank Merriwell's Foes; or, An Uphill Fight.* 1902. Ed. Jack Rudman. New York: Smith, 1972.

Stanley, Linda C. *The Foreign Critical Reputation of F. Scott Fitzgerald: An Analysis and Annotated Bibliography.* Westport: Greenwood, 1980.

———. *The Foreign Critical Reputation of F. Scott Fitzgerald, 1980–2000: An Analysis and Annotated Bibliography.* Westport: Greenwood, 2004.

Stark, Bruce R. "The Intricate Pattern in *The Great Gatsby*." *Fitzgerald/Hemingway Annual* 6 (1974): 51–61.

Stavola, Thomas J. *Scott Fitzgerald: Crisis in an American Identity.* New York: Barnes, 1979.

Stegner, Wallace, ed. *The American Novel from James Fenimore Cooper to William Faulkner.* New York: Basic, 1965.

Stein, William Bysshe. "Gatsby's Morgan Le Fay." *Fitzgerald Newsletter* 15 (1961): 67.

Steinbrink, Jeffrey. " 'Boats against the Current': Mortality and the Myth of Renewal in *The Great Gatsby*." *Twentieth Century Literature* 26 (1980): 157–70.

Stern, Milton R. *The Golden Moment: The Novels of F. Scott Fitzgerald.* Urbana: U of Illinois P, 1971.

Stevens, G. A. *Garden Flowers in Color: A Picture Cyclopedia of Flowers*. New York: Macmillan, 1934.

Stewart, Lawrence D. " 'Absolution' and *The Great Gatsby*." *Fitzgerald/Hemingway Annual* 5 (1973): 181–87.

Stoddard, Lothrop. *The Rising Tide of Color against White World-Supremacy*. New York: Scribner's, 1920.

Stouck, David. "White Sheep on Fifth Avenue: *The Great Gatsby* as Pastoral." *Genre* 4 (1971): 335–47.

Susman, Warren I. *Culture as History: The Transformation of American Society in the Twentieth Century*. New York: Pantheon, 1984.

Tanselle, G. Thomas, and Jackson R. Bryer. "*The Great Gatsby:* A Study in Literary Reputation." 1964. Claridge 2: 181–94.

Tate, Mary Jo. *F. Scott Fitzgerald A to Z: The Essential Reference to His Life and Work*. New York: Facts on File, 1998.

Taylor, Douglas. "*The Great Gatsby*: Style and Myth." 1953. Claridge 2: 209–19.

Tenenbaum, Ruth Betsy. " 'The Gray-Turning, Gold-Turning Consciousness' of Nick Carraway." *Fitzgerald/Hemingway Annual* 7 (1975): 37–55.

Thale, Jerome. "The Narrator as Hero." *Twentieth Century Literature* 3 (1957): 69–73.

Thornton, Lawrence. "Ford Madox Ford and *The Great Gatsby*." *Fitzgerald/Hemingway Annual* 7 (1975): 57–74.

Thornton, Patricia Pacey. "Sexual Roles in *The Great Gatsby*." *English Studies in Canada* 7 (1979): 457–68.

Trask, David F. "The End of the American Dream." Piper, *Fitzgerald's* The Great Gatsby 213–17.

Tredell, Nicolas, ed. *F. Scott Fitzgerald:* The Great Gatsby. New York: Columbia UP, 1997.

Trilling, Lionel. "F. Scott Fitzgerald." *The Liberal Imagination*. New York: Viking, 1950. 243–54. Rpt. in Donaldson, *Critical Essays* 13–20.

Turnbull, Andrew. *Scott Fitzgerald*. New York: Scribner's, 1962.

Tyson, Lois. *Critical Theory Today: A User-Friendly Guide*. 1998. New York: Garland, 1999.

———. *The Psychological Politics of the American Dream*. Columbus: Ohio State UP, 1996.

———. "The Romance of the Commodity: The Cancellation of Identity in F. Scott Fitzgerald's *Great Gatsby*." Tyson, *Psychological Politics* 42–62.

Updike, John. "*Remembrance of Things Past* Remembered." *Picked-Up Pieces*. New York: Knopf, 1975. 162–68.

Vanderbilt, Kermit. "James, Fitzgerald, and the American Self-Image." 1965. Claridge 4: 457–68.

Veblen, Thorstein. *The Theory of the Leisure Class: An Economic Study of Institutions*. 1899. New York: Dover, 1994.

Verene, Donald Phillip. *The Art of Humane Education*. Ithaca: Cornell UP, 2002.

Viel, Michel. "Les lectures de Mrs. Wilson dans *The Great Gatsby*." *Études Anglaises* 50 (1997): 434–41.

Wagner, Joseph B. "*Gatsby* and John Keats: Another Version." *Fitzgerald/Hemingway Annual* 11 (1979): 91–98.

Wagner, Linda W. "Ernest Hemingway, F. Scott Fitzgerald, and Gertrude Stein." *Columbia Literary History of the United States*. Ed. Emory Elliott. New York: Columbia UP, 1988. 873–86.

Wagner-Martin, Linda. *Zelda Sayre Fitzgerald: An American Woman's Life*. New York: Palgrave, 2004.

Washington, Bryan R. *The Politics of Exile: Ideology in Henry James, F. Scott Fitzgerald, and James Baldwin*. Boston: Northeastern UP, 1996.

Wasiolek, Edward. "The Sexual Drama of Nick and Gatsby." *International Fiction Review* 19 (1992): 14–22.

Wasserstrom, William. "The Goad of Guilt: Henry Adams, Scott and Zelda." *Journal of Modern Literature* 6 (1977): 289–310.

Watkins, Floyd C. "Fitzgerald's Jay Gatsby and Young Ben Franklin." *New England Quarterly* 27 (1954): 249–52.

Way, Brian. *F. Scott Fitzgerald and the Art of Social Fiction*. New York: St. Martin's, 1980.

Weinstein, Arnold. "Fiction as Greatness: The Case of *Gatsby*." 1985. Claridge 2: 369–86.

West, James L. W., III. *The Perfect Hour: The Romance of F. Scott Fitzgerald and Ginevra King, His First Love*. New York: Random, 2005.

Weston, Jessie L. *From Ritual to Romance*. 1920. Princeton: Princeton UP, 1993.

Wharton, Edith. *The Age of Innocence*. 1920. Mineola: Dover, 1997.

———. *The Custom of the Country*. 1913. New York: Random, 2001.

———. *Summer*. 1917. New York: Doubleday, 1993.

———. "Three Letters about 'The Great Gatsby.'" E. Wilson 308–10.

Whitley, John S. *F. Scott Fitzgerald: The Great Gatsby*. London: Arnold, 1976.

Wilson, B. W. "The Theatrical Motif in *The Great Gatsby*." *Fitzgerald/Hemingway Annual* 7 (1975): 107–13.

Wilson, Edmund, ed. *The Crack-Up*. New York: New Directions, 1945.

Winter, Jay. *Sites of Memory, Sites of Mourning: The Great War in European Cultural History*. Cambridge: Cambridge UP, 1995.

Yezierska, Anzia. *Salome of the Tenements*. 1923. Urbana: U of Illinois P, 1995.

Young, Philip. "Scott Fitzgerald's Waste Land." *Kansas Magazine* 23 (1956): 73–77.

Young, Thomas Daniel, ed. *Modern American Fiction: Form and Function*. Baton Rouge: Louisiana State UP, 1989.

INDEX

Modern Language Association of America
Approaches to Teaching World Literature
Joseph Gibaldi, series editor

Achebe's Things Fall Apart. Ed. Bernth Lindfors. 1991.
Arthurian Tradition. Ed. Maureen Fries and Jeanie Watson. 1992.
Atwood's The Handmaid's Tale *and Other Works*. Ed. Sharon R. Wilson, Thomas B. Friedman, and Shannon Hengen. 1996.
Austen's Emma. Ed. Marcia McClintock Folsom. 2004.
Austen's Pride and Prejudice. Ed. Marcia McClintock Folsom. 1993.
Balzac's Old Goriot. Ed. Michal Peled Ginsburg. 2000.
Baudelaire's Flowers of Evil. Ed. Laurence M. Porter. 2000.
Beckett's Waiting for Godot. Ed. June Schlueter and Enoch Brater. 1991.
Beowulf. Ed. Jess B. Bessinger, Jr., and Robert F. Yeager. 1984.
Blake's Songs of Innocence and of Experience. Ed. Robert F. Gleckner and Mark L. Greenberg. 1989.
Boccaccio's Decameron. Ed. James H. McGregor. 2000.
British Women Poets of the Romantic Period. Ed. Stephen C. Behrendt and Harriet Kramer Linkin. 1997.
Charlotte Brontë's Jane Eyre. Ed. Diane Long Hoeveler and Beth Lau. 1993.
Emily Brontë's Wuthering Heights. Ed. Sue Lonoff and Terri A. Hasseler. 2006.
Byron's Poetry. Ed. Frederick W. Shilstone. 1991.
Camus's The Plague. Ed. Steven G. Kellman. 1985.
Writings of Bartolomé de Las Casas. Ed. Santa Arias and Eyda M. Merediz. 2008.
Cather's My Ántonia. Ed. Susan J. Rosowski. 1989.
Cervantes' Don Quixote. Ed. Richard Bjornson. 1984.
Chaucer's Canterbury Tales. Ed. Joseph Gibaldi. 1980.
Chaucer's Troilus and Criseyde *and the Shorter Poems*. Ed. Tison Pugh and Angela Jane Weisl. 2006.
Chopin's The Awakening. Ed. Bernard Koloski. 1988.
Coleridge's Poetry and Prose. Ed. Richard E. Matlak. 1991.
Collodi's Pinocchio *and Its Adaptations*. Ed. Michael Sherberg. 2006.
Conrad's "Heart of Darkness" and "The Secret Sharer." Ed. Hunt Hawkins and Brian W. Shaffer. 2002.
Dante's Divine Comedy. Ed. Carole Slade. 1982.
Defoe's Robinson Crusoe. Ed. Maximillian E. Novak and Carl Fisher. 2005.
DeLillo's White Noise. Ed. Tim Engles and John N. Duvall. 2006.
Dickens's Bleak House. Ed. John O. Jordan and Gordon Bigelow. 2009.
Dickens's David Copperfield. Ed. Richard J. Dunn. 1984.
Dickinson's Poetry. Ed. Robin Riley Fast and Christine Mack Gordon. 1989.
Narrative of the Life of Frederick Douglass. Ed. James C. Hall. 1999.
Early Modern Spanish Drama. Ed. Laura R. Bass and Margaret R. Greer. 2006
Eliot's Middlemarch. Ed. Kathleen Blake. 1990.

Eliot's Poetry and Plays. Ed. Jewel Spears Brooker. 1988.
Shorter Elizabethan Poetry. Ed. Patrick Cheney and Anne Lake Prescott. 2000.
Ellison's Invisible Man. Ed. Susan Resneck Parr and Pancho Savery. 1989.
English Renaissance Drama. Ed. Karen Bamford and Alexander Leggatt. 2002.
Works of Louise Erdrich. Ed. Gregg Sarris, Connie A. Jacobs, and
    James R. Giles. 2004.
Dramas of Euripides. Ed. Robin Mitchell-Boyask. 2002.
Faulkner's The Sound and the Fury. Ed. Stephen Hahn and Arthur F. Kinney. 1996.
Fitzgerald's The Great Gatsby. Ed. Jackson R. Bryer and Nancy P. VanArsdale.
    2009.
Flaubert's Madame Bovary. Ed. Laurence M. Porter and Eugene F. Gray. 1995.
García Márquez's One Hundred Years of Solitude. Ed. María Elena de Valdés
    and Mario J. Valdés. 1990.
Gilman's "The Yellow Wall-Paper" and Herland. Ed. Denise D. Knight and
    Cynthia J. Davis. 2003.
Goethe's Faust. Ed. Douglas J. McMillan. 1987.
Gothic Fiction: The British and American Traditions. Ed. Diane Long
    Hoeveler and Tamar Heller. 2003.
Grass's The Tin Drum. Ed. Monika Shafi. 2008.
Hebrew Bible as Literature in Translation. Ed. Barry N. Olshen and
    Yael S. Feldman. 1989.
Homer's Iliad *and* Odyssey. Ed. Kostas Myrsiades. 1987.
Ibsen's A Doll House. Ed. Yvonne Shafer. 1985.
Henry James's Daisy Miller *and* The Turn of the Screw. Ed. Kimberly C. Reed
    and Peter G. Beidler. 2005.
Works of Samuel Johnson. Ed. David R. Anderson and Gwin J. Kolb. 1993.
Joyce's Ulysses. Ed. Kathleen McCormick and Erwin R. Steinberg. 1993.
Works of Sor Juana Inés de la Cruz. Ed. Emilie L. Bergmann and
    Stacey Schlau. 2007.
Kafka's Short Fiction. Ed. Richard T. Gray. 1995.
Keats's Poetry. Ed. Walter H. Evert and Jack W. Rhodes. 1991.
Kingston's The Woman Warrior. Ed. Shirley Geok-lin Lim. 1991.
Lafayette's The Princess of Clèves. Ed. Faith E. Beasley and
    Katharine Ann Jensen. 1998.
Works of D. H. Lawrence. Ed. M. Elizabeth Sargent and Garry Watson. 2001.
Lazarillo de Tormes *and the Picaresque Tradition*. Ed. Anne J. Cruz. 2008.
Lessing's The Golden Notebook. Ed. Carey Kaplan and Ellen Cronan Rose. 1989.
Mann's Death in Venice *and Other Short Fiction*. Ed. Jeffrey B. Berlin. 1992.
Marguerite de Navarre's Heptameron. Ed. Colette H. Winn. 2007.
Medieval English Drama. Ed. Richard K. Emmerson. 1990.
Melville's Moby-Dick. Ed. Martin Bickman. 1985.
Metaphysical Poets. Ed. Sidney Gottlieb. 1990.
Miller's Death of a Salesman. Ed. Matthew C. Roudané. 1995.
Milton's Paradise Lost. Ed. Galbraith M. Crump. 1986.

Milton's Shorter Poetry and Prose. Ed. Peter C. Herman. 2007.
Molière's Tartuffe *and Other Plays.* Ed. James F. Gaines and
    Michael S. Koppisch. 1995.
Momaday's The Way to Rainy Mountain. Ed. Kenneth M. Roemer. 1988.
Montaigne's Essays. Ed. Patrick Henry. 1994.
Novels of Toni Morrison. Ed. Nellie Y. McKay and Kathryn Earle. 1997.
Murasaki Shikibu's The Tale of Genji. Ed. Edward Kamens. 1993.
Nabokov's Lolita. Ed. Zoran Kuzmanovich and Galya Diment. 2008.
Poe's Prose and Poetry. Ed. Jeffrey Andrew Weinstock and Tony Magistrale. 2008.
Pope's Poetry. Ed. Wallace Jackson and R. Paul Yoder. 1993.
Proust's Fiction and Criticism. Ed. Elyane Dezon-Jones and
    Inge Crosman Wimmers. 2003.
Puig's Kiss of the Spider Woman. Ed. Daniel Balderston and Francine
    Masiello. 2007.
Pynchon's The Crying of Lot 49 *and Other Works.* Ed. Thomas H. Schaub. 2008.
Novels of Samuel Richardson. Ed. Lisa Zunshine and Jocelyn Harris. 2006.
Rousseau's Confessions *and* Reveries of the Solitary Walker. Ed.
    John C. O'Neal and Ourida Mostefai. 2003.
Shakespeare's Hamlet. Ed. Bernice W. Kliman. 2001.
Shakespeare's King Lear. Ed. Robert H. Ray. 1986.
Shakespeare's Othello. Ed. Peter Erickson and Maurice Hunt. 2005.
Shakespeare's Romeo and Juliet. Ed. Maurice Hunt. 2000.
Shakespeare's The Tempest *and Other Late Romances.* Ed. Maurice Hunt. 1992.
Shelley's Frankenstein. Ed. Stephen C. Behrendt. 1990.
Shelley's Poetry. Ed. Spencer Hall. 1990.
Sir Gawain and the Green Knight. Ed. Miriam Youngerman Miller and
    Jane Chance. 1986.
Song of Roland. Ed. William W. Kibler and Leslie Zarker Morgan. 2006.
Spenser's Faerie Queene. Ed. David Lee Miller and Alexander Dunlop. 1994.
Stendhal's The Red and the Black. Ed. Dean de la Motte and Stirling Haig. 1999.
Sterne's Tristram Shandy. Ed. Melvyn New. 1989.
Stowe's Uncle Tom's Cabin. Ed. Elizabeth Ammons and Susan Belasco. 2000.
Swift's Gulliver's Travels. Ed. Edward J. Rielly. 1988.
Thoreau's Walden *and Other Works.* Ed. Richard J. Schneider. 1996.
Tolstoy's Anna Karenina. Ed. Liza Knapp and Amy Mandelker. 2003.
Vergil's Aeneid. Ed. William S. Anderson and Lorina N. Quartarone. 2002.
Voltaire's Candide. Ed. Renée Waldinger. 1987.
Whitman's Leaves of Grass. Ed. Donald D. Kummings. 1990.
Wiesel's Night. Ed. Alan Rosen. 2007.
Works of Oscar Wilde. Ed. Philip E. Smith II. 2008.
Woolf's To the Lighthouse. Ed. Beth Rigel Daugherty and Mary Beth Pringle.
    2001.
Wordsworth's Poetry. Ed. Spencer Hall, with Jonathan Ramsey. 1986.
Wright's Native Son. Ed. James A. Miller. 1997.